AMERICAS OVERLAND

The Driving Handbook

Greene and Greene

For self-driving journeys from the USA through Mexico, Central America and South America

Americas Overland – The Driving Handbook

Copyright © 2008 Kim and Don Greene

Plan your trip carefully, but remember: Procedures and schedules change, routes improve and deteriorate and camping areas come and go. So if you find things have changed, have different contacts for shipping, route suggestions, camping ideas or GPS information, please tell us and help make the next edition even more accurate and useful.

Visit our Web sites at www.AmericasOverland.net or www.QuestConnect.org for ordering books and for updates to the information contained in this book.

ISBN 978-0-557-00712-7

Photos by Donald and Kim Greene except where indicated otherwise.

Front Cover Photograph: Laguna Colorado, Bolivia
Country Maps courtesy of:
    Central Intelligence Agency - The World Factbook
    Canadian International Development Agency

Latin America

CONTENTS

Preface

In our opinion, many adventure books and magazines present the stereotyped image that a journey through Central and South America is an adventure way outside the boundaries of normal human life. That it should only be undertaken with many precautions and is one for which you need all kinds of specialized equipment. Yes, you definitely must be prepared, but truth be told, it is a fabulous experience that can be undertaken by anyone who does their research and knows what they want out of their adventure.

Fear of crime is probably the biggest deterrent to most of those who contemplate this journey. Crime exists everywhere in the world and you have to take the appropriate precautions to try to prevent it. That said neither we nor anyone we've met on the road has been the victim of anything but the same types of petty crime that can happen at home.

Yes, accidents do unfortunately happen – we have seen photos of unlucky drivers that have ended up in ditches or flipped their vehicles. We have personally experienced such high winds on one stretch of *Ruta 40* in Argentina that we had to drive on the wrong side of the cambered road to prevent being blown over. Accidents do happen and when you least expect them. Being diligent is the best way to prevent them.

Not being fluent in the native language also adds a whole different level of "survival" to your day-to-day experience. But it isn't too difficult to learn the basics – hello, goodbye, thank-you, how much? or I'm lost. Hand signals also work really well. Learning the necessities will tell the locals that you are interested in their culture. What an icebreaker "How are you?" can be in a native language! Try it and see for yourselves.

This book is intended as a handbook to help you drive through the countries of Mexico and Central and South America. It is not intended as a guidebook for those countries and does not contain all the information that you will want to have at your disposal. Make sure to buy a guidebook such as Lonely Planet, Moon, Rough Guides, Brandt or any of the other guides available for your areas of intended travel.

Have a great journey!

Kim and Don

Chapter One

Why A Self-Driving Journey?
- Driving Options
- What Type of Vehicle
- Four Wheel Drive or Two Wheel Drive
- Our Expedition Vehicle
- The Build Out

It started out as just an idea, a dream really. Wouldn't it be nice to drive our own vehicle around the world?

After many years of traveling the world on public transport such as buses, trains and boats, we had discovered that the times we had rented cars, motorcycles, boats or bicycles, we had been able to see and do more, stopping whenever and wherever we wanted to.

Driving Options

There are four main options available for traveling into Mexico, Central and South America with your own transport.

One, is to join a caravan. There are several companies that lead trips into Mexico and there are others that lead caravans to Central America, but these all turn around once they reach Panama. As of 2007, there was only one company that specialized in leading self-drive caravans into South America.   But it is not free or even inexpensive to join a caravan. Caravan travel is offered not so much due to security issues but rather for the camaraderie of group travel.

Two, Overland truck tours are another option, but they really are not even close to the self-driving option. Overland trucks are generally little more than a private bus fitted on a truck chassis and filled with upwards of 35 people. Itineraries are pre-set and facilities are a combination of camping and inexpensive "backpacker" accommodations. Again, camaraderie is a major attraction of these tours.

Three, rental of a car or motor home works well if you will be visiting one country, unless you can obtain permission to cross borders with the rental. Moreover, if you want to travel for an open-ended period of time, a rental could get very expensive.

So if you want to travel with the unlimited freedom to go where you want, when you want and to spend as much or as little time in a place as possible, then self-driving is the way to go.

This leads us to the option we chose, **Four**, travel with your own vehicle. Having our own vehicle meant that there would be no more night buses, no more sharing seats with chickens and un-diapered babies. No more climbing over sacks of onions and potatoes to exit trains. No more live goats tied to the roofs of buses. No more hitching rides from the side of the road in the middle of nowhere. No more fighting to get on already overcrowded buses. No more maniac bus drivers. No more women going into labor in the back of a minibus. No more poorly tied cargo falling off the top of the bus. No more wondering if our bags would end up in the same place we did. No more locked passenger compartments on ferries. No more drunks on minibuses. No more bus drivers behind locked doors. No more bus drivers leaving the rest stop while you're still in the bathroom.

Oh yes, there were many reasons to consider having our own vehicle. Not that most of those experiences didn't make for good stories, but we were ready for different types of stories.

What Type of Vehicle

This book is written for those of you who want to travel by motorized transport. Self-powered transport, be it walking or bicycling, is covered in specialty books written by people who are enthusiastic about those forms of travel. Motorcyclists will find much of our information helpful, although you generally won't be primarily camping and your shipping experiences will generally be by air rather than by ship.

The first decision that we needed to make was what type of vehicle did we want? We like to camp, so we knew that we wanted a vehicle that could also be our "home away from home". We knew from past experience owning a small, slide-in, pop-up camper on a pickup truck that we would want a high clearance, 4-wheel drive vehicle. Our previous truck was a 4X4 and it could take us just about anywhere we wanted to go.

We also knew that it needed to be bigger than the pop-up, which was just too small for two people for extended periods of time, such as during long bouts with bad weather. Small vehicles are weather dependant, meaning that since you will be spending large amounts of your time outside, good weather and a lack of bugs are necessary when considering your ability to set up camp. Privacy is also an issue to be considered when thinking about small vehicles and tent camping options – can you camp anywhere? A larger vehicle affords more privacy thereby allowing you to camp anywhere, in a service station or even right on the street.

Your vehicle needs to meet **your** needs. Based on your budget and what you need to make you comfortable, you might decide that you need a large, self-contained vehicle like ours. Or you may decide that you can be comfortable with a van or SUV. There are pros and cons for both. A large vehicle can be difficult to maneuver in the small streets of colonial towns and it can prohibit you from accessing some spots like beaches and trails when access is limited by height or width. Small vehicles can limit what you can take and where you can spend the night. But that decision can only be made by you.

Thus the process begins with soul searching and research, lots and lots of research. Thank goodness for the Internet. I don't think we would have been able to accomplish what we have, from the small town we live in, without it.

Four Wheel Drive or Two Wheel Drive

So start off by asking yourself where do you want to go? Are you going with other vehicles or will you be by yourself? Do you want to explore off the beaten path or will you be traveling primarily on main roads? Do you need four-wheel drive (4x4) and do you know how to get the most out of it?

Two wheel drive vehicles will usually be sufficient for getting you around the regions and to get you to the major tourist sites. Even when we would think a 4x4 would be a good idea on a road, we would pass a VW van or even a taxi. Just because a road is rough doesn't mean that you need to avoid the road (although high clearance is always good to have.) Driving slowly, sometimes very slowly, is all that you need to do. And don't forget to tighten up those bolts and screws periodically.

We like to have the freedom to travel off the main roads. Since we travel most of the time by ourselves, we need to have the ability to "self-rescue" as we may not see another vehicle for days. For us, a 4x4 is a requirement.

If you decide that the 4x4 option is for you, take into consideration that driving with 4x4 engaged is very different from driving in two-wheel drive. If you have limited off-road experience or have never driven in 4-wheel drive please consider taking an off-road driving course from a qualified instructor. Learning the limits of your vehicle is an important factor when making choices about where you can drive.

Our Expedition Vehicle

We started by looking to see what kinds of 4x4 vehicles were available.

We first considered American-made pickup trucks (larger than the ½ ton truck that we had) and full size slide-in campers. We eliminated these from consideration because the overall length would have been around 24 feet, which we considered too long for the types of places we wanted to visit and the conditions we figured we might encounter. This type of combination would also create a long rear overhang that we felt would reduce our ground clearance as well as the approach and departure angle for off-road travel.

Next we looked to see if there were any specialty vehicles available that would fit our needs. We did find a couple, but the price tag was much higher than what we could afford. We then started considering building out our own vehicle.

After much more research, we decided it was feasible to build our own camper. We chose the 4-wheel drive Mitsubishi Fuso FG639 (2004) as our cab and chassis because of its short wheelbase, its ground clearance and its carrying weight ability. For our body we designed a 14½-foot long, 8-foot wide box that would become our camper.

First we looked at companies that could build the box from honeycomb type materials to lower the overall weight while increasing the strength of the unit. We were unsuccessful in finding someone with experience that would work with us. We finally found a company that would make our box from a one-piece fiberglass mold, thereby eliminating what we considered to be unsightly seams every four feet. Unicell Body Co. would even install our windows, vents and doors per our specifications. So we went to work designing our new home.

The interior design was based on our experiences with our little camper. Priorities included a standard queen mattress (no more wimpy little mattresses for us!), a self-contained bathroom (no more outside showers!) and plenty of storage space.

The Build-out

Starting at the front we added a heavy-duty roof rack loaded with driving and fog lights, 3 five-gallon containers for diesel fuel and a high-lift jack (for emergencies). On the driver's side, we added a 14-gallon gray-water tank connected to our shower. Next to the tank we added a high-grade weatherproof storage box for our air compressor, warning triangles, leveling blocks, jacks and toolbox. We mounted a door into the camper's side for our European-style cassette toilet and another smaller compartment door for our water inlet. Toward the rear is the "shore" power hook-up and a door to our storage compartment that goes the entire width of the body.

At the rear there is a custom bumper on which we mounted two spare tires, 2 five-gallon water containers and two floodlights. Behind the bumper and mounted directly to the chassis frame, we installed a two-gallon air tank (connected to the air compressor) and a 6-inch diameter ABS pipe to hold our wastewater drain hose. Looking up at the rear of the camper, about 9 feet from the ground, we installed the license plate – so we wouldn't have to worry about having it stolen or held by police for parking infractions.

Above the bumper is a five-foot wide compartment door for our "garage". Inside the garage we have stored some equipment and our toys: two folding mountain bikes and an inflatable kayak.

On the passenger side there are three storage compartment doors and the entrance door. The front storage compartment holds our propane tank for cooking. We also store our water hoses and our folded steps in this compartment. When in camp, the steps are removed and placed on a bracket beneath the entry door – making entry inside very easy.

Two more storage compartments are located toward the rear. One holds our battery bank of two 245-amp hr. AGM batteries, inverter/converter/charger, BBQ and some more tools. The other door is the entry to the "thru" storage compartment mentioned above. Beneath the body we have our 32-gallon fuel tank and another 11-gallon gray-water tank connected to our sink. Tucked away on the frame we installed the fuel pump for our diesel camper heater. Installed up at the roofline, we have a 12-foot long awning that can be pulled out to provide shade.

We like being able to look outside and to let lots of light into the living area, so we installed two windows on each side (excluding the front) of the camper body.

On the roof, we originally installed two 14-inch powered vents to provide air circulation, an eight-inch exhaust vent in the bathroom and a seven-inch solar powered vent as our refrigerator exhaust. We later removed one of the powered vents and installed a 12-volt evaporative cooler. Our solar power is also mounted on the roof. This consists of two 120-watt solar panels.

Inside we placed our queen size bed on a platform above the garage, with a storage box at the head of the bed containing our library of reading material and guide books on one side, and our music CDs (later updated to an MP3 player) on the other. Stereo speakers are mounted in the back corners. On the driver's-side wall above the bed is a monitoring board, containing our solar charge and voltage charge monitors, heater control and the remote for our inverter/converter.

The "kitchen" consists of a cabinet with seven drawers and an access door to the water purifier, heating duct and instant-hot water heater. On top of the cabinet are a two-burner propane stove, a counter and a double sink. Across from the sink is the eating/seating area.

The seating area has two bench seats facing each other with an 18-inch wide table in between. The table is removable when not in use. Each of the bench seats contains storage. The seat closest to the bed can be tilted forward for access to the fuse box and half of the clothes closet and the other seat hides a 65-gallon water tank. Cushions were made for the benches and curtains or reversible blinds installed on all the windows.

Between the water tank and the bathroom are two cabinets. One is mounted to the wall and the other is a slide-out cabinet holding our food pantry. Hidden behind the pantry is a second electric instant-hot water heater that supplies the bathroom. The bathroom is only three feet deep, but it contains our shower and toilet, separated by a shower curtain. We felt that there really wasn't any need to have a sink in the bathroom as the kitchen sink is only six feet away. Racks and a mirror have been hung in the bathroom to accommodate the necessities.

Across the front wall of the camper, between the bathroom and the passenger side is a storage closet containing 10 shelves for clothing, etc. and in the corner is our 8.5 cu.ft. refrigerator/freezer.

We were concerned about the availability of propane so we decided that the only item that would use propane would be our cooking stove. With our 35-gallon tank we can go nearly three months between fills.

Diesel powers our truck and provides the fuel for our camper heater. The refrigerator, lights, vents and pump all run off 12-volt DC electricity and are powered by our battery bank. The batteries charge primarily via solar, with alternator back up. If available, we are also set up to connect to 110v "shore" power (any exterior electrical supply). The shore electrical is then converted to 12-volt DC by a 2,000- watt inverter/converter to power our 110v appliances and to charge the batteries. 220v "shore power" requires a converter to change the electricity to 110v (necessary in South America).

The Mitsubishi Fuso FG is a commercial truck, and it rides like a truck. When we drove the truck back to our home in Arizona after getting the box installed, we learned the true state of the roads in the USA. The suspension on a passenger car is soft and absorbs most of the defects in the roads while our FG did not.

Every hole or bump was immediately transferred to the cab. Several times we were tossed up out of our seats, straining at our seatbelts. We decided that the first modification would have to be to replace the factory hard-bolted seats with suspension seats. Oh yeah – what a big difference. We also added a MP3/CD player and changer, and installed solar reflective tinting to the windows of the cab.

Chapter Two

Pre-trip Planning
- The Big Idea
- The Budget
- How to Finance Your Adventure
- The Route
- Guidebooks and Maps
- Internet

The Big Idea

So, you want to drive your vehicle southward out of the United States. It is a great idea, a BIG idea. Many of your friends and family won't understand, in fact, many of them will tell you that you must be crazy. They'll come up with all the stories – all the urban legends, that have been passed down for decades.

<u>Fear</u>
Here are some of the things you'll hear:

Police will be looking to stop you so that they can demand a bribe for some made-up infraction. Border guards are corrupt and will demand bribes to let you into their country. Your vehicle will stand out like the proverbial sore thumb causing everyone who sees it to think that you have valuable items in it that they must steal. If you get into an accident you'll be thrown into jail. Nobody speaks English. Everybody will be jealous of you or hate you. The stories just keep coming and coming. And what's worse, the stories are being told to you, with authority, by people who have never been south of the border or traveled in the same manner as you.

Don't let their fear infect you and make you change your mind. International travel is generally as safe as domestic travel. The cardinal rule is: Don't do anything that you wouldn't do at home. Don't disrespect the local laws, don't flash large amounts of money and don't walk down dark streets alone at night. The same way you live at home, you should live while on the road.

The Plan
Let's think about your plan. What do you want to see, where do you want to go, how much time do you have and how much money do you want to spend?

Getting ready for a trip of this magnitude takes a lot of planning and organization. No matter how much time you have to prepare for such a major journey you will probably still be running around like headless chickens right up to the time you drive away.

We had crossed over the border into Mexico many times over the years, exploring the country without ever venturing further south. But curiosity got the better of us and now that we have ventured further, all we can recommend is that you try to go as far south as you can. Whatever time you are able to spend will be worthwhile. The memories and experiences will stay with you forever.

The Budget

This is a Catch 22 situation. In order to decide how much money you need, you will need to know where you want to go and for how long you want to travel. However, in order to decide how far you can go, you need to decide how much money you need.

So where to start? Determine how much money you will have available to spend and then you can start the process of determining where and for how long you can go away (and whether you will need more money).

Our personal goal was to stay under $60/day for the two of us, plus the occasional extra like scuba diving, Spanish classes or a splurge on a great meal.

Fuel will probably be your biggest expense. With fuel costs averaging over $3.00US/gallon, the more miles you drive in a day translates out directly to higher per day cost. But we've had to rebalance our budget in places where we had to pay upwards of $5.00US a gallon for fuel which means a tank-full kills off a couple of days on the road.

The answer – slow down and take your time. Things tend to balance out when you stop for a few days on that perfect beach and spend money only for cold beers and fresh shrimp. Get the idea? If that means that you only visit one or two countries your first time out, that's OK. It'll just plant the hook to get you out on the road again when you have more time and/or more money.

When trying to decide how much time you have and how far you can go, an easy mistake is to calculate driving times based on US highway-driving speeds. Mexico and several South American countries have toll-roads that are similar to US highways, but many are not maintained to the same grade. The Pan American Highway (*Panamericana*) is mostly two lanes in each direction but most other Mexican and Central American roads are narrow with only one lane in each direction.

Our general rule of thumb is to calculate driving times based on an average of 45 miles per hour. This may sound ridiculously low, but when you take into consideration road quality, food and rest stops as well as photo ops, the time just flies by.

How to Finance Your Adventure

What would you do if you won the lottery? That is a common starting point in many conversations when brainstorming about what you would do if you had the money to do anything. Obviously, to win the lottery you'd first have to actually buy a ticket. And if you wait until you win the lottery to start planning your trip, you might be waiting a VERY long time.

One way to finance your trip is to sell everything you own and then travel for as long as the money holds out. Many people have done this. It probably works best when you are young and have fewer responsibilities.

Another option is to try and save as much money as possible. Reduce your expenses. Eat out less and don't buy the latest and greatest of everything that comes out.

You can also try to pay down your mortgage and rent out your house using some of the money to offset your travel costs.

Our choice was to buy a Laundromat and build it into a business that ran as well when we were traveling as when we were at home. Much of the management of the business could be accomplished via email and online banking services, but we still had to return home every couple of months to "put out the fires" and do the things that only the owner could do.

One of the great things about overland travel is that you don't need to have unlimited funds. Sure it would be nice to have the ultimate, "über vehicle", something so over-the-top that it includes every possible thing you could ever need (or not need, too). But the bottom line is that you only have to spend as much money as you feel comfortable spending.

On the road, there is the cheap method of spending only for the necessities, never eating out and never paying for camping or overnight parking. But this way you may miss out on some wonderful experiences. We prefer to spend money when necessary and conserve our cash by bush-camping, wild camping or free camping – different terms for the same concept.

Start saving today for your overland travel. Cut out one latte a day, don't buy another DVD to add to your collection, buy used paperback books rather than that discounted hard cover at the big-box store. Take the money you save every day and sock it away in a piggy bank, shoe box or even in an actual bank account.

Only you can decide which idea works best for you, but if you make the trip a priority, you can find a way to achieve the dream.

The Route

Planned routes are strange beasts as they actually have a life of their own. If you try to stick to the route, hard and fast, it will control you and cause you grief. Yet without a route, you won't even be able to leave home. Routes are great suggestions, but remember that you have to be flexible. You may find yourself running short of time and having to pass up places, or you may find yourself ahead of schedule and looking for places to spend a few days. You may find new friends with whom you will want to spend extra time, or who may have heard of exciting places to visit that you were unaware of.

Another detail to factor into the route is local festivals. Festivals, holidays, patron saint days and fairs are exciting times to visit. Yes, there will be bigger crowds, but how often will you get a chance to view the locals carrying their patron saint on their shoulders, under the weight of a float that could weigh a thousand pounds. Or you could witness the grandeur of an ancient Inca celebration or the beauty of flower festooned carpets. Be sure to find out if any celebrations will be happening along your intended route. These will be the source of some of your best memories.

In the country-specific chapters we list our favorite places along with suggestions for you to consider when planning your route.

When to Go

The weather is an important factor when planning your route. Be sure to do your research on when to travel in a country and, more importantly, when not to travel. Check out the weather so that you don't arrive in the middle of the wrong season.

One common mistake is thinking that summer is always the best time of year to travel. Instead, do not think in terms of summer or winter but rather in terms of wet and dry.

In the tropics you will have to take into consideration humidity, hurricane season and rainy seasons. These do not always correspond to the standard seasons found in the northern hemisphere.

Guidebooks and Maps

There are numerous guidebooks available that will provide you with a wealth of background as well as tourist information on cities, countries, parks, native animals and birds and just about anything else you can think of. The purpose of this Handbook is to make you feel comfortable and secure enough that you will drive yourself to these wonderful places.

A quick search on the Internet for guidebooks will bring up names like Lonely Planet, Moon, Footprint , Rough Guides or Bradt Guides, as well as dozens of independent guides providing so much good information that you will have difficulty deciding which guides to take with you.

Americas Overland

Most guidebooks are oriented to the independent traveler yet very few will have any information directed to the self-driving traveler. Some guides will even suggest not driving yourself. Hah, you know better than that!

For many countries we took along two different guidebooks so that we would get two views on the places to visit, but also so that we could use their city maps, as country maps don't usually include city maps other than for the largest cities.

Maps

Looking for a good quality road map is like looking for the proverbial needle in a haystack. There are so many different maps available, yet very few are really produced for the overland driver. Most are designed as supplemental to a guidebook for tourist travel.

You need to be able to view a sample of the map before you buy it. For this, the Internet helps tremendously. You may have to look at more than a few sites, but eventually you will find a site that has a sample of the map that can be viewed.

Whenever possible, review and compare maps. Be sure to check out the publication dates. Newer maps are generally better, however some companies have been known to reprint older maps without updating the information.

Look for a map that has the smallest scale. For example, a map that has a scale of 1 to 200,000 will show twice the detail than a map with a scale of 1 to 400,000. With better scale comes better accuracy.

Review the color schemes of the maps to find one that is easy on the eyes and where place names are easily readable. More color can be pretty, but it can make details harder to find when you are driving. You do want to have some topographical detail so that you can see whether your route will be going up or down, but you don't want the elevation lines to confuse you because they look like roads or rivers. Also make sure that your map shows distances.

In some cases, we found maps produced by the transportation or highway departments for a country were better than any map we could find from a map company. Best of all, these maps were free to download and print and can be used to help plan your route.

In other cases, we bought the best or only map available, then looked for maps at every fuel station that we visited. Eventually we would find a supplemental map to buy. Having more than one map for an area comes in handy because, let's face it, not all maps are accurate and it's good to have a second opinion.

When you arrive in the country, you can stop at fuel stations and ask if they have highway maps available. Compare their maps with the one you have brought. If you want you can always purchase a second or even third map as an option.

Despite having maps, directions and even a GPS, you will get lost. It may be just a matter of time but it will happen. Signage is at best, terrible. Much of the time there will not even be a sign, even at major intersections. Just grin and bear it. You might just stumble across some celebration in a small village. Practice your Spanish directional words and ask for directions sooner than later.

In the country sections we list the maps that we used.

The Internet

The Internet is a fabulous reference source. The problem with it is that there is just too much information. You must decide what it is that you are looking for.

There are the travel blogs, the tourism sites, the tour company sites, individual websites, UNESCO and official country tourism sites – just to name a few.

Most sites have something that you might want to use. We like to start our planning with the commercial tourism sites, just to see what they consider to be a country's highlights.

By starting with a computer printed map, we'd highlight the places that are recommended. Then we would search out more details. There might be other nearby sites that would be worth a look, but the big companies avoid them because of time constraints that we don't have.

Personal sites can offer you other routes, camping information, costs of travel, even up-to-date road status. If possible, email the authors with specific questions you have. Travelers are a great source of information, both before you leave home and when you meet on the road.

There is so much information out there that you almost have to set yourself a time limit so that you don't spend all of your time online, reading other people's travel stories.

Our educational website, Adventure Learning Foundation at www.QuestConnect.org has a detailed Internet Resources listing and contains the journals and photographs from our expeditions through Mexico, Central and South America. It is a good place to start your research.

Unpacking supplies after a return trip home

Chapter Three

General Trip Preparation
a. Documents
b. Insurance
c. Visas
d. Carnet De Passage En Douane
e. Language
f. Vehicle Preparation and Equipment
g. GPS

Documents

The decision has been made, you have decided to go and you're working on setting up your route.   Now you've got to take a moment to clear the dreams from your eyes and consider some of the practicalities of travel.

Make a list of the documents you will need to take with you. Here's a list of the personal and vehicle-related documents that we bring.

Passport
Personal insurance documents
Vaccination Card
Driver's License
International Driving License (if required – like for Brazil)
Vehicle Title
Vehicle Registration
Vehicle Insurance documents

We like to use an expanding file folder (what we call the Document Folder) to carry the documents. This way, every time we go through customs and immigration, we are organized and can easily find the documents the official is requesting.

In addition to the originals we take copies of our passports and of all the vehicle-related documents, generally two or three of each for each country to be visited. Having the copies ready ahead of time will save you considerable stress.

Imagine this example, you have just waited in a long line on a hot and humid day only to be told that you need multiple copies of everything and, so sorry, but the copy machine is out of paper – or maybe the line for copies has 10 people waiting. Now you say, no problem, how many copies do you need?

Being prepared will usually impress the customs agent and make the entire border crossing process that much easier.

Then you have your personal documents to consider. Take your Vaccination Card, copies of any lens or medical prescriptions and anything else you think you might need.

Make up some business cards with your name, address and email. Print them on your home computer or order some free ones online. They make exchanging names with the people you meet really easy. They are also helpful when you need to get a business card from someone you are working with, like a customs agent. When you give them a card, they may look at you as someone more important than they originally thought.

Another reason for making copies of your documents is so that you never have to give an original document to the police who stop you on the road – just in case the stop is not legitimate. Our favorite is to make up a set of color copies (five or so) of our driver's licenses and then have them laminated. This will make the copies look more official.

Insurance

There are two categories of insurance to consider, vehicle and personal coverage.

Vehicle Insurance

When it comes to third party liability and comprehensive insurance for your vehicle, you will have to make the difficult choice of whether to purchase it or not. Accidents do happen but fortunately they are rare. It comes down to a personal choice whether or not to spend the money for the coverage. Many countries offer third party liability coverage at their borders and in several countries, coverage is mandatory.

Start with your local agent to find out if he or she can offer international coverage, and then check the Internet. Many North American insurance companies refuse to offer any coverage for vehicles once they have departed the United States. Other companies offer coverage at high rates.

When driving in Mexico, auto insurance is easily obtained at the border. You can even get full coverage similar to that available in the US. Since our vehicle was new, we decided to splurge on full coverage insurance for Mexico. By the time we entered Central America, we felt comfortable driving our beast (what we lovingly called our camper) on various quality roads so we opted to only purchase liability insurance in the Central and South American countries.

For your journey, determine what coverage you need to make you feel comfortable. For countries that require liability insurance, there will usually be a booth offering short-term policies right at the border. These policies are offered with low premiums, but will not cover damage to you or your vehicle.

If you do purchase insurance to cover you during your travels in Central and South America, be sure that somewhere on the insurance document it says what it is in Spanish, *"Seguros Internacional"* should be sufficient.

Personal Insurance
If you have homeowners or renters insurance, check to see if the policy covers your personal possessions out of the country, surprisingly many do. You can also find companies that provide coverage at various rates.

One thing you don't really want to go without is medical coverage. Our option was to keep our medical insurance (it covered us outside the US) to use as a major medical policy with a high deductible, and to purchase a supplemental travel policy to make up the difference should we get sick or injured and require evacuation back home.

Visas

Once you have an idea of what countries you want to visit, go to the US State Department website to check on requirements for tourists. In addition to visa requirements you will find general country background information and security warnings.

Security warnings are just that – warnings. It doesn't mean that everyone will be subjected to the same problems that have been reported. Other than minor pick pocketing, the only crime we've ever been victims of occurred in the United States.

As a direct example of "tit for tat", many countries that never had fees or visa requirements for US citizens now require $100.00 visas to visit their countries. This is due to the fees instituted to help pay for Homeland Security expenses. Grin and bear it, they are a one-time only expense to be amortized over the duration of your journey.

If you need to obtain a visa you can take the time to visit the local embassies or you can hire a company that specializes in obtaining visas. If you don't have a consulate nearby, it may end up being less expensive to hire someone to process the application for you. There are times when you will find that visas can be obtained in neighboring countries or right at the border. This is helpful and saves time.

Taking a chance

We decided to get the visas we needed for Brazil while we were on the road because we found that we had to enter Brazil within 30 days of the visa's issuance. If we had obtained the visas before we departed the US they would have expired before we arrived at the border.

We decided to apply for the visas in Venezuela and hoped that we could get them the same day. First we visited the consulate in Caracas and were told that the process would take at least three days, but if we didn't want to wait, we could get visas at the border. We then tried the consulate in Ciudad Guayana and got the same answer. Neither city held enough appeal for us to spend the extra time in them.

So we took a chance and drove to the border at Santa Elena de Uairén. We showed up at the consulate before it opened so that we would be first in line. When the doors opened, we filled out the visa applications, paid our fees and were told to pick up our passports that afternoon. Whew! And we got the maximum time allowed!

Carnet De Passage En Douane

The Carnet is probably the most misunderstood document that overland travelers encounter. The Carnet has taken on a mystic connotation that compounds the fear and confusion that the name generates.

Even the issuing organizations indicate that they have received conflicting reports as to which countries require the Carnet.

So what is the Carnet? This document is the equivalent of a passport/bond for your vehicle. It is a financial guarantee that you will bring your vehicle back to its home country, and if you don't, then the money put up for the Carnet will be used to pay any duties and import taxes generated by the vehicle's sale in a foreign country.

For residents of North America, the only authorized issuer is the CAA – Canadian Automobile Association. For a fee of about $500.00 per year, the CAA will issue you a Carnet covering your vehicle.

However the fee is not the issue. The real expense is that you will have to post a cash bond for the value of the taxes due should your vehicle be sold based on the book value as determined by the CAA. In some countries that bond can be as high as 150% of the value of your vehicle. If your vehicle is older this won't be too big a problem, but if you have a new vehicle the cost can be prohibitive.

If you are lucky and can convince your bank to prepare it, a Letter of Credit will be accepted to cover your deposit. Now for the good news.

As of January 1, 2008 there were no countries in Central America that required overland travelers to hold a Carnet.

The issue in South America is slightly more confusing. The list of countries, used by the CAA, that require a Carnet show that Uruguay and Paraguay do, while a "deposit of duty" is required for Guyana. Other travelers have reported that they have not been required to show a Carnet when crossing land borders into these countries. Be sure to check the current status before you leave your home. Telephone the CAA for their current list and then telephone the consulates of those countries requiring a Carnet for verification. Once you have verbal confirmation, follow up your conversation with a letter or email to the person you spoke with requesting the confirmation in writing, preferably in Spanish. This way you have something in writing to show a border guard in case of a dispute.

Speaking personally, the expense and inconvenience of obtaining a Carnet makes travel to these countries less than appealing. We have not driven through these countries yet, but for reasons other than not having a Carnet.

If you want to visit and get refused entry with your vehicle, you can always arrange a secure parking option for your vehicle while you cross over for the day or for a more extended period. Tour companies and hotels are willing to work with you regarding temporary storage of your vehicle. Some times you can even park your vehicle at the border police station.

The remaining countries in South America, we know from personal experience, do not require a Carnet.

Language

Spanish is the most common language in Latin America (with the exception of Brazil where they speak Portuguese). This doesn't mean that you shouldn't go if you don't *"habla español"*. We know many travelers who have spent months or even a year south of the border never learning Spanish.

However, we think this is foolish as well as disrespectful. You are going south to experience the culture and to explore the countries. You should at the very least learn a handful of words and greetings.

Even better, should you have the time, spend a week or more in an intensive Spanish language class during your travels. There are many good schools to choose from. Pick an interesting city and stay for a couple of weeks. Maybe San Miguel de Allende, Mexico or maybe Antigua, Guatemala, Bocas del Toro, Panama or maybe even Buenos Aires, Argentina or Santiago, Chile.

Gaining the confidence to ask questions and understand the answers is wonderful. Besides, a little Spanish goes a long way to simplifying your border crossings and to generate a smile during negotiations for your presents and souvenirs.

Be sure to purchase an English – Spanish dictionary, and an English – Portuguese one if you plan to visit Brazil. It is much better to get them before you leave the US. It took us nearly two weeks of looking in different Brazilian cities before we found even a very basic dictionary. Don't leave home without one.

Vehicle Preparation and Equipment

The type of equipment you will need to take, can again, only be determined only by you. While some self-rescue equipment is always good to have, don't be fooled into buying items that you don't really need. There are lots of things that you can buy, but you need to look at where you want to go and what you want to do before handing over any cold hard cash.

If you won't be doing any off-roading, you won't need a lot of self-rescue equipment. A tool kit, some spare parts, a tow strap, a tire repair kit, jumper cables and a small compressor should be all you need. You won't even need any spare fuel containers because fuel is readily available on the main roads and in lots of small towns. Make sure that you have a tire jack and a strong lug wrench.

If you are going to spend a lot of time driving on sand, a good pair of sand rails (we use Maxtrax) and a 100% duty air compressor (for airing up your tires after you've deflated them) will be very important. A good tow strap is always important to have, not only to get you unstuck, but to help the other guy. We always stop and help because we never know when it's going to be we who needs the assistance.

If you plan to do major off-road excursions you will probably want to consider having a winch and a high-lift jack along with a jack plate and extra containers of fuel. The winch is just an option and we do not have one. We concluded that the times that we were most likely to get stuck would be in sand and that it was unlikely there would be a large tree or substantial anchor strong enough to attach to.

Other basic equipment that might come in handy is a shovel and an ax.

Your choice in what vehicle you drive will dictate which extra parts you will want to take with you. If you are driving a new vehicle, you most likely will only need extra filters. Oil and other fluids are readily available.

For an older vehicle you may want to take a whole shopping list of parts: alternator, brake shoes, master cylinder and other hard-to-find parts.

If you are planning to update your vehicle with new parts before you leave home, consider keeping your old parts and bringing them along as spares. You already know that they work and fit on your vehicle. You can also pick up used parts from an auto wrecker, as long as you verify that they work on your vehicle before you pack it up in your supply box. Imagine how you'd feel when you're in the middle of nowhere and you find that your spare part doesn't fit on your vehicle or doesn't work.

For all vehicles you should consider having some emergency repair items. A basic list should include: tire puncture repair kit, hose repair kit, fan belt repair kit and some liquid gasket. Why get stranded someplace if you can do a simple repair that will get you to the next garage?

If you think you will need some piece of equipment and you have the space to carry it, then take it along. Think of that equipment as insurance. If you have it, you probably won't need it but if you leave it home you will definitely need it.

Some states in the US do not require a front license plate yet you will find that most foreign countries do require one. This is to make the job of the police easier in identifying your vehicle. Coming from Arizona, we only had a rear license plate. Originally we made a second plate up by scanning our license plate and printing a color copy of it, then laminating it in plastic.

We had planned to place this "front plate" on our dashboard. We knew from past experience that placement of the plate in the front window was acceptable in Mexico. But what we ended up doing was finding a company that printed "novelty" plates for vehicles. We found a design that was the same as the Arizona license plates only in a slightly different color. For less than $10.00 we had a metal plate that we installed on the front bumper of our vehicle.

One simple yet very important piece of equipment that is all too often forgotten is a well placed "hide-a-key" container and a couple of spare keys. You may never lock yourself out, but what would be the consequence if you did?

> **Locked Out**
> Don't take the chance of getting locked out of your vehicle like we did. We went swimming and accidentally took the wrong key. When we got back to the vehicle, we were lucky to find that we had left a window ajar and were able to borrow a ladder to climb through, all this while wearing our bathing suits! After that, we got a "hide-a-key", just a plastic box with a very strong

> magnet, in which we placed a key for both the cab and the camper and secured it to a safe spot that we felt could not be found. This is very cheap security that will save you time and money in the long run.

A list of our equipment and supplies are provided for reference purposes in Chapter 24 – The Information Index.

GPS

If you are considering taking along a GPS unit then we will presume you know how they work and that you know how to use your unit. As part of the Internet research that we discussed earlier, you have probably identified websites of other overlanders (people who drive vehicles vs backpackers) who have traveled at least a portion of the route you are considering. Many overlanders like to keep a list of GPS points from their travels.

Like us, many of them will have a list of their camping locations in GPS format. Finding the way to some of these camping locations without a GPS might still be possible but would be more difficult.

Others may include useful information such as propane filling stations, good restaurants and maybe interesting sites to visit. Generally speaking, you do not need GPS locations for most archaeological or tourist sites as most guidebooks will have specific location information detailed for you.

In some places, having GPS waypoints for routes are not just helpful but absolutely necessary. One example is the Southwest Circuit in Bolivia which includes crossing the Salar de Uyuni, the largest salt lake in the world. Without waypoints you could easily go astray and end up breaking through the salt crust getting you and your vehicle stranded days away from rescue.

If you are familiar with using a GPS in the US, you have likely used a unit with maps to help you find your way. Once you leave the US, finding reliable GPS maps for Central and South America becomes more difficult. As time goes by and the demand for GPS maps grows, you will find more mapping options becoming available. One option is to look for European GPS websites as there seem to be more mapping options available from them.

Consider bringing along a compass in addition to your GPS. You can use the compass when you are stopped, and it can be a handy backup if your GPS fails. If you'll be using a GPS, make sure that you have a 12v connection so that you can plug it into your vehicle and leave it on whenever you are driving.

A good place to start your research into GPS points is the database accumulated by Doug and Stephanie Hackney at www.hackneys.com/travel/index-gpssawaypoints.htm.

The Equator in Brazil

To convert GPS coordinates into or out of Degrees/ Minutes/Seconds, Degrees/Minutes, or Decimal Degrees use a good GPS Coordinate Calculator like the one found on Road Notes at www.roadnotes.com/gpscalc.htm

Chapter Four

Day to Day Life on the Road
   a. Road Quality
   b. Rules of the Road
   c. Night Driving
   d. Police
   e. Food & Water
   f. Camping
   g. Toilets & Gray Water
   h. Health
   i. Laundry
   j. Money
   k. Local Customs
   l. Communications
   m. Vehicle Repairs
   n. Security & Safety

Road Quality

The quality of the roads that you will encounter will
cover the entire spectrum of what is possible. Modern
highways and toll roads are always a surprise but are
common, especially around major cities. But just
because you'll be paying for the privilege of driving on
the road, don't expect it to be in great condition or to be
free of potholes.

You will be sharing the roads with more than just other
vehicles. Expect horses and donkeys, ox-carts, bicycles
and push carts. There can and will be, animals on the
road as well as rocks, branches, trash and who knows
what. Sometimes that branch or rock will be a warning

to you of a disabled vehicle on the road ahead, just around that blind turn. And then there is our favorite – missing sewer and manhole covers. If you're lucky someone will have taken the time to stick a branch into it as a warning, but most times there is just a gaping, vehicle eating hole in the middle of your lane.

The most common type of roadway is the basic two lane paved or chip-sealed road with no shoulder and barely wide enough for two buses to pass each other. These roads are usually the main highways.

In many places, especially in mountainous regions and in remote regions like Patagonia, the main road is gravel – what the locals call *ripio*. *Ripio* is subject to extreme washboard or corrugation conditions. In some places even reducing the air pressure in your tires won't help to make driving a smooth experience. Sometimes we've had to drive as slow as 10mph for an hour or more.

Wrecked in Patagonia
Have you ever been in that frozen moment of time, when you understand that disaster is on top of you, no avoiding it. Time really does slow down. Or maybe time doesn't slow down at all. Maybe it's slow because looking back on things later, that is the moment when it went wrong. You can recall that precise second when it was very clear that you were in trouble.

Rewinding from that instant you second-guess what could have been done differently. Going forward, the disaster plays out second by second, feeling, light, pain. And you run it again and again in your mind with macabre fascination, like picking a scab, to understand this thing that has upset the world as you know it and scattered all the plans so carefully laid.

The day after Christmas, just after crossing the border from Chile back into Argentina, on a gravel road in an empty stretch of Patagonia, the Land Rover rolled.

Five kilometers after the border on a sharp right turn with a soft gravel shoulder, in seconds, the accident played out. "Don't turn so hard!" "Huh?" The Land Rover slid briefly in the loose gravel shoulder and then, the front wheels bit and it tumbled. Rolling over onto the left side, the driver's side, CRASH, and then CRASH again as we came to rest on the roof.

We owe so much to the many people that helped us out in the next couple of hours. Four Israeli travelers in a pickup saw Jody walking and picked her up. They came to the accident scene, helped us gather a few things, and took us to the Argentine border post. The soldiers at the border post virtually adopted us. Gently cleaning Guin's wounds, another of the guys dashed back to the truck to pick up Jody and most of our packed luggage.

They fed us, gave us their best chairs, and threw some more logs on the fire to warm us up. I went back with two soldiers to the truck and we tried to flip it over, no luck. A passing farmer saw our problem and got his two sons. We tied ropes around the truck and it eased it upright, changed the two blown tires, hauled the roof rack back on and towed the thing to the border post - one truck in front and one behind to brake.

Jeff Wilner, from www.Junglerunner.com
Overland Expedition Consulting

Many countries are actively working to improve their roads. Unfortunately this often means that you will be driving through miles of construction work. The good news is that if you ask the locals along your route, they may be able to direct you onto either new roads or

newly paved roads. Inquiring about the conditions of
your route is helpful especially when venturing into
remote regions. Truck drivers and taxi drivers may be
the best source of road conditions.

The bad news is that locals are always trying to be
helpful and may not really know the conditions of the
roads where you want to go. We have been told by
police, the people who you would expect to have the
best road information, that a road was paved only to find
that the pavement ran out halfway to our destination
and the remainder of the drive was under construction.

We have also found that federal roads will generally be
in better condition than the roads that pass through
cities or villages. Don't be surprised if the good road
you've been driving on turns into a pitted mess when
you reach the municipal limits.

When visiting colonial towns consider the size of your
vehicle before attempting to drive into the city center.
These towns were built before motorized vehicles were
even thought possible. The roadways are extremely
narrow, the paving is often cobblestone rather than
asphalt and roofs often overhand the road! Look up and
you might see damaged rooflines overhanging that
perfect parking spot.

Part of the attraction of these colonial towns is the lovely
landscaping. Yet once again, old trees reach over the
roads only to be pruned by passing trucks, buses and
unaware tourists.

After getting stuck in one of these towns, you will find
that just as in battle, discretion is the better part of valor.

Find a parking spot outside of the colonial center and take a bus or taxi into town.

Rules of the Road

When driving in Mexico, Central and South America remember to always be watchful. You should never expect things to be as familiar as they are at home, and always expect the unexpected.

Drive slower than you do at home. The roads are rarely in as good of condition as you'd like. Beware of surprises and more importantly remember that you are traveling to enjoy the countries, not just to get through to the other side. You can see a lot more at 50 mph than at 70 mph, enjoy the drive!

Different road rules apply outside of the United States. Sure the laws are pretty much the same, but it's whether they are enforced by the police or are just considered to be merely suggestions by local drivers.

On the highway, anticipate that there might be an oncoming car, bus or even truck in your lane as you enter a curve. Just because they are unable to see on-coming traffic is not a good enough reason for them not to overtake another car or to avoid that massive hole in the pavement. Besides, they reason, the oncoming car can always pull over onto the shoulder to let them go by. Quite often the rule of the road is that the biggest vehicle has the right of way.

And what does that turn signal really mean? Is that vehicle turning or is the driver telling you it's safe to pass? In many of the countries south of the border, drivers use their turn signals to indicate to drivers behind when it is safe to pass. Never pull out blindly based on this information, but use it as a guide and acknowledge the other driver after you have safely passed. And remember that some countries use the left blinker and others use the right. Got it?

City driving is completely different. Take your relaxed driving mentality and toss it out the window. City driving can be total chaos. In time you will develop the same skills as the locals, and you'll be surprised to find that you can squeeze into that "extra" lane too. Courtesy often means that other drivers will stop to let you go only after you have pulled out and blocked their vehicle.

Just relax, take a deep breath and go for it. In no time at all you will be prepared for anything and everything. You will have one of the greatest experiences of your life.

An Unfortunate Lunch Stop

Looking for a lunch stop in Peru these drivers found a promising flat area off to the side of the road. This driver pulled in and then reversed to make room for the second vehicle. As the van gently tipped over onto its side, the driver radioed to the second van: "I think I've fallen off the road".

Although the driver was then suspended by the seat belt in the cab, she was unhurt and still in excellent humor! The van engine was still running and the rear wheels were turning in mid-air.

But what tipped the van over? The answer was: a deep drainage ditch that had been virtually invisible to see from even from a few meters away.

The police arrived on the scene soon after. Spare tires were placed under the side of the van and a chain was attached to a large truck then strung around the up-in-the-air front axle of the van and quick as a blink, the vehicle was upright and out of the ditch.

Was the vehicle ok? It is almost unbelievable, but yes it was. It was still drivable as it had not lost any fluids, and the bodywork, though dented, was in far better condition than might be expected. Inside not even one egg was broken and the only casualties were a spilled saltshaker and a butter dish that landed on a cushion.

One necessary skill to develop is what we call "slalom driving". This is the art of avoiding potholes in the roadway. After a while you will become quite skillful in this driving method and will laugh as you see the oncoming vehicles driving the same way.

And while you may be driving on the wrong side of road to avoid a vehicle sized hole, the truck coming towards you will be doing the same thing on your side of the road. Just don't try to pass each other on the wrong side of the road! Also be aware of vehicles catching up to you from behind, as they will sometimes try to pass you while you are doing the slalom. We have unintentionally cut off drivers who tried to pass without giving us any warning.

Night Driving

Our recommendation? Don't do it. Most roads are not lit at night and all those obstacles that you avoided during the day are still there, but now you can't see them, and besides, isn't this supposed to be fun? Driving in the dark is not fun.

Yet despite your best efforts, at some point you will find yourself on the road after dark or maybe with an early departure before sunrise. Just slow down, maybe you'll be able to follow another vehicle, or you'll just turn on all of your driving lights and illuminate the road like it was daylight. If possible, look for an overnight parking or camping spot as quickly as possible. Driving that extra hour just isn't worth the risk.

Police

Expect that you will have more interactions with the police than you ever had at home. This does not mean that your experiences will be bad. Nor does it mean that you will be continuously stopped for false reasons, harassed or asked for bribes. These things do happen, but they are rare and getting rarer.

Ask around and you will hear stories about bad cops, we probably all have one. But if you ask for good experiences, you will hear many. The largest cities are usually the setting for the stories about the police asking for bribes.

Out in the country we have had nothing but good experiences with the local police. Remember, overlanders are the exception to their "usual". Our vehicles look different and we may be camping overnight in places where nobody else does. This inevitably calls attention to us and invites the occasional visit from the authorities.

Just be polite, shake their hand and introduce yourself. You'll get the normal questions, where are you from, where are you going, how long will you stay, do you like our country, etc. Ask them about the town, for restaurant recommendations or places to visit.

The same goes for police or military checkpoints. The checkpoints are there to keep the roads safe by establishing a police presence in the area.

But just in case, never give up your original documents when asked. Always give them a photocopy so you don't have to worry about getting stuck paying to get your document back. With a copy, you know that you have the upper hand.

Food

As surprising as it may sound, many people consider developing countries so backward that they are surprised to find that there is food available to eat or purchase. One very common question that we get asked is "What do you eat there?" Our reply is – we eat just about anything.

So where can you buy food to prepare? Most cities have supermarkets (*supermercados*). In the bigger cities, you can find large western-style markets full of choices. Some cities will have *hipermercados* that could easily compete with Wal-Mart for size and selection of products. In fact, these *hipermercados* may take HOURS to get through.

The most common type of market will generally be the generic *supermercados*. Now, not every store called a *supermercado* will be big, or even have much choice, but they will probably have what you are looking for, or at least enough for a dinner and breakfast.

Whenever possible, we prefer to buy bread products from the bakery (*panadería*), vegetables from the local outdoor marketplace (*mercado*) and meat from the butcher (*carnecería*). We prefer to interact with the locals and we feel that we get a fresher product from these smaller businesses. But when there is a western style supermarket available, it is usually where we head first because of the variety of choices.

The outdoor markets or municipal marketplaces are not just great places to shop; they are one of the experiences not to be missed. The local growers and sellers are interesting and eager to talk, the fruit and vegetable displays are fresh and colorful and this is your opportunity to see exactly where your meat comes from. These markets are so fascinating that you will search them out to do your shopping.

Whether buying food in the *hipermercados* or the local shop, vegetables and fruit should be washed thoroughly in a lightly soapy mix and rinsed with purified water and if possible peeled as well. We also wash off our meat before cooking.

How about those little food stalls you'll find on the street or in the street markets, if the food edible? Yes! Most of the food has been bought right there in the market that morning and you can see that it is being cooked just for your order. We like to find a restaurant stall that is busy with other customers. That way we feel more confident that the food is constantly being turned over and what we get will be fresh. Sometimes we'll even wait at the busiest stall until a couple of seats open up.

Eating in the Marketplace
One of our favorite things to do when we travel is to eat in the local marketplace. In Oaxaca, we had one of our best experiences. Walking through the market, we came upon a stall where people were eating *carne asada* tacos. Thinking that they looked good, we decided to try a meal.

When we indicated to the cook what we wanted, he told us that he only had the meat, and that we needed to gather the other ingredients from other vendors. Telling him that we'd be back, we set out to find the tortilla seller, the vegetable seller and the drink seller. Finally assembling everything we needed, we headed back to the original stall and gave the cook our ingredients.

He proceeded to cook everything up for us on his grill. The ingredients included thin slices of beef, small chorizo sausages and grilled green onions and peppers, slathered onto fresh cooked tortillas. With all the other customers watching to see how we would react to this meal, we dug into it with relish and had one of our best market lunches ever.

Typical local dishes like *ceviche* – raw seafood – can also be very tasty and safe to eat, but try to get it early in the day and from a busy food stall.

If you have some special foods that you like to eat and know that you don't want to go without, be sure to take some along with you. Not all types of food or drink are easily found outside of North America. You don't need to bring along a case of anything but having a bit of comfort food can make any experience, good or bad, better.

To provide yourselves with more choice for preparing your food, try to find space to bring along a small BBQ, either gas or charcoal. If you clean it and store it in a plastic bag, you will find that even a disposable BBQ can last for months. Charcoal is available in the larger markets of nearly every country. Don't count on finding wood to burn as many of the local cultures collect firewood to use or sell, although you may be able to buy wood from them. It is just easier to buy charcoal.

With our limited space we decided not to include an oven as we would lose two drawers from our kitchen.

We have found that this is not a detriment as we use a small gas BBQ that can be connected directly into our gas line through a special split fitting.

In addition we rely heavily on a pressure cooker to prepare thicker cuts of meat, like ribs or roasts and squash and beans. Pressure cookers are great time savers which also translates into using less propane, thus extending the period between tanks fills.

Don't forget to include some money for eating out in your budget. This way you can ask for the *comida corrida* or *comida criolla* or the equivalent of the meal of the day.

This is what the locals are eating and it is the best way to sample the local dishes inexpensively. Once in a while you may not want what you end up with, but chances are it will be a quick and tasty dish.

By the way, don't forget to bring along a cookbook or two so that you can fix a few new meals to spice up your day.

Water

There are several choices for carrying drinking water. You can buy water in plastic bottles of up to several gallons at most markets. Or you can fill up with tap water, chlorinate it and/or pump it through a purifier. We have even filled our water tank with river water!

We would recommend that you use regular household bleach to kill any contaminants in the water you fill up with. The recommended dose is one teaspoon of bleach for every 10 gallons of water. Iodine is another option but we feel that it gives a bad taste to the water. Using a water purifier simplifies things immensely. This permits you to fill up from just about any water source. We have used water taps at fuel stations, hotels, marinas, private residences, churches and parks. The purifier will also remove any bleach you add to the water.

There are many types of water purifiers on the market. A good choice is one that has a dedicated counter faucet to use. When attached to the water pump in your vehicle, it will provide good clean water. Carry a spare filter too. We have used Nature-Pure water purifiers by General Ecology for over 15 years with no ill effects.

If you are going to use local water, you will need a holding tank. Our water tank holds 60 gallons as we can easily go through 5 or 10 gallons of water per day. Before you leave home, purchase a couple of inline water filters for your fill hose. After letting water run through the spigot for a 10 count, (to dislodge any insects or other undesirables) attach the filter right to the spigot to remove any large impurities or sand from the water. We use these filters even when filling up with water in the US as some communities and campgrounds use well water and can have sediment that can clog your sink filters. You should carry a hose that you can dedicate only for drinking water.

If you will be using your own hose, be sure to get adaptors for various size faucets. Depending on the size of your hose bib, you should carry adaptors in ½", ¾" and 1" that you can screw onto your hose and any faucet. We also carry an attachment called a "hose thief" that allows us to attach to faucets that have no hose threads or where the threads have been damaged or stripped. Carry several screened washers that you can use between the faucets and your filter. No reason to clog an expensive filter if you can catch debris in a cheap screen.

Camping

South of Mexico it is difficult to find anything that resembles an American RV campground. That said there are numerous options for overnight camping or parking.

Be aware that south of Mexico the word camping is usually understood to refer to sleeping in a tent. If you ask for permission to camp somewhere that isn't a camping area, you will likely be turned down. However if you ask only for a place to park for the night you will receive permission. So remember that if you are self-contained, you are not camping, just parking overnight.

Some of the types of places available are: restaurant parking lots, fuel stations, hotel parking lots, church parking lots, police stations, schools and soccer fields. There is wild camping or bush camping on beaches or on small side roads away from the highway. And there is city camping, which is basically parking on a city street under a street light, near a police station, or in a public or private parking lot.

If you are camping on private property, always ask permission to park overnight and agree on a price that you will pay. This reduces the possibility of being charged a higher fee in the morning.

When visiting a city we prefer to find a private parking lot if we plan to spend a large portion of the day in town. Then, if it gets late, we just stay overnight in the parking lot, maybe for free or for just a couple of extra dollars. Not only is this option cheap, it is usually centrally located and includes security. As a bonus, there are often water taps available for topping off our water supply and a toilet to dump our cassette into.

When is a No not a No?

When an employee seems uncertain as to whether to give you permission to park for the night, ask to speak to the manager. When they say "the manager isn't here right now", ask them to telephone him/her so you can ask for permission. When they say "the manager doesn't have a phone", ask when will the manager be back? When they say "he/she won't be back until tomorrow", say "OK, I'll just park out of the way down there and ask the manager when he shows up". At this point walk away. This works well in large complexes where you can park out of their sight, or look around for the *vigilancia,* the security guard and introduce yourself and ask him where would be the best place to park.

This may sound outrageous, but after a long day driving and a dearth of other camping options you may just not want to accept the fact that someone won't take responsibility and let you spend the night. And what usually happens is that the desk clerk's shift will end and their replacement will just accept the fact that since you are already there, you are OK. Of course, if they ask you to leave, do so politely, but our experience has been that if you aren't in the way, they won't bother you.

Wild or bush camping is our favorite. While our friends at home think that we are pushing the limits by camping alone on some dark beach or in the middle of nowhere, the quiet and the view of the stars are astounding. Besides, we feel that if someone is out and about looking for someone to bother, the chances are they will not be going into the middle of nowhere because people generally aren't found there. They will look for easier targets closer to home.

So if you find that you are in the middle of nowhere in need of a camp spot and the day is getting late, look for a small dirt side road or track leading away from the road. Try to get far enough away from the road that your vehicle can't be seen. If you can't get that far away, remember that it'll be dark soon and then you'll be pretty much invisible from the road. Additionally, traffic really dies off at night, as the locals don't like to drive at night any more than you do.

Some times your camp spot may not be ideal and you may have radios, dogs or even roosters keeping you awake. At times like these you can shut out the noise by using foam earplugs. These are readily available in the US at any pharmacy.

Toilets and Gray Water

Regardless of the type of vehicle you plan to drive on your journey overland, you should consider taking some type of a toilet. If you are in a small camper, a van or even a car, you should consider a small porta-potty. Having some kind of toilet facility will grant you greater flexibility in where you can spend the night.

Not having to rely on finding a camping ground or service station enables you to spend extra time just about anywhere. You can also have greater peace of mind knowing that you are not contaminating a great camping spot for the next people who follow you. This may sound like a difficult thing to do, especially when you see other people not being considerate or because you find a spot already dirty, but that doesn't mean that it should be OK for you to add to the mess.

For those of you traveling in self-contained vehicles, you will probably have both a gray-water and black-water holding tank. Do yourself a favor and try to drain the gray-water tank on a daily basis. Again, don't dump in your camping spot or in front of someone's home, find some other more appropriate (remote) place to do this.

The black-water tank will be more difficult to empty. Your best choice is to empty the tank every few days using some type of 5 gallon container that you can transfer the contents of the tank into, then carry (or roll) that container into a toilet to dump. A ten-gallon container may sound like a better solution, but remember that a ten-gallon container full of waste may weigh as much as 100lbs (45k). Save your back and use a smaller container.

Another option is to carry a portable macerator RV waste pump that connects directly to your RV's waste outlet. This enables you to dump at longer distances and directly into a toilet via a garden hose discharge port. They aren't supposed to be messy as they are self-cleaning and use a remote on/off switch.

Also, remember to leave your formaldehyde-based chemicals at home. Many toilets outside of North America are on septic systems and the chemicals will adversely affect their efficiency. Use some type of oxidizer or other "green" toilet treatment.

Don't even consider doing a "jungle dump" where you dump the tank on the side of road or some other inappropriate spot. Think about the contamination you would be creating.

Health

There are a number of books written specifically on the topic of staying healthy while traveling so we will not go into specifics on the diseases and illnesses that you might be exposed to while traveling. The best place to get a handle on illnesses and necessary vaccinations would be the Center for Disease Control (CDC). Their website has a country-by-country discussion.

Basic good health while traveling begins with good hygiene. While it is not necessary to go overboard with cleanliness, at a minimum be sure to keep your hands clean. For us, we keep a small bottle of hand sanitizer in the cab. That way when we stop at a restaurant we can be sure that our hands are clean when we eat.

The hand sanitizer also comes in handy when out shopping in the markets. You'll be handling lots of used money that has been handled by the vendors and butchers. It isn't uncommon that the same person who just cut your chops or handled your chicken, will take your money and give you change without so much as wiping their hands! We've been known to have them drop the money into the same bag as the food, and then wash it off when we get back to our vehicle.

If you get sick or injured while on the road you'll be comforted to know that there are competent doctors and clinics to be found in almost every community. If a doctor isn't to be found, the pharmacist is a good back up. They usually have some medical training and can sell you appropriate medication for most illnesses.

You should prepare a good first aid kit and know how to use the items. Consider enrolling in a basic first aid course as part of your trip preparation. If you don't have the time, buy a first aid guide to use as a reference. Remember to read it before you actually need it. If you wait until there is an injury, the stress you'll encounter will make it difficult to find the section you are in need of.

Carry a couple of cold packs or ice packs in your fridge and freezer. They come in handy for that occasional smashed thumb when you are doing a repair or changing a tire.

If you are planning to go explore well off the beaten track consider taking along some type of medical book with more detailed information than your first aid manual. We carry the book _Where There Is No Doctor_ as our reference manual. In years of travel we have never had to use the information to treat ourselves or any injured local. It's just good to be prepared.

Laundry

Laundromats (*lavamaticas*) as known in North America are hard to find in Mexico, Central and South America. It is much more common for the laundries, the *lavanderías*, to be a drop-off laundry facility. You drop off your clothes and pick them up later in the day or the next day. The best option is to have your laundry done in places where you will be spending a couple of days. We've even dropped off laundry and picked it up several days later when we backtracked through town.

Just be sure to check and verify that you have all of your clothes returned before you drive away. Sometimes an item may be misplaced but is likely to be sitting forgotten in the shop.

On a day-to-day basis, we find that washing a few personal items makes laundry day more manageable and helps to extend that major drop-off laundry day a bit further off.

Creative options for doing small amounts of laundry abound. We've learned to have a small container or bucket with a top that we can fill with water and detergent and a few clothing items. Then the container can be placed in the bathroom, tied to the bumper or strapped to the roof, using the motion of the car to agitate and wash the clothes. At lunch, empty the soapy water, put in the rinse water and at the end of the day you can hang the clothes up on a line to dry.

We've also heard of the hand washer where you use a toilet plunger (clean, of course) to agitate your clothes in the bucket. This helps to save your back rather than if you washed everything by hand.

Bathing

If you are not in a self-contained vehicle that includes a bathroom, you must find places to bathe. In Argentina this is easy as most towns have free or inexpensive municipal camping grounds. If you are bush camping you can use a solar shower. In other countries large fuel stations are truck stops and have shower facilities for truckers that you can use.

If there are no truck stops, you can often find hotels that will let you park on their grounds and use a shower in a room for a nominal price. When all else fails, spend the night at a backpacker hostel and use their facilities.

Money & ATMs

Long gone are the days of the good old "don't leave home without them", traveler's checks. Fortunately, the proliferation of ATMs throughout the Americas has made it simple to get money almost anytime you need it.

While you are making your other plans for this trip, open a bank account at a bank that will reimburse you or credit your account for ATM fees from other banks. There are many institutions that will do this to attract your business. At $5.00 a pop, these fees can add up and cost you several days traveling expenses. And check your guidebook for information on what types of cards and passwords (usually 4 digits) are accepted.

The other important thing to do is to give yourself at least two months time to set up, get familiar with and make sure that your bank's online banking system works for you. Setting up your regular expenses to be paid by automatic billing (EFT) saves you the worry that a bill will not be paid while you are on the road.

If having a stash of traveler's checks handy makes you feel more comfortable, by all means do it. But they are becoming more and more obsolete and difficult to cash.

And you should always have some cold hard cash available in reserves that you can exchange at borders or use when you just have a day or so left to travel in a country. Building in a hidden safe in your vehicle is an excellent idea. Using a locking box like those from Tuffy Products works well.

We would also recommend taking along at least two different credit cards and ATM cards. This will give you flexibility in purchasing items and in obtaining cash. Credit cards come in very handy should your vehicle require major repairs.

Purchases outside of your home country can trigger fraud alerts with your bank causing the bank to freeze your card. Be sure to call each bank whose credit card or ATM card you are carrying, **before** you leave home, and notify them that you will be traveling out of the country and may be using your card.

Respect Local Customs

How you choose to conduct yourself in a foreign country is obviously up to you. But here are some tips that we feel will be helpful.

Photography
Please remember that not everyone likes to have their photo taken, especially members of some indigenous cultures. While you might be dying to have that perfect photo of the colorful people in their traditional clothing, these people are not on display and sticking a camera in their face is considered rude and sometimes culturally inappropriate.

However, if you would like to take a photo, for example, of a woman working at a colorful food stall, purchase something and ask for permission to take a photo. More often than not she will agree. She may even smile. However, indiscriminately walking through an outdoor market taking photos may get rotten food thrown at you. If you want to take photos of the general scene, try to be discreet.

Always be careful about taking photos of children. Some parents can be very touchy so make sure you ask their permission. Some people may want to charge you a fee to take their picture. It is up to you how you want to handle that, however we feel paying sets a bad precedent and makes it difficult for travelers who follow.

Environment
Regardless of how you see the locals treating the environment, you should always treat it with respect. Always place trash in a proper receptacle, even if this

means carrying it around with you for a couple of days (gas stations always have trash receptacles). This includes "bio-degradable" trash like orange peels and apple cores. Always dump your gray water and black water appropriately. Never show the locals that you do not respect them or their community by trashing it.

Actions

Respect the locals also by showing them that you care what they think about you. Dress appropriately for the area that you are going to be in. Try to be clean and neat. In most big cities, people dress nicely. In small villages, most people dress more conservatively.

There are always exceptions of course, like the young women who dress very scantily to try to attract attention, however it may not go over very well with the locals if the scantily clad person is you. Especially in indigenous villages, long pants and loose fitting shirts are more appropriate. When visiting churches or places of worship, remove any hats and take your cue on how to act by watching what the locals do.

Treat all officials with respect if you expect to be treated respectfully in return.

Please do not give candy or other unhealthful gifts to children (or adults). If you would like to share something with them, try offering fruit. As you will undoubtedly find, giving items away (such as candy or gifts) gives the recipient the impression that you have money to burn and prompts the recipient to ask every traveler following for something. Refrain from giving money to beggars. If you really feel that they are in need and you want to help, try offering food or unneeded clothing.

In some areas, children (or adults) may offer to watch your vehicle for you while you shop or wander around town. We usually pay about 50 cents.

Children, especially, may follow you around asking over and over again for *"un peso"* or some other small amount of money. Do not give into the temptation to give them money just to make them go away. This will only perpetuate their belief that travelers can be pestered into giving them something, making it that much harder on the next traveler who follows you.

Tipping
Tipping for service is appropriate in some areas and not done in other areas. Consult your guidebook. Check your restaurant bill, as service charges may automatically have been included.

Often times you are expected to tip small change to the child who packs your bags at the grocery store and the fellow who washes your window at the gas station and it is always appropriate to offer a dollar or two to a security guard who watches over your vehicle at night.

Bargaining
Negotiating is an art and is not to be taken lightly. A lot of times you will feel that the item you are interested in is already so ridiculously low priced, you would be insulting the person by trying to negotiate. Not so. Negotiating is a time-honored tradition and is expected in many places.

Always decide beforehand how much you want to pay and start someplace lower. You will quickly get a feel for how interested the seller is in making a sale. Don't be surprised if after you decide against negotiating any further and turn away, the merchant comes after you with a lower price.

If you are unaccustomed to bargaining you can start out by asking the merchant for their best price. This will usually result in a reduced asking price.

As we mentioned previously, never behave in a manner that you wouldn't behave in at home. Don't be a target. Don't get drunk and walk down dark alleys. Don't pick up strangers. Don't flash large wads of money and don't wear flashy jewelry.

Communications:
Cellular and satellite phones, phone-cards and the Internet

Telephones
You will need to have a GSM cellular telephone in order to make and receive calls and text messages.

With the type of coverage and companies that provide cellular coverage constantly changing, it would be worthwhile to check with your phone carrier to see if they can help obtain coverage for you. At the time of research only AT&T and T-Mobile were offering GSM network coverage in the United States.

If you have your own phone and have service with a US based cellular company you will need to notify them that you need international coverage and they will add this service your line. You will get charged high rates for this service.

If you own your own GSM phone, be sure that it is a quad-band phone as different countries use different bandwidths. A quad-band phone will be able to access the networks in all GSM countries, pending arrival of the next generation GSM.

Owning your own unlocked telephone will also give you the option of buying prepaid services in each country you travel through.

An alternate option is to purchase disposable pay-as-you go telephones in each country that you visit. However this option can quickly become very expensive.

Satellite Phones
Satellite telephones are basically a high-end purchase for the person who wants to be 100% prepared. That said there are times where a sat-phone can be very handy as emergency equipment.

If you are planning to travel into remote regions, or if you plan to travel on 4x4 trails, having a sat-phone available in case of breakdown or medical emergency can be helpful if not down right necessary.

Sat-phones can be rented which make sense for short-term travel. For longer journeys you can find good prices on used telephones by researching online. Once you purchase the phone you will have to set up an account so that you are billed each time you make a call. These calls are not cheap, but if you use your telephone only for emergencies then the cost is not an issue.

There are sat-phones available that offer the option of Internet or email access, but with the proliferation and low cost of Internet cafés it isn't necessary to purchase one of these high-end devices.

Phone-cards
The best option available is to purchase a local prepaid calling card should the need arise for you to make phone calls. Calling cards are available from nearly every supermarket even in small towns. Unlike in the United States where the public telephone booth is rapidly disappearing from street corners, the public telephone is still to be found in Central and South America.

Calling cards are inexpensive, being offered in denominations as small as $2.00US, perfect to carry just in case you need to place a local call. For international calls we find that calling cards are still a good offer. Using a card, we have been able to telephone the United States for as little as a penny a minute.

Internet
Another option we use is an online calling option. There are many VOIP options (voice over Internet protocol). One of the services available is Skype. The services basically all work the same; download and install on your laptop the free software, open an account and make a payment to establish a prepaid balance.

After you purchase a headphone with a microphone, you will be ready to make calls from your computer whenever you get online. Many Internet cafes already have Skype installed on their computers, so if you have an account already set up, you can make calls on your account from any computer anywhere in the world. Getting online to make Internet calls, check emails, update websites, pay bills or for any other reason has become extremely easy while traveling.

In Mexico, Central and South America personal ownership of a computer is not yet the norm. For the majority of the population, access to the Internet is accomplished at the local Internet café. You will find these places all over and not just at tourist locations. Sure, at tourist hot spots you will likely find an Internet café on every street corner, but even in most of the smaller towns there will be at least one place where you can get online.

It used to be a challenge to find an open network connection at the cafes to hook up your laptop computer. This is changing and most locations will have a cable available for you to connect through. Just be sure that your anti-virus program is up to date and that you have your computer set so that other users cannot access your files while you are online.

If you are unable to find a connection for your laptop, be sure to carry a USB memory stick. This way you can have your emails already written so that all you have to do is cut and paste them online at the Internet café, or so that you can upload photos or download your emails onto it so that you can put them on to your personal laptop. Nearly all Internet café computers have USB ports that you can use.

Internet connections are surprisingly inexpensive. In most places you can get online for as little as 50 cents or a dollar an hour. And after using an Internet café remember to delete temporary files, history, cookies and passwords from any public computer.

Vehicle Repairs

At some point in your travels you will probably need to get service done on your vehicle, even if it is just a tire repair or an oil change. But don't worry, there are mechanics everywhere, we have even found tire repair services in the middle of nowhere.

Whether or not you are an experienced mechanic you should include in your repair kit a service manual for your vehicle. Manuals can be extremely large books so if you can get a copy on a disc or install it on your laptop computer, even better. This way you will know exactly what the mechanic you have hired needs to be doing to fix your vehicle.

Over the years we have used the services of a variety of mechanics, some we found on the side of the road while others were at name-brand dealerships. We have yet to feel that we were in any way taken advantage of. In fact, at nearly every service call, the mechanics we found were willing to drop whatever they were working on and to begin work on our vehicle immediately. We can't remember ever having to make an appointment.

When was the last time you could get immediate service at your local mechanic?

If we needed major service requiring work for more than one day or if work wasn't completed until after dark, we were allowed to make camp in the parking lot of the service shop. We've done this in Brazil, Chile, Guatemala and Belize.

Although you should carry whatever spare parts you expect to need, there will be times where something unexpected occurs. We once had a suspension bushing fail for which we had no spare. The manager of the repair shop took us around town to what seemed like every parts shop looking a replacement. When none could be found, he machined a substitute that held until we were able to obtain a factory replacement.

Our view is that we have received exceptional service from every shop, large or small, that we have used. An additional benefit of having regular service performed while on the road is that wages are less in developing countries. This means that you can have work done at the cost of anywhere from $5.00 to $20.00US an hour.

Broken Windshield

The road to Ushuaia, the southern-most city in the world, used to be entirely graveled. During the past few years the government has been working to get it paved, and we only had a gravel section of about 25 miles to travel. Just as we were approaching the end of the gravel, we had a crazy driver approach too fast from the other direction and start to lose control of his car. Fortunately, he missed us and regained control, but unfortunately for us his tires kicked up a rock that slammed into our windshield leaving a large smashed area.

Continuing on to Punta Arenas we were surprised to see a billboard for a windshield repair company, just the thing we were hoping to find. When we got into town, the shop was easy to find and they fixed our cracked window for just $4.00US.

Actually it wasn't really "fixed", but they drilled a hole into the outer pane of glass on either side of the crack to stop it from continuing across the window. It was very disconcerting to be sitting in the cab and watching the technician drill holes into the windshield. But it looked like it would work and the by the end of the day the crack hadn't grown. Two years later the repair has proven itself and the crack has remained its original size.

Stopping the windshield crack

If your vehicle requires any special tools for you to perform general service, be sure to buy a set to have with you. It will be unlikely that mechanics would have equipment accessible for a vehicle that they never work on. In our case, our vehicle did not come with any tire changing equipment. We needed to purchase a jack, sockets for our lug nuts and a wrench to use with the sockets. Whenever we needed tire work done, none of the mechanics had our size sockets and had to use our set.

Something else to consider is learning how to change the tires on your vehicle. Sure you already know how to change a flat tire, but have you changed a tire on your new vehicle yet? Be sure to practice. You may find that the jack is too small or that the lug wrench doesn't fit or is too small or weak.

Or you may find, like we did, that the lug nuts on our tires were so tight that we could not loosen them in the field. When we took our vehicle to the dealer to have the nuts loosened, they were barely able to get them off with their impact wrench! If we had failed to practice tire changing we would have been stranded on the side of the road even though we had the right parts.

You can reduce the number of flat tires that your vehicle may sustain by replacing your stock tires with the highest ply rated tires that will fit on your rim. We use a minimum of 10 ply tires on our vehicle.

Changing a tire or doing any type of vehicle maintenance will be dirty work. A simple trick we have learned is to wear a pair of coveralls whenever doing any type of repair. We don't care if we get oil, grease or anything else on them. Just go and browse at your local used clothing or thrift store and chances are you'll find something you can bring to wear and save yourself some money at the same time.

Include a couple of pairs of gloves for both you and your traveling companion. Gloves can save you from scraped knuckles or worse when doing repairs. We also use them every time we get fuel. Pumps and nozzles don't always work perfectly, so why get fuel all over your hands. Don't forget about using gloves when you're dumping your toilet and some hand sanitizer will come in handy here too.

You can save yourself from some major repairs by promptly washing off the mud that will collect on the bottom of your vehicle and on the backsides of the wheels. After one long off-road trip that took us through more than a few mud bogs we stopped in the nearest town to find a car wash. Unfortunately it was a Sunday and most businesses were closed. So we drove around looking for an accessible hose connection and found one at a movie theatre. After getting permission, we washed off what had to be nearly 50 pounds of mud.

We have subsequently spoken with other overlanders who failed to promptly wash their vehicles and who had electronic parts fail and front ends go out of alignment due to unbalanced wheels that were filled with hard, dried clay. They also had to chisel the clay off of their transmissions and drive shafts. Take the easy way out and wash your vehicle off ASAP.

A list of the tools that we include in our repair kit is detailed in the Information Index at the back of the book.

> ### Dead Refrigerator in Patagonia
>
> Arriving in Puerto Varas, Chile, we expected to find our new refrigerator shipped down from the United States for us. Arriving at the hostel where the refrigerator was supposed to have been shipped, we found that it wasn't there, but the owner telephoned around and found that it was being held in a warehouse in Puerto Montt about 30 minutes away.
>
> The warehouse guys were really nice and let us drive the Fuso into the warehouse (it was raining outside) to work on replacing the fridge over the next couple of hours. Of course the new refrigerator wasn't a perfect fit, so having some tools handy made the job a little easier. And one of the truck drivers even got into the act and became a helpful assistant, helping Don remove the old fridge and lifting the new one into place.
>
> Everything went well and we had a new, updated, WORKING refrigerator for the first time in over two months!

Security and Safety

Make window coverings for your vehicle so that no one can see into it. Don't leave valuables in sight – that way there are no temptations.

If you have any equipment bolted to a rack or to your bumper, be sure to lock them as well. We bought different lengths of plastic coated cables and made custom sized cable locks to use to secure our extra fuel and water cans to their racks. We have also used cables to lock our bikes and our kayak to the vehicle at night.

When using padlocks, spend the extra money for a good quality, waterproof, outdoor lock. The locks will be exposed to all types of conditions and the keyholes could become clogged with dust or mud. Try to get multiple locks all keyed alike so that you don't have to mess with a bag of loose keys.

Burglar alarms seem like a good idea yet most bystanders are so used to hearing alarms go off that they just ignore the sound. On one occasion, we found that a gardener who was working near our previous vehicle accidentally bumped the vehicle and set off the alarm. After the alarm was reset, he started to show his friends how easy it was to set off our alarm and got us running back to check on it several times before we figured out what was happening.

Carry at least one fire extinguisher in the cab of your vehicle and one additional one near your kitchen cook-top. Even better, try to find a fire blanket that you can use in your kitchen area rather than a fire extinguisher as the force of the extinguisher can not only make a huge mess but it can even spread a grease fire.

Having a fire extinguisher and a couple of safety triangles not only make good sense, they are required by police in many countries. At some police stops you may actually be requested to show the officer these items. Be prepared.

Don't put yourself in compromising or potentially dangerous situations. Don't get into arguments. Arguments can escalate very quickly and can turn ugly. If you get into a situation where a crowd begins to assemble, get out as quickly and quietly as possible.

Don't take along any weapons. It is illegal to import them without a permit and getting a permit is extremely difficult. If you would feel more comfortable having some sort of protection, consider pepper spray. We carry a small air horn. We have yet to be in a situation where we've had to use any type of self-protection.

Public laundry, Livingston, Guatemala

Chapter Five

Border Crossings
   a. Documents
   b. Language
   c. Tramitadores
   d. The Dry Run

In general, you will be crossing borders more often in Central America than you will in South America as the countries are smaller than their South American counterparts. Although border crossing formalities are mostly straight forward, our experience has shown that the Central American borders will be more personally taxing as it is usually hot, the officials require more details and the instructions can, at times, be confusing. Just be patient and things will go just fine. Detailed border crossing information can be found in each of the country chapters.

After the CA4 Agreement went into effect in 2006, border crossings between Guatemala, Honduras, El Salvador and Nicaragua became much easier. Once you have entered one of these countries your passport stamp grants you ninety (90) days to visit all four countries. If you want to stay longer you must obtain an extension. The best part of this is that you no longer have to get your passport stamped at each border. The border officials will check your date of original entry and send you off to *Aduana* (Customs) for your vehicle permit.

Documents

Get your expanding Document Folder that we talked about in Chapter 3 with all of your documents and copies. As we said earlier, you should have the following documents and copies ready for the border crossing experience:

> Passport
> Driver's License
> International Driving License (if required – like for Brazil)
> Vehicle Title
> Vehicle Registration
> (Vehicle License Plate Number)
> Vehicle Insurance documents

It is necessary to provide *Aduana* with the vehicle license plate number. As our Title does not include the license plate number we choose to provide them with a copy of the Vehicle Registration that does include the plate number.

Language

The biggest barrier facing you at the border is the language. Don't expect the officials to speak or understand English, many do but you shouldn't expect it. You should learn some of the specific words for the documents that you will be asked for.

Here is a small list to help you complete your paperwork and to understand the customs inspectors at the international borders.

Americas Overland

English	Spanish
Immigration	Immigración
Customs	Aduana
Name	Nombre
Last/family Name	Apellido
Type of Vehicle	Tipo de Vehículo
Title	Título
Registration	Matrícula
License Plate Number	Número (No.) de Placa or Matrícula
Vehicle Identification Number (VIN)	Número (No.) de Chasis
Driver's License	Licencia
Color	Color
Make	Marca
Model	Modelo
Year	Año
Number of doors	Número (No.) de Puertas
Capacity	Capacidad
Country/Origin	País/Origen
Insurance	Seguro
Passport	Pasaporte
Nationality	Nacionalidad
Entry	Entrada/Ingreso
Exit	Salida
Destination	Destino
Border	Frontera
Foreign	Extranjero
Tourist	Turista
Signature	Firma
Date	Fecha
Type of Fuel	Tipo de Combustible
Number of Cylinders	Número (No.) de cilindros
Motorhome/camper	Casa Rodante/Carro Casa/ Casa Movil

Tramitadores

Tramitadores is the Spanish word for the informal and quasi-formal people who will swarm you and your vehicle as soon as you arrive at the border and offer you their services to guide you through the border crossing procedure.

While it may be tempting to surrender your self-will and to hire one of these pesky, pushy individuals we strongly recommend against it. There are a number of reasons not to hire them, starting with the fact that they won't be doing anything that you can't do yourself.

The *tramitador* might speak English and might tell you that they only work for tips. What you won't realize is that in addition to your tip they will be overcharging you for any fees, legitimate or not.

If you hire one you will not learn the process for clearing yourself or your vehicle. You will be pushed and rushed from place to place and in the end you will feel that you have surrendered control of your life for the duration of the documentation process.

It may take you a few minutes longer to decipher the process by yourself but it will still go quickly. Most importantly, don't rush, don't get flustered and don't get angry. The process makes sense and you will become used to it. From the time that you arrive at the departure border to the time that you leave the new entry border your experience will average an hour and a half. It's part of the experience, enjoy it.

A tramitador experience

We had heard that the Nicaraguan borders were the most difficult to pass through so on our first trip south we decided to avail ourselves of a *tramitador*. As soon as we crossed out of Honduras our vehicle was besieged by about a dozen people all waving little official looking badges and offering to help us for free. We chose an English speaking youth to be our assistant.

The first thing he wanted was for us to give him all of our documents so that he could process them by himself. NO WAY! Never let your documents get out of your sight. What would you do if something got lost, or you had to pay (a bribe) to get the documents returned to you. Additionally, there are several documents that you personally need to sign so you have to go to each window.

We insisted that we would take the documents and personally give them to whatever official was requesting them. Thus began a whirlwind rush around the border offices with everyone speaking so fast that we couldn't follow what was going on. We were told to do this, do that, pay this and pay that.

Whoa, things were moving at such a fast pace we felt that we could easily be taken advantage of. We requested to see the price list *(la tarifa)* showing the fees that we were being charged and requested a receipt for every payment. When these demands elicited negative comments from the *tramitador* we knew that we were being overcharged. We fired our assistant and finished the job ourselves.

Stories abound online about travelers being charged hundreds of dollars in fees to cross borders. *Tramitadores* claim that these "fees" are necessary otherwise the official won't process the documents.

Other stories circulate about the necessity to pay bribes to get across the border and that the *tramitador* knows who to bribe and how much to pay. This is not the case!

It is illegal for any official to demand a bribe to handle your paperwork and illegal for you to offer one. If you feel that you are being improperly charged, ask to see the official list of fees. If none is offered and the charge is not rescinded, get the official's name and even take his photograph, then ask to see his *jefe* or supervisor.

The Dry Run

Each border experience will be slightly different, yet they will all follow a similar pattern. This is what you can expect:

Arrival
1) Most Central American countries require that your vehicle be fumigated when you cross the border. This usually entails driving through a spray booth that automatically sprays the exterior of your vehicle. You will be charged for this "service", usually something less than $5.00US. Remember to have any windows closed and your vents/air conditioner off.

2) Drive to the Immigration office and park. Lock your vehicle and take your Document Folder and a pen with you. Obtain an arrival card from the official, fill it out and return it with your passport to be stamped. Sometimes you will be asked how long you intend to visit, maybe even where you intend to exit the country. If you aren't sure about how long you may want to visit, ask for 90 days as this is generally the maximum amount of time

given to visitors. The Customs Official will usually grant your vehicle permit for the same period of time as stamped in your passport.

3) Ask where the *Aduana* office is, then take your passport and your vehicle documents to that office. Tell the official that you would like to have a temporary vehicle import permit and give him your documents. Give him the original and a copy of your vehicle title, registration, passport and driver's license.

You may be requested to buy third party liability insurance. If you have proof of insurance provide it to the official. Otherwise follow his directions and go to the appropriate office to purchase insurance.

4) Collect your documents. Verify that you have all of your originals. Compare the Vehicle Identification Number on the permit to the number listed on your title to ensure that it is correct. If it is wrong you may not be allowed to exit the country with your vehicle.

Put all of your originals away before you walk away from the window. Ask the official where you can get a photocopy of your permit. If possible, get a photocopy of the permit before you leave the border.

5) Drive to the exit gate where you will be asked for your passport and vehicle permit. When you get the documents back, put away the originals and use the copies if you ever get stopped at a checkpoint. Welcome to your next country.

Departure

1) Arrive at the border and find a place to park your vehicle. In some cases you may find a long line of trucks blocking the highway for hundreds of yards as they get their paperwork processed. Do not stop in line behind the trucks. The rules for commercial vehicles are very different than for the temporary importation of private vehicles.

Go around the trucks, even if you must drive on the wrong side of the road or along the shoulder. Once you get to the border the police or a guard will probably show you where to park. If not, ask the guard where Immigration (*Immigración*) and Customs (*Aduana*) are located then park as close to the immigration building as possible. Lock your vehicle and take your Document Folder and a pen with you.

2) Go to the Immigration Officer to get your passport stamped. You may have to fill out an exit card similar to the entry card you filled out when you arrived in the country. You may even have to pay a departure tax. If so, get a receipt.

3) Go to the Customs office to surrender your Temporary Vehicle Importation Permit. You may get your passport stamped again or have the Permit cancelled in your passport. The official may gave you a slip of paper to surrender to a second customs official at the actual border as proof that you surrendered your permit.

Sometimes you may be required to surrender your permit before you get your exit stamp in your passport.

4) Convert any remaining local currency into the currency of the new country with a money changer. You want to have between $20.00 and $50.00US in the new currency to cover possible fees.

5) Drive to the border gate, have your documents rechecked, then drive across to your next country.

Each country has slightly different requirements when you enter and exit their borders. We have provided more detailed instructions in the country specific chapters.

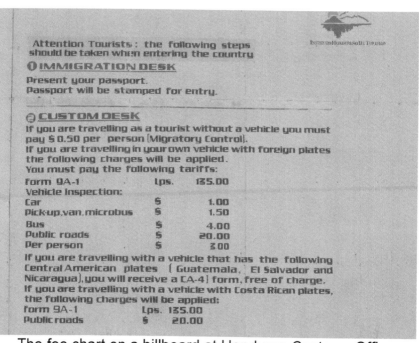

The fee chart on a billboard at Honduran Customs Office

Chapter Six

Shipping Information
   a. Shipping Methods
   b. Shipping Documents
   c. Shipping Companies
   d. Customs Agents

How do you get your vehicle from Central to South America? Yes, the Pan American Highway does run through both regions, but the road ends about 170 miles south of Panama City. From that point, at the town of Yaviza, your options are a dirt track through the jungle and dugout canoes, hardly sufficient for your vehicle.

It is true that in 1960 a group did drive their jeeps across what is known as the Darien Gap, but it took them nearly 5 months to travel the 180 miles, and they had to build their own bridges over the creeks and through the swamps. So you and I won't be driving through it any time in the foreseeable future.

And even though it did exist in the past, the ferry that once plied the route between Colón, Panama and Cartagena, Colombia halted at the end of the 1990's. As of 2008 there was no ferry traveling the route from Panama to Colombia or vice-versa.

Shipping Methods

The only option is to transport the vehicle around the Darien by ship and arrange an airplane ticket for your personal travel. We have not been able to find a shipping company that will allow passengers to travel with their vehicle.

There are three methods of shipping your vehicle from Central America to South America: RORO, which is roll-on-roll-off, LOLO, lift-on-lift-off and shipping in a Container. The choice is generally made based on the size of the vehicle. Motorcycles do have the option of paying for shipment by air-cargo.

If you are traveling in a vehicle that can fit inside of a container, consider yourself lucky. Container shipping generally is the least expensive way to ship. The other benefit of containerized shipping is that you are the person who loads your vehicle into the container and the person who seals it. The seal must remain intact throughout the voyage, so your vehicle is secure.

The down side of container shipping is that the container must generally be moved from the ship to some other location for you to collect your vehicle. Simply, this means that the port has some additional way to charge you extra money over and above the cost of the international transport.

OK, so you realize that short of chopping off the roof of your vehicle, it will never squeeze into a container. This means RORO should be your first choice. Your vehicle will be driven onto and off of the ship.

Why not LOLO you ask? Well, I know I'm uncomfortable having my vehicle driven onto a platform that is then lifted onto the ship by a crane. We are also familiar with other overlanders who have shipped via LOLO and had their vehicles sustain damage. If this is your only option, then the decision will have been made for you.

How big of a vehicle can you ship in a closed container? That depends on the size of the container. Containers come in standard 20-foot and 40-foot lengths. These lengths though refer to the outside length.

A 20-foot dry-container has the following dimensions:
- Interior Length: 5,897mm or 19 ft, 3 in
- Door Width: 2,338mm or 7 ft, 8 in
- Door Height: 2,278mm or 7 ft, 5 in

A 40-foot dry-container has the following dimensions:
- Interior Length: 12,024mm or 39 ft, 5 in
- Door Width: 2,330mm or 7 ft, 7 in
- Door Height: 2,278mm or 7 ft, 5 in

A 20-foot platform, for LOLO shipment, has the following dimensions:
- Length: 6,058mm or 19 ft, 10 in
- Width: 2,288mm or 7 ft, 6 in

A 20-foot open-top container has the following dimensions:
- Length: 5,897mm or 19 ft, 3 in
- Width: 2,338mm or 7 ft, 8 in
- Door Height: 2,278mm or 7 ft, 5 in

You'll have to measure your own vehicle to see if it will fit through the doors and into a container.

If you ship RORO, you must bring your vehicle to the port and after it is inspected, you must hand over the key to the ship's agent. When the ship arrives, someone will load your vehicle onto the ship and (supposedly) give the Captain your keys. More likely is that the key will stay in the ignition of the vehicle so that it doesn't get lost. And while it is sitting at the dock, or even while it is on the ship, someone may enter your vehicle looking for something to steal.

Make sure you remove anything of value from any accessible portion of the vehicle and you must make sure that your vehicle has some way to close off the living quarters from the driver's cab. Some vehicles have no passage at all or have a lockable passageway. Other travelers have built special walls that cannot be penetrated. If you have a roof vent that is large enough for someone to fit through, block it off. This is not to say that you will suffer theft, but the likelihood of if happening is very high if access is easy. If you have no choice but to ship with your living area accessible, you MUST remove anything of value.

Shipping options are available from Costa Rica or Panama to Venezuela, Colombia, Ecuador or Peru, and vice-versa. Most of the vessels that ship to/from Costa Rica travel to Ecuador and Peru. From Panama there are more options as to shippers and destinations. It does appear that shipping out of Panama is the slightly more expensive option.

Details about our shipping experience from Panama are found in the Panama chapter. Our experience shipping from Colombia is detailed in the Colombia chapter. Shipping a vehicle is completely different from simply crossing a border. If you are not confidently fluent in Spanish, hire a Shipping Agent to assist you. More than likely, your agent will have a working relationship with the shipping company that you are negotiating with and may even have been referred to you by the shipper.

So what does the Shipping Agent do for you? You are paying them to organize 1) The export procedure of your vehicle, and 2) The port procedures.

The export procedure of your vehicle should include having the agent:

(a)   Prepare all necessary documents for export, i.e. the Waybill or Bill Of Lading (BOL) for your vehicle. You will need the Original BOL when you retrieve your vehicle at its destination.

(b)   Obtain the cancellation of your temporary vehicle import permit, or provide you with instructions on where to get it cancelled. See Panama shipping information below.

(c)   Schedule any vehicle or customs inspections required at the port.

(d)   Determine the type and amount of any fees that you are required to pay before you arrive at the port.

The port procedures will differ depending on whether you are shipping RORO or by container.

RORO port procedures are actually easy and straightforward. The agent should meet you at the port and act as translator for you. You will need to complete the customs inspections as scheduled by your agent and then you are finished. You will be directed to drive your vehicle to the loading area where you will turn the key over to the ship's agent.

For containerized procedures, the agent should accompany or meet you at the port to be your translator.

a) He (or she) should have your container ready for you and accompany you to the warehouse or location where you will load your vehicle into the container. Be prepared with your own straps to secure your vehicle should there be none in the container.

b) There should also be a special lock for you to seal the container when you are finished.

c) The agent then coordinates the loading of the container onto the ship.

The Original Bill of Lading (BOL) will not be available until after the ship has sailed. You should try to arrange your departure so that you can travel with the BOL. If this is not possible, have your agent email you a copy so that you can have it when you meet your other agent at the port of destination.

At the port of destination, if you are working with an agent that your shipping agent referred you to, be sure to have them give you a list of all fees that you will be expected to pay in order to get your vehicle released from the port and customs. This should help reduce the likelihood of additional, unanticipated fees being charged to you. You should also instruct the new agent to have a letter releasing your vehicle into your custody.

This ensures that all fees have been paid to the shipping agency, besides which, the port will not release your vehicle to you without this letter.

We prefer to arrive at the destination city with a couple of days to spare. This gives us time to contact the agent and to speak with customs to determine what inspections, if any, will be needed so that we can schedule them. Just because you are working with an agent, don't expect the agent to have everything under control. In a perfect world it would be great, but this way you won't be surprised if the agent "drops the ball".

With either method of shipping, one constant is true. Your vehicle must be clean. Our agents described this as "new clean", meaning as clean as a new car. If the vehicle is not clean, you could be subjected to a ridiculous fee to have the vehicle steam cleaned. In our case, shipping from Panama, we washed the outside, swept the inside of the cab and when it arrived in Venezuela, no one even checked it. But just to be on the safe side:

- Be sure to wash the exterior.
- Wash under the body of the vehicle, paying special attention to the wheel wells and the frame right under the body.
- Clean the interior of the cab, including under the floor-mat.
- Clean the interior of the camper.

Shipping Documents

Country specific requirements for shipping into and out of their ports are addressed in the chapters for each country.

Generally, you will need the Bill of Lading (BOL) – the original will only be provided after the ship has left port, but you can get a preliminary BOL from the shipping company or agent.

You will need a copy of your passport, visa (if necessary), tourist card, any temporary vehicle import document, vehicle title with the VIN clearly visible and vehicle registration.

You will also be required to present a letter on the agent's or shipping line's letterhead authorizing the port to release your own vehicle to you. We believe this is a CYA (cover your ass) document for the port authority, so that the agent/shipping line cannot later try to collect fees from the port.

Be sure to have this authorization letter with you when you arrive at the port. Otherwise the port will require you to obtain the document and return to the port. Considering the agents are rarely located at the port this could cause an unnecessary delay of an entire day running back and forth, not to mention unnecessary stress.

Shipping Companies

Below are links to shipping companies and agents that have been brought to our attention. The list is not a recommendation but should be viewed as a place to start your own research. Should you find our information outdated or if you have additional names and information, please take the time to write us and help make the next edition even more accurate and useful.

Wallenius Wilhelmsen Logistics - RORO
http://www.2wglobal.com

K-Line - RORO
http://www.kline.com/KAMCarCarrier/Contacts/Car-Carrier_RORO_Contacts_Central_America.asp

CSAV – RORO
http://www.csav.com

NYC-Line – RORO and Container
http://www2.nykline.com/

InterOcean Lines – RORO and Container
http://www.interoceanlines.com/

CSAV – Container
http://www.csav.com/index_en.htm

Hapag - Lloyd/TMM Lines – Container
http://www.tmmlines.com/en/offices/index.html

K-Line – Container
http://www.kline.com/,

Americas Overland

Maruba – Container
http://www.maruba.com.ar/MAIN-280403.html

Panalpina – Container
http://www.panalpina.com/www/global/en/about/organization/organization_structure.html

Maersk Line – Container
http://www.maerskline.com/link/?page=brochure&path=/local_websites

Evergreen Marine - Container
http://www.shipmentlink.com/

APL – Container
http://www.apl.com/

Marfret – Container
http://www.marfret.com/

Nordana - Container
http://www.nordana.com

Customs Agents

Grupo Humberto Alvarez – Costa Rica
http://www.grupoha.com/paginas_i/index.php

Barwil Agencies, SA – Panama City
http://www.2wglobal.com/www/officesAgents/searchOffice.jsp

Transworld Chartering – Colombia, Gustavo Barrios, Phone 6655780 or 310-3375109 or 316-7669837

NAVECUADOR S.A., Ana Patricia Trejo M,
(mailto:anna_patricia@hotmail.com) Ecuador
http://www.transoceanica.com.ec/

Paragua Maritima - Puerto Cabello, Venezuela. Our
contact there was Ms. Haydee Silva, email at
(haydee7s@paramar1.com).

Collecting our vehicle at the port in Manzanillo (Colon),
Panama

Country Information

Chapters Seven through Twenty-three contain important information on travel to help you choose possible routes and cross the borders of seventeen countries and regions.

Each of the following country chapters will provide ideas for driving routes, lists of camping opportunities, specific border crossing formalities, suggestions for maps and Internet resources as well as anecdotes from our travels.

Chapter Seven

Mexico

Routes
Maps
Camping
Border Crossing Formalities
- **Arrival**
- **Departure**

Routes

Baja Routes

Looking at the long, narrow peninsula that is Baja California, it is easy to pick the most obvious route from Tijuana to Cabo San Lucas and then crossing the Gulf of California to Mexico's mainland. This route will take you close to most of the sites to be found in Baja, but you need to get off of Highway 1 in order to see the "real" Baja. In addition, the ferry to the mainland is very expensive so if you have more time than money, we'd suggest driving back up to Mexicali to cross over to the mainland so that you can explore northern Mexico more fully.

Following Hwy 1 south, be sure to detour off to the ocean where you can find quiet beaches. Just remember to top off your fuel tank whenever you see a Pemex. On Baja, stations can be few and far between.

There are so many great places to explore, here's a list of our favorites:

- The fish market at Ensenada
- The blowhole at La Bufadora south of Ensenada

Ensenada Shrimp Tacos
One of the joys of exploring Mexico's Baja Peninsula is the availability of fresh seafood. 90 miles south of the California border we stopped at the fish market at the port in Ensenada. At the market we could stock up with just about any type of seafood available, tuna, cod, lobster, clams, squid, octopus or shrimp.

Surrounding the fish market are numerous restaurant stalls selling fish and shrimp tacos cooked to order with fresh made salsa and a secret sauce that we have never been able to duplicate. You know that the food is fresh as it is bought right next-door at the fish market.

We chose one of the busier stalls feeling that the food would be the freshest. We grabbed a seat, ordered our drinks and then lost count of the number of tacos that we ate, which is very easy to do when the tacos only cost a buck or so each!

- The mountains at Rancho Meling and Parque Nacional San Pedro Mártir
- The onyx geyser and onyx schoolhouse at El Mármol
- The desert around Cataviña with its pictographs, giant cardon cactus, boojums, datilillo, organ pipe, ocotillo and elephant trees
- The missions and ruins of missions built by the Jesuits, Franciscans and Dominicans scattered throughout the peninsula
- The spectacular rock art sites in the Sierra de San Francisco

Cave Paintings

The Baja Peninsula contains some impressive cave paintings. Most of the paintings are found in deep, nearly inaccessible arroyos (water run-offs). Many of the caves contain large colorful murals of figures, spirits and animals, so large that they are actually larger than life-size. So impressive are these paintings that in 1993 UNESCO included them on The World Heritage List.

The most spectacular of the murals are found in the canyons of the Sierra de San Francisco and the Sierra de Guadalupe. Roughly, this covers the mountainous regions both north and south of the town of San Ignacio in Baja California Sur.

Access into the canyons is either by walking or by mule. We chose to descend the steep canyon on mule-back and burros carried our supplies. The descent into the canyon was steep and the trail not maintained. The mules and burros have blazed the trail over years of use, but it is full of rocks, loose gravel and in places is just slick rock. The mules were very sure footed however and they carefully picked their way down. Our mantra soon became "trust the mules" and after a while the movements of the mules became a second nature feeling. But this adventure is definitely not for the faint-hearted. Many times during the day we had to tell ourselves not to look down.

Reaching the bottom of the canyon, we made camp and then set off hiking to the caves. The painted caves and overhangs are located anywhere from 150ft to 250ft above the canyon floor and the trails that exist are not maintained and are little more than animal trails. We had to look at every spot we placed our feet, but our guide, who has lived in these mountains his whole life, just about ran up the cliff side.

Our appreciation for the beauty of the canyon, the artistry of the murals and the ability of our mules and burros was enhanced by the difficulty of the journey.

- The bay at San Quintín with its oyster farms and beaches full of clams and sand-dollars
- The beach and bay at Bahía de Los Angeles
- The deserted beach at Malarimo as you drive to Bahía Tortugas

Lobster Feast

After spending two days exploring the lonely windswept Malarimo Beach in Baja California Sur and looking at the myriad type of flotsam from around the Pacific that washes up on the sand, we went wandering in search of a fishing village to buy fresh fish or, with luck, lobster.

Driving down the beach we followed tracks that lead us to the type of temporary village that we were looking for. There were several pickup trucks filled with fishing equipment and lobster traps. In the past, the Baja fishermen have warmly welcomed us into their camps so we trusted that it would not be difficult to approach this group and negotiate a purchase.

After trying to make small talk in our broken Spanish we asked if they had any fish we could buy. Sorry, we were told, they had no fish, only lobster. Oh boy! Yet when we asked if we could buy some lobsters for our dinner we were turned down. This was such a surprise, as we had never been refused in the past. Our disappointment turned into pleasure when it was explained that the lobsters would not be sold to us because we were being invited to join them as they barbequed the lobsters right on the beach. We spent a wonderful evening practicing our Spanish, drinking cold beers (which we contributed) and, of course, eating loads of lobster.

- The salt pans and whale nursery at Guerrero Negro
- San Ignacio and the whale nursery at Laguna San Ignacio

To Touch a Whale
We chose to visit the whales at the large Laguna San Ignacio as we hoped that this birthing lagoon would be full of whales of all sizes. To reach the lagoon we first had to negotiate a 40-mile drive down the "world class washboard" road that goes to the water. We averaged 20 mph so it took about 2 hours to get there. The worst part was right before we arrived at the whale watching camp when we had to cross washboard and mud at about 2 mph.

We boarded our boat and as we headed out we could see the whales blowing from a distance but they all seemed to disappear as soon as our boat stopped the required 100 feet away.

But suddenly a mama with her baby appeared. Just as curious about us as we were about them, mama surfaced next to the boat followed closely by baby. Over the next 1/2 hour, mama and baby went back and forth between us and another boat that had arrived nearby, coming alongside us to be scratched or just to hang out. After a while we moved away and the two whales followed us! We slowed down and let them catch up.

For the next hour, these two whales stayed with our boat, coming alongside, diving below, hanging out at the surface and spyhopping (sticking their heads straight out of the water). The baby in particular liked to come up at the rear of the boat as if he liked the sound or movement of the motor. Everyone got a chance to pet the whales and feel a close communion with them.

It is an absolutely incredible experience to see a 40 ft. whale come up next to and underneath an 18 ft. panga with the ultimate in grace and dexterity. This was an experience we will never forget.

- Reserva de la Biosphera El Vizcaíno
- Santa Rosalia, Mulegé and Bahía Concepcion – an area so peaceful you may have trouble dragging yourself away
- Loreto with a detour into the mountains to San Javier and the hidden waterfalls along the old Camino Real
- The estuaries along Bahía Magdalena
- La Paz

Perhaps a loop from the mining ruins at El Triunfo around the tip visiting los cabos – Cabo Pulmo, San José del Cabo and Cabo San Lucas, and if you have time or are returning up the peninsula, Todos Santos.

Baja Ferries operates the ships that traverse the Gulf of California from La Paz to Mazatlán or Topolobampo

(Los Mochis) or from Santa Rosalía to Guaymas. Prices just for your vehicle can run as high as $1,100.00US!

All throughout the peninsula are back roads and 4x4 trails that will take you deep into the desert landscape where you may not see another soul for days.

If you are doing a return trip through Baja, you can follow the back route from Chapala to San Luis Gonzaga, Puertecitos and San Felipe, then find your way across the Colorado Delta to San Luis in Sonora State.

Ensenada Fish Market, Baja California

Mexico Mainland Routes

The Mexico/USA border measures nearly 2,000 miles (3,300km) in length. Needless to say there are numerous border crossings allowing you to choose to enter Mexico from California, Arizona, New Mexico or Texas.

Overlanders who wish to travel quickly through Mexico into Guatemala and Central America most often use the border crossings in Texas. These border crossings can also get you more quickly into the colonial center of the country, if you are already starting from the eastern half of the United States.

Following Hwy 180 along the Gulf of Mexico you can detour inland at Tampico to enjoy the cool mountain air and the waterfalls at Tamasopo. Then drive south on the old Panamericana from Cuidad Valles cutting across the mountains back to the coast to visit the mysterious square temples at the ruins at Papantla.

Then back onto Hwy 180, through Veracruz. If you are heading to Guatemala then you can head south through Oaxaca or Tuxtla Gutiérrez. The attractive mountain/indigenous city of San Cristóbal de Las Casas will give you an introduction into the Mayan lifestyle before you enter Guatemala.

If you are heading to the Yucatan Peninsula from Veracruz, continue on Hwy 180 along the coast to Laguna Catemaco and El Salto de Eyipantla. Your next stop would be to view the giant basalt Olmec heads in Villahermosa. From Villahermosa it will be on to the great ruins at Palenque. From Palenque you can head into the Yucatan Peninsula. The Yucatan Route can be found below.

New Mexico and Arizona are good starting points for journeys down the full length of Mexico. If you have unlimited time you can wander throughout the country and see most of the major sites.

From Yuma/San Luis you can travel along Hwy 2 through the Desierto de Altar (also known as the Gran Desierto) and through the stark landscape of Parque Nacional El Pinacate. Continuing across through Caborca, Magdalena de Kino and Agua Prieta you can explore several Kino Missions and view the relics of Padre Kino.

If you want to explore the beaches of the Pacific Coast, you would turn south at Magdalena de Kino and, after reaching Guaymas, follow the coast for some 1,800 miles until you head inland to Tuxtla Gutiérrez.

From Agua Prieta stop at Nuevo Casas Grandes to explore the ruins and small towns nearby. Heading south toward the Barranca del Cobre (Copper Canyon), detour into the hills around Madera to view wonderful ruins built by the Paquimé people.

Then detour down the Hermosillo road to the amazing waterfalls in Parque Nacional Cascada de Basaseachic. Take the back road through the mountains to San Juanito and then into Creel. Take a few days to explore the Copper Canyon. The road out of the canyon leads to Hidalgo del Parral, from where you can head south to Durango.

From Durango you can travel down to the coast near Mazatlán, but the more interesting route is to the old silver city of Zacatecas. From Zacatecas head to Guadalajara from where you could detour off to Tequila, before heading east to Lago de Pátzcuaro and Isla

Janitzio. Then it would be through Morelia and northward into the heart of Colonial Mexico. Exploring the cities of Guanajuato, Dolores Hidalgo, San Miguel de Allende and Querétaro could take days.

Butterfly Migration
One of our objectives for visiting the state of Michoacán was to see the annual migration of Monarch butterflies. But the different literature we had read had conflicting information as to when the butterflies would start arriving, so we feared that we might be too early. Confirming our fears, the tourist office in Morelia informed us that the butterflies had not yet arrived. Disappointed, we decided to visit San Miguel de Allende, where we set up camp in a campground. After spending the afternoon visiting the town, we took a stroll around the camp.

After a few minutes we saw a butterfly and made a joke about it being a Monarch. But Don, who studied butterflies in his youth, said no joke, it was a Monarch. As we looked around, we noticed more butterflies and that they were landing in the trees at the edge of the campground. We walked over and discovered that the butterflies were clumping together as units, for protection perhaps? As time went by, more and more butterflies arrived and as darkness fell, thousands and thousands of butterflies had gathered. We were in awe and felt extremely privileged and fortunate to have witnessed this stop on the annual migration to the mountains of Michoacán.

As you head east, the road takes you to Mexico City with its 20 million people. Do yourself a favor and do not drive into the city. If you must, wait until Sunday when the city quiets down before you try to tackle the drive. It is possible to camp on the north side of the city from where you can explore the city by bus and visit the extensive ruins at Teotihuacán.

Now that you have climbed one of the three tallest pyramids in the world, continue on to Cholula so that you can climb your second (which is considered to be THE largest pyramid in the world).

Leaving the Aztecs behind, you will continue south into the land of the Zapotecs – Oaxaca. Oaxaca is another one of Mexico's great colonial cities and if you happen to be here at the end of October for the Day of the Dead celebrations, you get to enjoy one of Mexico's greatest parties! Don't forget to leave plenty of time to visit the small Zapotec villages and impressive ruins nearby. You can take a break at the beach at Puerto Angel before leaving the Pacific behind. It is now time to drive into the highlands where the Zapatista Revolution began. San Cristóbal de Las Casas, an attractive colonial town with a large indigenous population was ground zero for the revolution on New Years Day 1994. Explore the nearby indigenous villages, then head to Palenque – just brace yourselves for the highest number of topes on any stretch of road in Mexico.

Topes

Tope is just one of the Spanish names for what in the US we call speed bumps. They are also called vibradores, reductors and tumalos (in Belize they are called pedestrian ramps.) You will find them in most Central American countries but none of those countries have quite the same love affair with topes as they do in Mexico.

Most small towns and villages have at least one set at both edges of town to slow down drivers. They are a normal part of the driving experience. The downsides are that they slow traffic considerably, especially when the villages are only a few miles apart and many of the topes are unmarked and can cause havoc or damage when drivers have to slam on their brakes to avoid hitting them at anything above walking speed.

One of the worst stretches of highway for topes that we've encountered is in Chiapas on the main route between San Cristóbal de las Casas and the Mayan ruins at Palenque. This is a distance of approximately 170 miles through beautiful winding mountain roads. After counting over 100 topes in the first 25 miles we lost count. The topes were not just placed at the edges of the villages they were also in the center of town, near schools and at intersections. They were also placed in groups, sometimes as many as 10 in one location. Additionally we had to deal with illegal topes, these are the ones constructed of dirt, trees or even old tire treads placed in the roadway by vendors trying to sell food or other wares to passing motorists.

There were so many topes and so much traffic that drivers put on their emergency flashers to warn other drivers that they were slowing so that they didn't cause accidents. As a result of these topes it took us over five hours to traverse this route.

Leave time to explore the ruins at Toniná, the waterfalls at Agua Azul and Misol-Ha before you arrive at Palenque. We'd highly recommend a detour of a couple of days to the ruins at Bonampak and Yaxchilán. When you finally pull yourself away from Palenque, travel to Villahermosa and walk through the jungle park to see the giant Olmec heads. Then follow the Gulf of Mexico to the walled city of Campeche.

Now that you are in the Yucatan Peninsula you will be traveling through the area with the highest number of accessible Mayan sites in Mexico. Take your time and visit as many as you can, they are all different and all are interesting. By exploring some of the smaller sites you may found that you have them all to yourselves, unlike the famous sites of Uxmal and Chichén Itzá. Visit Edzná, Kabah, Sayil and Labna before arriving at Uxmal.

If your timing is right, explore the Reserva Especial de La Biosfera Ria Celestún by boat to witness the beauty of huge flocks of flamingos. Explore Mérida before heading to the most famous of Mexico's Mayan cities – Chichén Itzá. Now head to the Mayan Riviera for some quality beach time. You can visit the ruins of Cobá either on your way toward Cancún or as a detour from Tulum.

Cancún is another one of Mexico's gigantic beach resorts, so after taking a quick drive through, head to Isla Mujeres, Playa del Carmen, Akumal or Tulum. If you snorkel or scuba dive, take a couple of days to enjoy Cozumel. There are secure parking lots in Playa del Carmen to leave your vehicle.

While you head south toward Belize on Hwy 307, stop off for a swim in the freshwater lagoon at Bacalar. When you reach Chetumal fill up on fuel and supplies, as everything will be a bit more expensive in Belize. But remember, Belize Customs Inspectors will search your vehicle for meat, cheese and alcohol.

Traffic and Police
One of the joys of driving south of the border is getting to experience different road conditions and driving styles. In Mexico, many of the roads are narrow and winding. Some drivers will negotiate these roads at breakneck speeds, crossing over the centerline on curves and passing when there is no clear line of sight. Other times you will be stuck behind a slow moving truck or worse, stuck in a line of traffic behind a slow moving truck. Don't expect that the truck driver will pull off the road to let anyone by. If you're lucky he might move to the right or signal when it is clear to pass, but he won't pull over.

One day when driving a mountainous road, we came around a corner and encountered a very long line of cars, all trying to get around a truck. Very slowly and torturously we moved ahead in the line, all the while getting passed by even more impatient people from behind. Eventually, we were right behind the truck. Our chance came and we took it. Finally! We pulled back into our lane, only to find a police car right on our tail with his lights flashing. What? Did we pass illegally? Uncomprehendingly, we pulled over and complied with the police officer who requested our paperwork. After surveying our documents and checking our windshield permit, he handed the papers back and wished us a good trip.

We then had to pull back into that long line of traffic and start the process again, apparently just to satisfy one curious police officer.

One word of advice, when stopping for fuel at the government Pemex Stations, always – did I say always, keep an eye on the total Peso amount on the pump. Even though the pumps are new electronic/digital pumps, some of the attendants will try all sort of ways to overcharge you. Sometimes they will even try to short-change you, so be sure of how much you pay and how much they owe. Not all or even most attendants are like this, but we have had more than our share.

Maps

Check the government highway website at www.sct.gob.mx.

A pretty good map book published in Mexico is the *Guía Roji*. Although we have found errors and mistakes on some of the pages, the map book remains standard equipment for our travels in Mexico.

Rough Guides Mexico map, scale 1:2,250,000 and Baja California map, scale 1:650,000
A great map book for Baja California is the Baja Almanac but it was out of print when we last checked. You may be able to borrow a copy at a library then make copies of the pages that pertain to your journey.

The American Automobile Club (AAA) has large scale folding maps of both Baja and the mainland available that are helpful in seeing the entire country for planning purposes.

Camping

There are several good books that detail places to camp throughout Mexico and many of the places where we have spent time are listed in these books. We would recommend that you review the list below and purchase one or more of them to take with you as a reference.

In Baja California it is still possible to bush camp along the beaches and elsewhere in the countryside, although we would not recommend it near the borders. Check with the locals. In the cities you will most likely be safe if you park on the street – we like to pick a spot under a street lamp. You can also park in public/pay parking lots.

In mainland Mexico the same rules apply for city camping. However in the bigger cities the streets will likely be rather noisy. It may be best to park in a secured parking lot or at a trailer park.

The camping choices in Mexico are so many and the country is so large that to prepare a list of possibilities would take up hundreds of pages. When all else fails, and you have not been able to find a good free camp, when there is no Pemex Fuel Station available or for when your request to spend the night in a parking lot has been rejected, we would recommend that you begin your search for a site with one of the camping books listed below. They are especially helpful if you are interested in camping in or near a major city.

These books are:

Mexico
Mexico Camping by Mike and Terri Church

The People's Guide to Mexico by Carl Franz and
       Lorena Havens

Baja
Exploring Baja By RV by Peterson and Peterson

Central America
99 Days to Panama by Harriet and John Halkyard

Border Crossing Formalities

There are multiple vehicle border crossings from the United States into Mexico. You can enter from California, Arizona, New Mexico or Texas.

<u>Crossing the border into the Border Zone (usually up to 20k (12.5m) south of the border) requires no paperwork and is usually an easy thing – stop at the red light, wait</u> for it to turn green and wave to the border police who wave back. Sometimes the border police will want to inspect your vehicle, but not usually.

<u>Arrival</u>
When crossing the border (if going further than the border zone), find the immigration building and ask for a tourist card – the Migratory Tourist Form (FMT). When you apply for the card, be sure to ask that it be validated for 180 days. It's always better to have extra time rather than find yourself looking for an extension. The officer will fill out the form, stamp your passport and instruct you where to pay the fee, which is approximately $25.00US.

If you are entering mainland Mexico from Nogales, Arizona, the Mexican Government has made getting the required documents a streamlined process. At KM 21, there is a set of offices where you go to get your Tourist Card and the Permiso De Importación Temporal De Casa Movil which is the Temporary Import Permit. The Permit is valid for a period of ten (10) years.

This is usually a pretty quick process, filling out the immigration forms and then the payment of a fee for the temporary import permit. You will need the original and one copy of the following documents:

- Vehicle Title
- Registration
- Driver's License
- Passport
- Migratory Tourist Form (FMT)

You should also have to have a credit card available to cover the bond that is your guarantee that you will not sell your car in the country. Credit cards are preferred, and if you do not have one, you will have to pay a cash bond based on the value of your car. Your credit card will not be charged the bond fee unless you fail to return your permit before it expires. The credit card must have the same name as the owner of the vehicle.

The fee for the permit is paid at the bank (easiest if you choose a border crossing with a Banjercito) and you are given a receipt. The vehicle permit has to be attached to the windshield of your vehicle. The fee for a car or truck, including tax, is $29.70US. The fee for a larger vehicle that can be considered a motor home (*casa movil*) is $50.00US.

Migratory Tourist Form (FMT)

Americas Overland

Temporary Import Permit

To be safe, remember to get two photocopies of the temporary import permit before you drive away. Sometimes the customs inspector who verifies your documents will request a copy from you before allowing you to drive into the country. You should use a copy to show any police who may stop your vehicle at highway stops or for traffic violations.

We also had to fill out a "Contents" form for our vehicle. This was a pre-printed form where we had to check off, Yes or No style, if we had certain items in our vehicle.

 **BANJERCITO**
Al Servicio de las Fuerzas Armadas

 ADUANA MEXICO

SERVICIO DE ADMINISTRACION TRIBUTARIA
ADMINISTRACION GENERAL DE ADUANAS

Folio:	121387
Holograma:	12239281
Fecha:	16/03/2008

Listado General de los Accesorios, Bienes y Equipos que forman
parte de la Casa Rodante

Register Form for Accesories & Equipment for the Motor Home

Accesorios, Bienes y Equipos (Accesories & Equipment)	Si	No	Cuantos (How many)
Computadora (Computer)	✓		✓
Televisión (TV)		✓	
DVD		✓	
Equipo purificador de agua (Purifired water)	✓		✓
Equipo de aire acondicionado (A/C Air Condition)	✓	✓	✓
Equipo de banda civil (Radion C. B.)			
Equipo de sonido (Sound System)	✓		✓
Estufa (Stove)	✓		
Horno de microondas (Microwaves)		✓	
Lavadora de platos (Dish Washer)		✓	
Secadora de platos (Driyer Dish)		✓	
Lavadora de ropa (Washer Machine)		✓	
Secadora de manos (Hand Dryer)		✓	
Herramientas (Tools)	✓		✓
Gato (Jack)	✓		✓
Otro (Other)			
Otro (Other)			
Otro (Other)			
Otro (Other)			

Número del Permiso de Importación Temporal y Holograma Permit & Hologram number	12239281
Fecha de Ingreso	16/03/2008
Fecha de Máximo Retorno (Expiration date)	16/03/2018
Numero de VIN de la Casa Rodante (VIN of Motor Home)	JL6
Marca (Make)	OTROS
Modelo (Model)	2004

Por Banjercito

OPERADO
CAJERO No. 1
SUC. OAXACA
SUAREZ LOPEZ

Sello, Firma y No. de Gafete

Por el Importador

Nombre y Firma

Vehicle Contents Declaration

Departure

Leaving Mexico is much simpler. If you do not plan to return to Mexico with this vehicle within the next ten years you need to surrender your temporary import permit and get your passport stamped. If you are planning to return to Mexico within 10 years with your vehicle, you can keep the permit on your windshield to simplify your return. If you fail to surrender your permit before it expires, or if you sell your vehicle without returning your permit, you may be prevented from bringing in a different vehicle later on.

Guanajuato, MX

Chapter Eight

Belize

Routes
Maps
Camping
Border Crossing Formalities
- **Arrival**
- **Departure**

Routes

Belize is an easy country to explore. Not only because the language is English, but because there is only one vehicle border crossing with Mexico and only one crossing into Guatemala. For such a small country you can find so many places to visit that after two or three weeks you'll be surprised to find yourself still in Belize!

Just south of Chetumal is the crossing into Belize. If you've just stocked up on food for your journey south beware of the Customs inspection for food and alcohol.

Drive to Corozal and spend the night on the bay. Continuing along on the Northern Highway you can take the main route to Orange Walk or explore off the beaten path by crossing the New River on a hand-cranked barge and then driving to Orange Walk via El Progreso.

Belizean Bridges
One of the more charming and interesting experiences of driving in Belize is crossing their one-lane bridges. These bridges date back to when the roads were also one lane wide and some of them can be quite narrow. Most of them also look their age. Today the roads are two-lane and they lend a certain challenge to the drive when coming around a curve you suddenly find a bridge with another vehicle already coming across it in your direction.

Just south of Orange Walk you can choose from several operators of boat tours to the Mayan ruins at Lamanai. Most of the operators will let you camp for free. If you are a birder, or don't know that you are one yet, camp at the Crooked Tree Wildlife Sanctuary to be amazed at the number of birds in the lagoons there.

To get close to large numbers of howler monkeys, a visit to the Community Baboon Sanctuary is a must. If you plan to go to Caye Caulker or Ambergris Caye, then you will need to leave your vehicle in a secure parking lot in Belize City and take a water taxi to the islands. If you plan to go to one of the islands in the south, like Tobacco Caye, you can take the bypass and give Belize City a miss.

Heading down the Western Highway visit the excellent Belize Zoo, then detour down the old dirt Coastal Highway to Gales Point to visit a friendly Garífuna village and maybe spot a manatee.

Continuing south, Dangriga is the spot to grab a water taxi out to beautiful Tabacco Caye. Continuing on the Southern Highway, you can drive to the end of the road at Punta Gorda. Other interesting places are Hopkins and the Sittee River, and the Cockscomb Jaguar Sanctuary.

Dominoes Anyone?
One day in Hopkins, Belize, we were waiting for a fish lunch when Don wandered over to watch several men playing dominoes. They invited Don to join them, but he explained that he didn't know how to play. "No problem, we'll teach you." They explained the basics and Don sat down to play. And promptly won the next two games. Fortunately lunch came and he was saved from losing his shirt when the players then wanted to start playing for money.

Placencia is at the end of a long, very washboarded road that runs along a peninsula separating the lagoon from the sea. If you make it down the road, you'll want to stay for a few days just to recover from the drive.

Cockscomb Jaguar Sanctuary
Hoping to escape the heat and the bugs on the coast we headed into the foothills, up to the Cockscomb Jaguar Sanctuary. This sanctuary has the highest numbers of jaguars in the country but it is unlikely that you'll see one, as they are nocturnal and very shy.

The Sanctuary has a wonderful campground but they don't allow vehicles in it. However, the park ranger allowed us to park on the helipad, presuming that no helicopters would be landing, I guess. It turned out to be a great spot.

It was still hotter than blazes and humid to boot. We decided to do a hike anyway and ended up seeing a number of birds that we had never seen before. When we got to Stann Creek we met a couple tubing down the river. Now that looked like a great way to spend a hot afternoon. So we hiked back to the visitor center and rented a couple of tubes. Hiking upstream for about 20 minutes we came to the tubing put-in.

Very ungracefully, we hurled ourselves backwards into the tubes and started floating. We knew the float would be over pretty quickly, so we tried various ways of slowing it down. We back-paddled for a while and then we got out and walked back upstream, but our favorite way of extending the time was to find a shady, shallow spot in the slow moving creek and just stop for a while. The quiet, broken only by the sound of birdsong, was heavenly.

Heading back along the Hummingbird Highway after you've learned the proper way of driving across dozens of one-lane bridges, you can stop and relax by doing a bit of cave tubing along the Caves Branch River.

Cave Tubing
Caves Branch Cave is one of several subterranean sites that were carved out of the limestone foothills of the Maya Mountains by the Caves Branch River. Archaeological investigations indicate that the ancient Maya used the site for several hundred years between 300 and 900 AD making pilgrimages with offerings to their gods.

Our visit to the caves started with a ride standing in a trailer with about 25 other people and 25 inner tubes. After about a 1/2 hour ride through beautiful orange groves, we arrived at the river. Never having "tubed" before, we really didn't know what to expect. We were given instructions however on how to properly use our tube, so placing it in the water (valve side down, thick edge to the back) we ungracefully plopped down into it. Cold water splashed down our backs as we gasped and laughed.

The entrance to the cave was upstream, so we all turned backwards and back-paddled with our hands toward the entrance. We entered the cave and were immediately swallowed up by blackness. Turning on our headlamps, we continued into the dark. Stalagmites and stalactites greeted us at every turn and dripping water glistened on the ceiling and walls. Beautiful sights that probably existed when the Maya visited this cave humbled us.

Periodically we would climb out of our tubes and explore dry caverns where the Maya performed their rituals. Evidence of fires and broken pottery were everywhere. Some of the rooms still held unbroken pottery that was quite magnificent. One of the caves even held a sculpture that had been carved and plastered by the Maya. It was very impressive.

Then it's back onto the Western Highway towards Guatemala. However, before you get to the border there are several more detours to check out.

Explore the Mountain Pine Ridge Forest Reserve on your way to the Mayan ruins of Caracol. The mountains are refreshing after the heat of the coast. Passing through Santa Elena you can do a fun tube or canoe float on the Belize River ending at Clarissa Falls. Turn off the highway in Benque Viejo and head to Chechem Ha where you can explore the cave loaded with Mayan ceremonial pots sitting as they were found.

Chechem Ha
One of our favorite experiences in Belize was visiting the private farm at Chechem Ha to visit the cave on the property. Many years ago the owner was chasing after his dog when the dog disappeared into a hole in the ground. Curious, the owner enlarged the hole to discover an 820ft. cave under his property. Even more amazingly, the owner discovered 96 Mayan pots that had been ceremonially stored in these caves and untouched for hundreds of years. Rather than selling the pots, the owner invited archeologists in to study them and then opened his property to visitors.

The pots are stored on ledges in the caves and we could only view them by climbing up hand-made ladders. There were several sets of these ledges and the pots ranged in size from volleyball size to washtub size. Many of them still contained the remains of ceremonial offerings.

When you finish up, cross the border and head to the Mayan city of Yaxha in Guatemala.

Maps

Rough Guides Guatemala and Belize Map, scale 1:500,000

Freytag and Berndt, Belize/Guatemala with a scale: 1:400,000

Nelles Map, Mexico – Guatemala - El Salvador and Belize, scale 1:2,500,000

ITMB, Guatemala travel reference map, scale 1:250,000

Sign at the Community Baboon Sanctuary, BZ

Belize Camping

Location	Description	GPS Coordinates	Cost
Corozal Town	Caribbean Village RV park, across from the water just south of town. Really run down but has hook ups and water, walking distance to town.	N18 22.99 W88 23.75	Pay
Corozal Town	Best spot is the malecon across from the RV park and Hotel Maya. Beachfront and within walking distance of town.	N18 23.078 W088 23.60	Free
Orange Walk camping possibilities	Go south from town past the sugarcane processing plant and just before getting to the toll bridge crossing New River. Camping possible on either side of the hwy at either Reyes & Son Tours or New River Cruises. Past the bridge is Lamanai EcoAdventures, also possible to camp.		Free with river boat tour payment.
Crooked Tree Wildlife Sanctuary	Free camping along the shore of the Lagoon just north of the Visitors Center. Pay your entrance fee first.	N17 46.55 W88 31.87	Free
Burrel Boom	Black Orchid Resort parking lot.	N17 34.267 W88 23.743	Pay
Community Baboon Sanctuary in Bermudian Landing	Camping at restaurants/bars just before the CBS Visitors center. Camping on the hill just above the river. Camping also available in the parking area of the visitor center.	N17 33.38 W88 31.86	Pay

Location	Description	GPS Coordinates	Cost
Belize City	Cucumber Beach Marina, 5 miles sw of Belize City, safe place to store vehicles while visiting the Cayes. If spending the night in the city, ask at the central Police Station or the Cruise Ship Terminal for overnight parking options.	N 17 28.383 W 88 14.95	Pay
Along the Western Hwy, between the Zoo and Belmopan	Amigos Restaurant/Bar free camping in the parking lot but order some food.	N17 19.131 W088 34.223	
Gales Point	Just ask around town for a parking spot or ask for Hubert @house #1350 for permission to park, friendly Garífuna village near manatees.		Free
Dangriga	Free camping at park next to Val's Hostel, beachfront, free wifi.	N16 57.938 W088 13.001	Free
	Possible to park at the fire station next to the Municipal Market, across river from boats to Tobacco Caye.		
Along the Hummingbird Hwy	Camping at Ian Anderson's Caves Branch, free camp with tour.		Pay
Hopkins/Sittee River area	Camping at Sittee River Toucan right on river, elect & water.		Pay
Hopkins/Sittee River area	Camping in Hopkins at Tipple Tree Beya		Pay
Cockscomb Basin Wildlife Sanctuary	Nice camping area, ask to camp on the helipad. Great birding area, also has tubes for rent for floating the river.		Pay
Caesar's Place	At mile 60, has camping and rv hook ups.		Pay

Americas Overland

Location	Description	GPS Coordinates	Cost
Caracol Road	You can camp anywhere in the Mountain Pine Ridge Forest Reserve.		Free
Douglas Da Silva Forestry Station.	Great camping area behind the soccer field along the "road" to the Río Frio Caves. Screened room available for eating.		Free
It looks possible to camp either at the Caracol ruins or just outside the entrance, ask first.			
5 Sisters Lodge along the Caracol road.	No camping at the lodge, but it is OK to park outside the lodge in the visitors parking area. The parking area is part of the reserve and camping is ok and free.		Free
Clarissa Falls, San Ignacio	Clarissa Falls Resort, on Belize River, restaurant, water, some electrical outlets	N17 06.713 W089 07.668	Pay
San Ignacio	Inglewood Camping Grounds, 2.8 miles west of town		Pay
Chechem Ha Cave	Poorly signed turn off in the village of Benque Viejo del Carmen just before the Guatemala border. 8 miles on a good dirt road, camping at the grounds before the cave. Great cave with lots of Mayan pots still in place. Excellent.		Free with price of tour

Border Crossing Formalities

There is only one vehicle border crossing between Mexico and Belize, as well as one with Belize and Guatemala.

<u>Arrival</u>
After driving over the bridge from Mexico into Belize there is a small building which houses the Insurance Corporation of Belize where you can buy mandatory vehicle insurance (if you don't already have an international policy). Do this before you drive to the building complex housing immigration and customs. If you can't find the building, stop and ask.

Be sure to purchase the insurance as you will be stopped at least once at a police check point and they will ask for proof of insurance. Don't be caught out and risk a fine.

Entering from Guatemala, the insurance office is after you leave the Customs and Immigration compound. Mandatory liability insurance costs $58.00B for two weeks or $69.00B for thirty days. Belize Dollar to US Dollar exchange rate was 2B to 1US, subject to change.

Americas Overland

INSURANCE CORPORATION OF BELIZE LIMITED

MOTOR COVER NOTE
No. PMV/0115941

DOGRBQV0002

MR/MRS/MS:

INSURER INSURANCE CORPORATION OF BELIZE

DEPOSIT PREMIUM 58.00

DATE OF ISSUE 07 March 2008 12:15 P.M.

I DONALD BARRY GREENE having proposed to the Insurer for Insurance of the Motor vehicle described in the Schedule and having paid the Deposit Premium the applicable thereto subjected to the Special Conditions or Restrictions (if any) indicated below for the period of Cover stated. Unless the insurance be terminated by written notice to the proposer at the above address, in which case the insurance will thereupon cease and a proportionate part of the annual premium will be charged for the time the insurance has been in force.

PERIOD OF COVER 2 Weeks from Date of Issue at the Exact same time.
SCHEDULE

Make, model and type of Body	Engine/carrying capacity G.P.W	Registration, Chassis or Engine number
MITSUBISHI MOTORHOME 3DRS WHITE 2004	4 Cyl 3 Passengers	
Cover: Third Party Commercial	Used only for the following purposes as per overleaf	Use Clause

Special Conditions or Restrictions *As per overleaf*

CERTIFICATE OF MOTOR INSURANCE

I HEREBY CERTIFY that this Cover Note is issued in accordance with the provisions of the Motor Vehicle Insurance (Third Party Risk) Ordinance 1980.

INSURANCE CORPORATION OF BELIZE LIMITED
(Authorized Insured)

Countersigned by

Managing Director

INSURANCE CORP. OF BELIZE LTD
Benque Viejo Border
Cayo District
Phone: 823-2319 Fax: 803-2595

You must also stop to have your tires sprayed with insecticide, and you are required to pay a fee of $10.00B for this service. Then continue down the road until you reach the Immigration building.

Border crossing into Belize from Mexico

At the immigration office fill out your tourist card, get your passport stamped, then go next door to obtain the Motor Vehicle (Temporary Importation) Permit for your vehicle. The Customs officer will stamp your passport to reflect the fact that you are traveling with a vehicle.

You will need the original and one copy of the following documents:

- Vehicle Title
- Registration
- Driver's License
- Passport

Americas Overland

After you receive your Permit a customs officer will inspect your vehicle. Depending on the number of people in line this process can take anywhere from ten minutes to over an hour.

Be forewarned, Belize does not allow importation of cheese, meat, fruit, vegetables or alcohol.

When you leave the Customs and Immigration building, your vehicle documents will be inspected once more before you are allowed into the country. Passengers must walk around the building to be picked up by the vehicles on the other side.

The best thing about this border crossing was that everyone we worked with was friendly and welcoming. The formalities take time because everything is hand written into logbooks manually without the use of computers. This may change by the time you arrive.

Departure
Leaving Belize is even easier and quicker than entering. Belize immigration requires payment of exit fees in the total amount of $37.50B. Customs will collect the original Motor Vehicle Permit and then cancel the passport stamp as evidence that you have removed your vehicle out of the country and away you go.

Conch fisherman in the cayes

Chapter Nine

Guatemala

Routes
Maps
Camping
CA-4 Border Control Agreement
Border Crossing Formalities
- **Arrival**
- **Departure**

Routes

If following the Panamericana from Mexico, you would enter Guatemala at La Mesilla. This is a busy border crossing, yet it is the most direct route into the Guatemala Highlands. You could also arrive from Mexico through one of the smaller border posts close to the coast. If you do cross here, skip down the page to Huehuetenango to pick up the route south.

We would suggest that you take the longer route through Mexico's Yucatan Peninsula, spend some time exploring Belize, and then enter Guatemala through Benque Viejo del Carmen. This route puts you right in the Petén close to the Mayan ruins of the classical period.

Along this route, make your first night at the huge Mayan complex at Yaxha. From here you could drive to Parque Nacional Tikal and the fabulous Tikal ruins. If you have the time, take a break along Lago de Petén Itzá before continuing to Flores.

Terrific Tikal

For years we'd heard "You have to see Tikal, there's nothing like it!" Well after exploring most of the "top" Mayan sites in Mexico and Belize we were a little skeptical. We were wrong.

The towering pyramids rising above the canopy in the Guatemala jungle are nothing less than spectacular. These steep-sided temples are the most striking feature at Tikal. And I do mean STEEP. The temples range from 32m (100ft) to 66m high (200ft)! The stairs are so steep that it is dangerous for tourists to climb them so the archeologists have built ladders going nearly vertically up the sides. To climb the tallest temple, Temple V, we had to ascend 300 steps.

Tikal is different from many other sites because it is surrounded by jungle and there are tons of birds, howler monkeys and spider monkeys. Many of its plazas have been cleared of trees and vines with many of the temples at least partially restored. As you walk between the buildings you pass beneath the rain-forest canopy. The smells, the jungle and the animal noises all contribute to an experience not found at most other Mayan sites.

From Flores you now have two routes to choose from. The most direct route south follows CA13 to Poptún and Río Dulce from where you could take a boat to explore the river Río Dulce and the Garífuna village of Livingston. You could then bypass central and western Guatemala and head directly to Honduras via El Florido and the ruins at Copán.

The other option is to follow the newly paved CA5 from Flores to Cobán, stopping off to explore the ruins accessed from Sayaxché as you travel through the heart of the Petén. From Cobán you can detour out to explore the Grutas de Lanquín and the amazing natural bridge and pools at Semuc Champey.

Bats and a Natural Bridge
At the end of a dirt road past Cobán are the Grutas de Lanquín and Semuc Champey. The Grutas is a cave system with lots of interestingly shaped dripstone formations. But the real highlight is the bats, millions of them. At dusk they exit the cave through the small opening where we can stand and feel the bats brush by you on their way out.

A few miles past the Grutas are the pools at Semuc Champey. The river rushes down through limestone rocks where it dug itself a tunnel and goes underground for 300m (390ft). This has created a "natural bridge" over the water, on top of which there are crystalline pools fed by springs coming out of an adjacent mountain.

These pools tumble downhill over small waterfalls eventually joining up with the river where it comes out from underground. We swam in the pools and wondering where the fish came from, marveled at the gorgeous scene that we were part of. There are also several hiking trails to partake of and camping is available outside the park entrance.

Leaving Cobán you can visit the Parque Natural El Quetzal where you might glimpse a reclusive Resplendent Quetzal. From here you can continue south to CA9 which will take you into Guatemala City, or you can reverse back toward Cobán and take the rough and narrow road across the mountains to the highlands, arriving in Huehuetenango. This road is under construction and will, in a couple of years, be completely paved. However in 2008 we had to drive through 35 miles of construction.

This is a beautiful route through the remote highlands giving you the opportunity to explore less visited areas like the Nebaj triangle. If you can fit on the small bridge at Sacapulas you could head south toward Chichicastenango and bypass Huehuetenango. But doing that will cause you to miss the hot springs of Fuentes Georginas near Quetzaltenango (Xela).

Hot Springs Camp

Fuentes Georginas is the most beautiful natural hot spring in Guatemala. Just getting there is a delight for the senses. The narrow road winds up a mountain through fields of onions, radishes and carrots and is made all the more colorful by the dress of the indigenous people gathering the produce. Arriving at the huge entry gate we were admitted to use the springs and camp for the night. We passed a pool near the entrance and parked nearby.

We then headed up to the main pools to spend some time. There were quite a few people there in a number of different pools of varying temperatures. We checked out a couple and spent about an hour soaking. We then decided it was time to visit the spring closest to the car and found it to be an absolute gem. It was the perfect temperature, it was in a beautiful natural setting, it was large enough to actually swim in and we had it all to ourselves. We soaked for another hour and reluctantly got out when we were completely pruned.

In the morning the skies were clear and we could see the tallest mountain in Central America, Volcán Tajumulco at 4,220m (13,926ft). The view was incredible and we celebrated by taking another solitary soak before driving back down the mountain.

From Fuentes Georginas you would follow the Panamericana to Chichicastenango, trying to arrive on Wednesday or Saturday afternoon so that you won't have to fight the traffic on the Thursday or Sunday market days. After market day, head to Sololá and Panajachel to explore and relax along the scenic Lago de Atitlán. Some travelers stay here for weeks!

Heading to Antigua, take the back route from Panajachel through Patzún. This is a beautiful drive

that is also quicker than returning to the Panamericana.
If you can arrange to be in Antigua during Easter you
will experience an amazing spectacle of faith.

Semana Santa
Visiting the town of Antigua for Semana Santa is one of
the most beautiful experiences we have ever had.
Semana Santa is the week before Easter and
observances are held daily all around the city and in
every church. These observances include decorated
altars in the churches and re-enactments of the Last
Supper and Trial of Jesus and the Crucifixion, but they
also include processions through the streets. Each day
a different church hosts a procession and the statues of
the saints from inside the church are affixed to large
wooden floats to be carried through the streets.

The residents begin preparing for the processions the
night before by gathering together the materials
necessary to create carpets (called *alfombras*) along the
street. The materials might consist of pine needles,
flowers, sawdust, leaves or anything they can think of or
find to use as a decoration. No one is allowed to walk
on the carpets until the procession comes by.

In the morning, the floats, weighing thousands of
pounds, are hoisted onto the shoulders of as many as
fifty purple-robed men (or women if it is a float for the
Virgin Mary) and carried through the streets of the city.
Drummers and copal (incense) bearers accompany the
floats. Regularly, the carriers are changed as the floats
are carried several miles through town. The devotion of
all of the participants is evidenced by the care with which
they prepare the beautiful *alfombras* and the sweat
rolling down the faces of the float carriers. The most
spectacular procession took place at night and was
accompanied by burning torches. An absolutely magical
experience.

Americas Overland

After spending a few days exploring the city, getting lost in the markets or maybe even studying a bit of Spanish, you can arrange to climb the Pacaya Volcano and roast marshmallows over the red-hot lava.

Hike to Flowing Lava

The Pacaya Volcano is the only one of Guatemala's volcanoes where it is possible to see flowing lava. Despite statements about how easy the hike would be it turned out to be a very difficult climb up to the crater. We should have guessed at how difficult it would be as the locals rent horses to the hikers for the ride up. About half way up, with the trail getting steeper with every passing step, we spotted a horse handler coming down the volcano empty. We negotiated a price and Kim got to ride the rest of the way up.

Reaching the top, we then had to negotiate the steep and sharp lava down into the crater. Finally getting close to the fresh lava, it was quite an interesting sight, and very hot if you got too close. So hot in fact, that other tourists pulled marshmallows out of their packs and started roasting them over the lava. It was hysterical to watch.

Then it was time to go back up out of the crater, as it was getting dark. Once more at the top, we put on our headlamps (and our jackets) and started hiking down. After a short distance, Kim stepped badly on a rock, twisted her ankle and fell. After picking herself up, covered from head to toe in dust from the fall, she determined that the ankle was usable, but very sore. It took us a couple of hours to make it down with the help of our guide. Finally making it off the mountain we were surprised to find the bus still waiting for us. We had figured that the bus driver would have to stick to his schedule and leave us behind, but he waited and nobody seemed to mind the extra wait.

If you are heading to El Salvador, you can bypass Guatemala City by taking the new road from Antigua to Escuintla, then follow the roads to the border crossing near Las Chinamas, El Salvador.

If heading to Honduras, you can either enter after exploring El Salvador, or you can brave Guatemala City so that you can enter near Copán Ruinas through the El Florido crossing.

Maps

Rough Guides Guatemala and Belize Map, scale 1:500,000

ITMB, Guatemala travel reference map, scale 1:470,000

Freytag and Berndt, Belize/Guatemala with a scale: 1:400,000

Nelles Map, Mexico – Guatemala - El Salvador and Belize, scale 1:2,500,000

Americas Overland

Guatemalan Maya

Share the road with the "Chicken Buses"

Guatemala Camping

Location	Description	GPS Coordinates	Cost
Yaxha Ruins	Campamento Yaxha, on the lake below the ruins, included with price of admission.	N17 7.00 W089 24.065	Free
Tikal Ruins	Great campground, bathroom and showers, in the park itself.		Pay
El Remate along Lago Petén Itzá	Gringo Perdido, lakeside, private, water, restaurant. North side of lake past the Cerro Cahui Reserve.	N16 59.658 W089 42.934	Pay
Flores	On the malecon as soon as you cross over the causeway.		Free
Sayaxché	Café del Río, free camp w/boat tour to Mayan ruins. Overlooking the river at the ferry crossing, grassy, restaurant.	N16 31.995 W090 11.346	
Candelaria/Raxruja	KM319 on RN5. Closed hotel, ask caretaker for permission. Lots of karst formations nearby.	N15 52.360 W090 06.370	Free
Semuc Champey	Multiple options, entry road has some steep sections. Beautiful.		
Lanquín	Hotel El Retiro, tight entrance, space for two vehicles, on the river, restaurant.	N15 34.867 W089 58.542	Pay
Lanquín	Grutas de Lanquín, great spot to watch the bats leave at dusk.	N15 34.820 W089 59.430	Pay
Cobán	PN Las Victorias, close to center, very quiet, entrance at 11a AV and 3a Calle.		Pay
Cunen	Big turn out at the summit between Sacapulus and Cunen, great views 7,000'.	N15 19.768 W091 02.897	Free

Americas Overland

Location	Description	GPS Coordinates	Cost
Huehuetenango	Maxi Bodega parking lot, not flat.		Free
Huehuetenango	Hotel San Francisco, Internet & restaurant.	N15 18.698 W091 29.093	Free
Fuentes Georginas, Zunil	Great hot springs, park just inside entrance next to semi-private pool, great views. 7,900'.	N14 45.030 W091 28.804	Pay
Siquinala	Texaco Station on CA2, great "port in a storm", free parking, water, toilet, shower, restaurant.	N14 17.835 W090 57.309	Free
Patzún	Backroad into Panajachal on RT1, camping ground w/pool on river, between KM 92/93.		
Panajachel	Vision Azul Hotel, lakeside camp, entrance is the GPS point. From Sololá entrance is steep.	N14 44.693 W091 09.774	Pay
Panajachel	Tzanjuyu Bay Hotel, closer to town but next to ferry port and more than a bit run down.		Pay
Chichicastenango	Casa del Rey, just on the edge before town.	N14 56.140 W091 06.605	
Chichicastenango	Parqueo, fenced and secure. Continue into town about 2-3 blocks past the Hotel Santo Tomas (at 7 Av). Black gate on left w/sign Parqueo. Do not try to access on market day.	N14 56.664 W091 06.576	
Poptún	Camp at Finca Ixabel. Great camping area, electricity and water available, many activities to spend days doing.		Pay

Location	Description	GPS Coordinates	Cost
Río Dulce	Possible camping and temp storage of vehicles (for visiting Livingston) at the marinas located under the Río Dulce Bridge. We parked our truck at Bruno's Hotel/Restaurant/Marina. Possible camping at Hotel La Ensenada possibly changed its name to Planeta Río.		Pay
Near Quiriguá Ruins	Possible to camp just outside the ruins at the guard shack. Better camping at the town of Mariscos 8 miles north of the highway (20min) on the southern shore of Lago de Ixabal. Camping at Playa Escondida.	N15 25.43 W89 04.65	Pay
Río Hondo	Possible camping at the Hotel Nuevo Pasabien.	N15 39.44 W89 40.28	Pay
Chiquimula	Comfortable camping in the secure public parking lot across from the Posada Don Adan. 2 blocks from the central plaza.	N14 48.12 W89 32.69	Pay
Antigua	Private parqueo behind the bus station/market near the private hospital.	N14 33.580 W090 44.483	Pay
Antigua	Secure, free parking at the Tourist Police Yard. Ask at the Tourist Office to call ahead. Near the bus station.		

Central America-4 (CA-4) Border Control Agreement

In June 2006, the Central America-4 Border Control Agreement was put into effect between Guatemala, El Salvador, Honduras and Nicaragua. Under the terms of the agreement, citizens of the four countries may travel freely across land borders from one of the countries to any of the others without completing entry and exit formalities at Immigration checkpoints.

U.S. citizens and other eligible foreign nationals, who legally enter any of the four countries, may similarly travel among the four without obtaining additional visas or tourist entry permits for the other three countries. Immigration officials at the first port of entry determine the length of stay, up to a maximum period of 90 days.

Foreign tourists who wish to remain in the four country region beyond the period initially granted for their visit are required to request a one-time extension of stay from local Immigration authorities in the country where the traveler is physically present, or travel outside the CA-4 countries and reapply for admission to the region. Foreigners "expelled" from any of the four countries are excluded from the entire CA-4 region.

Border Crossing Formalities

There are three vehicle border crossings between Guatemala and Mexico. There is one vehicle crossing with Belize, four crossings into El Salvador and three into Honduras.

Arrival
At the Belize/Guatemala border, we changed some US
dollars for Guatemalan Quetzals and paid 40.00Q
(about $6.00US, subject to change) to have our tires
sprayed with insecticide. This included our spare tires
too! Then we were directed to park at the border gate
itself so that the guard could keep an eye on our vehicle
while we did our Guatemalan paper work.

Immigration was quick, just a stamp in the passports. If
you are entering Guatemala from one of the CA-4
countries, immigration will verify your original date of
entry into the region and not stamp your passport.

Then inside the SAT office (Guatemala Customs) where
we completed our vehicle documents and had our
vehicle title checked. The inspector will direct you to the
bank to pay 40.00Q for taxes, the *Impuesto de
Circulación*.

At the *Importaciónes y Exportaciónes* window provide
SAT (Customs) with the original and one copy of the
following documents:

- Vehicle Title
- Registration
- Driver's License
- Passport
- Receipt for tax payment

Americas Overland

Declaración de Ingreso de Vehículo Automotor por Turista

SAT-No. 8093 No. VN-8-0262330

FORMA
114-3-SAT-CCC-S-V

Aduana y fecha de Ingreso del vehículo: VALLE NUEVO FEB-15-2008

1. Nombre completo del Turista: GREENE DONALD	
2. Nacionalidad: UNITED STATES	3. No. de Pasaporte:
4. País de Expedición: UNITED STATES	5. Motivo de la Permanencia: TURISMO
6. Dirección en Guatemala: HOTELES	
7. Tipo de Vehículo: CASA RODANTE	8. Marca: MITSUBISHI	9. Línea: F I6 TK
10. Color: BLANCO	11. Modelo: 2004	12. No. De Serie (VIN): 014
13. No. De Placas: OO	14. País de Expedición de las Placas: UNITED STATES
15. Desplazamiento c.c.: 0	16. Aduana de Salida del Vehículo:

17. Declaro bajo juramento que los datos consignados son ciertos y exactos, de lo contrario me someto a las disposiciones que establece el artículo 459 del Código Penal. Además me comprometo a retornar al extranjero el vehículo antes de vencer el plazo de permanencia autorizada, de no ser así tendré la obligación de ponerlo en conocimiento de la Autoridad Aduanera más cercana, con el objeto de hacer efectivo el pago de impuestos de importación en base al artículo 18 del Decreto 117-96 del Congreso de la República de Guatemala.

18. Firma del Turista:

19. Código de Barras:

20. Firma Electrónica de Internación:

54PB27HXN

21. El Administrador de la Aduana VALLE NUEVO HACE CONSTAR Y DA FE: Que por la misma ingreso el vehículo anteriormente descrito y para demostrar la propiedad del mismo se tuvo a la vista el documento consistente en: TITULO DE PROPIEDAD para el cual se autoriza la calcomanía de la serie: TIRISTA con registro numero 188061 y cuyo valor es de Q40.00

22. Fecha de Expiración de la permanencia: MAR-28-2008

23. Firma y sello del Administrador de la Aduana:

24. Vehículos Adicionales Autorizados:

Descripción	Marca	Modelo	Número de Serie	Número de Calcomanía
NO DECLARO VEHICULOS ADICIONALES				

Ejemplar: Turista
Ejemplar: Aduana

Autorizado por la Contraloría General de Cuentas, según resolución número Br.;845 Clas.; 2001-12-B-A-17-2002 de fecha 06-02-2003. Número correlativo de autorización de impresión 57/03 de fecha 03-03-2003; Rango de numeración del 001 al 500,000. Número de envío fiscal 4-ASCC-1824 de fecha 03-03-2003.

You will receive the vehicle permit – *Declaracion de Ingreso de Vehículo Automotor por Turista* together with a registration stamp. You do not need to adhere the registration sticker to your windshield, just leave it attached to your vehicle permit.

Be sure to have a photocopy of the vehicle permit made before you leave the border.

If arriving from Belize, or exiting into Belize you will be stopped at the entry into Melchor de Mencos, the border town, and required to pay a fee of 50.00Q just to enter the town. This fee is demanded from all foreign vehicles and you will not be allowed to pass if you do not pay it.

There was no mandatory insurance requirement as of 2008.

Departure
When leaving Guatemala you will need to pay an exit fee of 10.00Q at the Immigration desk, then surrender your *Declaracion de Ingreso de Vehículo Automotor por Turista* together with the registration stamp at the *Aduana* desk.

Semana Santa celebration in Antigua

Chapter Ten

El Salvador

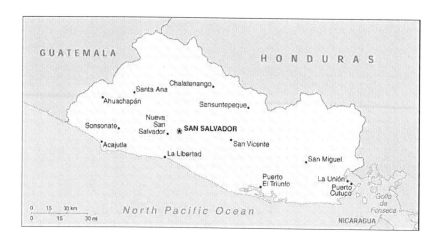

Routes
Maps
Camping
Border Crossing Formalities
- **Arrival**
- **Departure**

Routes

Following the coastal route from Guatemala you will enter El Salvador at La Hachadura. This is fine if you are hurrying through the country and wish to continue down the coast and bypass San Salvador. This would also be the route to follow if you wanted to visit all of the beaches.

If you are driving south from Belize and wish to avoid Guatemala City you would likely enter at Anguiatú. However most overlanders will likely use one of the routes off the Panamericana.

The Panamericana crosses the border at San Cristóbal, which will likely be the busiest place to cross as most of the trucks and buses follow this route right into San Salvador.

Our favorite crossing is the small border post near Las Chinamas. Commercial vehicles are prohibited from using this entry so the process here is very relaxed. After climbing into the highlands, the highway, CA8, deposits you on the Ruta de Las Flores know for its colorful wildflower displays in the fall and winter months.

Continue along CA8 past Izalco where you can turn off to hike the volcanoes at Parque Nacional Cerro Verde. Then follow the edge of the crater housing Lago de Coatepeque. Dropping off of the crater rim, meet up with the Panamericana which will take you to the archaeological site of Joya de Cerén.

Cerro Verde National Park
The early morning drive to Parque Nacional Cerro Verde was quite attractive with nice views of the crater lake, Lago de Coatepeque. We needed to arrive at the park before 11:00am when the only guided hikes of the day occur.

We had wanted to climb Volcán Santa Ana, but when we arrived we found out that since the eruption in 2005, the volcano was closed to hiking. This is the very same volcano that some friends of ours had hiked only a month before the eruption. Their email to us at the time said "it was an awfully active volcano for one that hasn't erupted in 100 years".

Our only other option was to hike Volcán Iralzco which is a cinder cone that rose out of the ground 200+ years ago and is still steaming. That sounded like a good idea until we were standing at the base of it looking almost straight up. After the steep hike down from the parking lot to the base (whose idea was that?) we didn't relish another steep hike up, then down, then up again. So we had lunch at the base of the volcano and enjoyed the view before heading back up the hellacious mountain trail we had endured earlier.

Skirt around San Salvador to CA4 and take the back entrance to the village of Suchitoto. If you were entering Honduras you could continue north on CA4 to the border at Citila. After relaxing in Suchitoto follow the Panamericana further east and then detour back into the highlands through Berlin and Alegría.

From Alegría you could venture toward the coast to visit the crowded scene at Playa El Espino, or head north towards Honduras to explore the cool mountain region around Perquín that was the headquarters of the FMLN during the civil war. If you haven't explored Honduras yet, you could cross here, or you could retrace your steps out of the mountains and cross into Honduras along the Panamericana at El Amatillo.

Playa El Espino
It had been a long, hot, tiring day crossing from Honduras into El Salvador. We drove through the city of San Miguel and after getting lost, of course, headed south to Playa El Espino.

Upon reaching the end of the paved road, we turned left,

determined to find a spot on the beach. Which was difficult because every inch of the beach between the road and the ocean was covered by private bamboo structures designed to provide shelter to beachgoers for a fee. The biggest problem (for us) was that most of the businesses were small, narrow and had blocked the view of the ocean completely.

After traveling as far as we dared down the narrow and getting narrower road, we turned around determined to find a spot. Very soon after turning back, we found one where you could actually still see the water and had a big enough parking area for us. I'm not sure how we missed it on the way in, but there it was.

We negotiated with la senora for $5.00US/night and pulled in. And as it was shortly before sunset, the first thing we did was pull out our chairs and walk down to the beach. And a good thing we did too, because it turned out to be the best sunset we had seen on the trip. And when la senora brought us some pupusas, which are the Salvadoran national food, well, it made our day.

Maps

ITMB, El Salvador travel reference map, scale 1:250,000

Nelles Map, Mexico – Guatemala - El Salvador and Belize, scale 1:2,500,000

Weller Cartographic Services, www.mapmatrix.com, El Salvador Road Map

El Salvador Camping

Location	Description	GPS Coordinates	Cost
Playa El Espino	Small plots with restaurants and palapas on beach with room for one, maybe two rigs. Nicer places further from the pavement. Beach isn't one of the best.	N13 10.212 W088 17.087	Pay
Suchitoto	Camped on street in front of police station near the square.	N 13 56.727 W89 01.042	Free
Suchitoto	Also camped at El Mangal de Suchitlan Pool & Restaurant next to Centro Turistico Puerto San Juan. Has pool, restaurant, toilets, showers, electricity, and water.		Pay
Ciudad Arce	Puma Petrol Station on the highway.		Free
Perquin	Parking lot of the Museo de la Revolucion.		
Parque Nacional Cerro Verde	Parking area very quiet at night restaurant open during the day. Do not take the road access from Izalco. 6,600'.	N13 49.594 W089 37.435	Pay
Apaneca	Finca Santa Leticia. Parking near guard shack, quiet, restaurant and park setting, 4300'.	N13 51.128 W89 46.913	Free

Border Crossing Formalities

There are four vehicle border crossings between El Salvador and Guatemala. There are three vehicle crossings into Honduras.

Arrival

At the El Salvador border, we changed our remaining foreign currency into US Dollars as that is the national currency. We paid $3.00, subject to change, to have our tires sprayed with insecticide.

Thanks to the CA-4 Agreement, our passports were checked by an immigration officer to verify our original date of entry into the region and we were waved into the country without a passport stamp. Be sure to ask the officer for the location of the *Aduana* office to obtain your vehicle permit. Ask the officer if he can provide you with the paperwork so that you can have it prepared for when you arrive at *Aduana*. Sometimes they will have copies available. Trying to find the correct building to get our permit was a bit tricky, but we just kept asking until we found the right place.

Your vehicle permit in El Salvador is the *Autorización Para El Régimen De Importación De Vehículos Usados*.

You will need the original and one copy of the following documents:

- Vehicle Title
- Registration
- Driver's License
- Passport

Americas Overland

REPUBLICA DE EL SALVADOR C.A.
MINISTERIO DE HACIENDA
DIRECCION GENERAL DE ADUANAS
AUTORIZACION PARA EL REGIMEN DE IMPORTACION DE VEHICULO USADOS

01.Fecha Ingreso: 07/02/2008	02.Aduana de Entrada:09 - TERRESTRE EL AMATILLO						03.Autorización No;000145770
04.Nombre (Consignatario)	DONALD GREENE				06.Teléfono:	00	
05.Dirección : HOTELES DE EL SALVADOR							
07.Tipo de Régimen o permiso solicitado	03-Turista Extranjero			08.Nit:		00	
09.Código Importador:	00			10.Impuestos a pagar($):		0	
11.No. Pasaporte:				12. País de Procedencia:		HN - Honduras	
13.Documentos que el vehiculo presenta:			CT: Certificate of Title		S/N		
			CT: Certificate of Title		S/N		
			CT: Certificate of Title		S/N		

DESCRIPCION DEL VEHICULO

14. Chasis Grabado:	JL6	26. Cilindrada (cc):	3000
15. VIN:	JL6	27. Peso (Kilogramos):	3400
16. No. Motor:	N/D	28. No. de Puertas:	2
17. Año:	2004	29. No. Placa Extranjera:	CC
18. Marca:	MITSUBISHI	30. Estado/País Placa:	U.S.A.
19. Línea y Estilo:	F39	31. Condición Vehículo:	01-Limpio
20. Clase:	CAMIONETA FAMILIAR	32. Ubicación Volante:	01-Izquierdo
21. Color:	BLANCO	33. Fecha de Producción:	01/01/2004
22. Tipo Combustible:	52 - DIESEL	34. Modelo:	GE1H
23. Tipo Capacidad:	1-Asientos	35. Tipo de Cama:	00 - No Aplica
24. Capacidad:	5/7	36. Tipo de Ingreso Vehic:	Rodando
25. No. de Cilindros:	4	37. Uso del Vehículo:	Circulación

38. Observaciones:

Declaro bajo juramento que la información contenida en el presente documento es
expresión fiel de la verdad; por lo que asumo la responsabilidad correspondiente.   Nombre y Firma del Declarante

RESERVADO POR LA ADUANA			
	40. Permiso autorizando:		
	60 Dias:	X	No:000145770Reg.:Turista Extranjero
	90 Dias:		Placa:CC Vin:JL6
	180 Dias:		Consignatario:DONALD GREENE
	Especial:		Aut:07/02/2008 14:22:08 Ven:05/24/2008 User:ppedro
	41. Fecha de autorizacion:		ADUANA EL AMATILLO
	07/02/2008		R.L. C.A. SVCA
39. Nombre, Firma y Sello del Funcionario de la Aduana.	42. Fecha vencimiento		CONTADOR VISTA
	06/04/2008		Pedro A. J. Perez

Coming from Honduras we were told to provide a copy of the passport pages containing the vehicle entry and exit stamps from Honduras. An unusual request but easy enough to comply with, as there were copy shops nearby.

When exiting from the border zone into El Salvador the inspector required that we provide him with a copy of the vehicle permit.

There was no mandatory insurance requirement as of 2008.

Departure

Leaving El Salvador into Guatemala was so easy that it was over before we knew what was happening.

At the border an *Aduana* official collected our vehicle permit and waved us across the border. There was no inspection and no immigration responsibilities!

Playa El Espino

Chapter Eleven

Honduras

Routes
Maps
Camping
Border Crossing Formalities
- **Arrival**
- **Departure**

Routes

Of the three border crossings with Guatemala, the one most used by overlanders is El Florido as it enters the country close to the Copán Ruinas. Agua Caliente is a minor crossing and the crossing at Corinto near Puerto Barrios, Guatemala often refuses to allow vehicles to cross, so be prepared to turn around if you are refused passage here.

From El Salvador the main crossings are at El Poy north of San Salvador and El Amatillo along the Panamericana. The small crossing at Perquín is rarely used.

 After spending a couple of days at the town and ruins of Copán Ruinas you could drive north straight to San Pedro Sula and then to the Caribbean coast. The better route however is to follow the roundabout route to Gracias a Dios and then through the mountains to Lago de Yojoa. After birding and relaxing at the lake, the route will take you to the Caribbean at Tela.

Good Friday, Honduras Style
From the town of Gracias a Dios, we headed out over the mountains on a narrow, 50-mile long dirt road toward Lago de Yojoa. Along the way we passed through some small villages. In two of them there were Good Friday processions taking place, and they were happening right down the middle of the only road. Fortunately, both times we encountered large devotional groups of people on the road, there was room to pull over to wait for them to pass. One of the groups stopped twice before they got past us to kneel on the rocky road and pray. It was quite a show of devotion and an unforgettable experience. Some of the other bystanders watching the processions took up vantage points in the shade created by our truck.

Along the coast you can continue to La Ceiba where you can park your vehicle and fly to the Bay Islands. Along the coast you can detour off the road and visit some of the small Garífuna villages. If you haven't had your fill of the Caribbean just yet, continue on to Trujillo or just beyond into the Mosquitia - Mosquito Coast.

Scuba Diving in the Bay Islands
Wanting to dive in the Bay Islands, we got up at 6:00am, secured the expedition vehicle to leave at Finca El Eden and headed out to the highway to catch a bus. Within minutes, we were on our way to the airport in La Ceiba. Arriving at the ticket counter, we asked when the next flight was to Utila. 10 – 15 minutes came the reply. Can we get on the flight? Yes, no problem. Will our bags get on the flight? No problem. We paid, our tickets were issued, we got someone at the front of the long line to pay the airport tax to pay our tax for us and we rushed off to the gate.

The flight to Utila took all of 15 minutes and we were soon eating a second breakfast on the main drag of the tiny town. Utila is the cheapest place in the world to learn to scuba dive and the town was filled with travelers from all over the world learning to do just that. We checked into a hotel and then went to find out about diving. Easy as pie, we were booked onto a boat for two afternoon dives.

The diving was spectacular on the protected reef and the fish and corals were very colorful, but it was the surface interval (dive speak for required rest time between dives) that was really memorable. As we were moving between dive locations, we spotted a very large pod of dolphins. And then they spotted us, turned and made a beeline for the boat, jumping out of the water and playing in the bow wake.

We grabbed our masks and snorkels and as soon as the boat was able to come to a stop, we slipped into the water. The dolphins surrounded us and swam under, around and next to us for about 15 minutes. Then they were gone. We climbed back into the boat, started up and here came the dolphins again. There were only five of us on the boat (plus the captain, who stayed at the helm) so we were able to take turns lying on the front of the boat, hanging onto the bow line, reaching over to try to touch the dolphins as they came up for air. The divemaster identified them as bottlenose dolphins and they had the most beautiful designs on their backs. They hung out with the boat for about a half hour and we had a wondrous time with them.

If you want to follow any of the overland routes across the country to Tegucigalpa be sure to stop and ask if the roads are open and safe. Otherwise, retrace your steps back to Lago de Yojoa and then through Comayagua and past Tegucigalpa.

Bird-watching
Lago del Yojoa is the largest lake in Honduras. We found a nice place to stay on the shore at Finca Las Glorias, which is a large farm that has been turned into a tourist attraction. Our grassy camp spot was in an open area surrounded by large trees and allowed a terrific view of the birds.

Our first morning we saw four Turquoise-browed Motmots. These are beautiful multicolored birds with a tail that is long and featherless until the very bottom where there is a paddle shaped feather. We also saw several types of orioles, doves, flycatchers, tanagers, seedeaters, and woodpeckers. All in all, a wonderful bird-watching spot.

On the way to Nicaragua you must now choose from the mountainous route through Danlí or the coastal route through Choluteca. Chances are that the temperature will be a factor in choosing the route.

Three Police Stories

We traveled through Honduras during the Semana Santa holiday, which takes place during the week leading up to Easter, and often carries over for the next week. During this time the police and military had a huge presence on the highways that resulted in a high number of stops/check points being in action, so we had an unusually large number of police interactions.

Far and away, the majority of the stops by both the police and the military were brief and courteous. Seeing from our license plate that we were a foreign vehicle, many officials just waved us through without stopping. Others stopped us and asked the usual questions: where are you from, where are you going and how long will you be in Honduras. These questions are just normal curiosity and their attempts to be friendly. Surprisingly, many officers told us to be careful of other drivers since this was a holiday time and many people might be partying. We also received more welcoming handshakes than we ever received in other countries.

We did have three other types of interactions with the local police:

1. One officer stopped us at a checkpoint and began asking if we had our safety equipment, ie: fire extinguisher and safety triangle. When we answered yes, he hesitated then asked if we could help him out with a few dollars. In reply we smiled and said no, and he smiled and said ok and we drove away.

2. One night we decided to spend the night in a

beautiful park that seemed safe and quiet. While we were using our BBQ, a motorcycle officer coasted up behind us with his engine off to surprise us. Yes, we literally jumped when he said hello. Then he explained that the park wasn't safe, hadn't he just snuck up on us? He suggested we leave before it was totally dark and spend the night elsewhere. We left immediately and found a quiet hotel parking lot to spend the night.

3. Our final interaction with the police was one of only two times in 16 months that a bribe was demanded. We were told, variously that our vehicle wasn't allowed on the road, that we were too wide or too tall and that our license plate was improperly displayed. We pleasantly argued with the officers (there were three) for close to thirty minutes. We had to as they had Don's drivers license. Actually they thought they had his original license but this was exactly the type of situation for which we carry color copies of our driver's licenses. We refuse to offer up the original of any document and will only give officials photocopies.

When these police refused to reconsider their one hundred dollar demand, Don got back into the truck, waved to the police and drove away. Looking back at the police none were rushing to their cars to pursue, but the one holding the fake license was standing in the middle of the street waving it at us.

Maps

ITMB, Honduras travel reference map, scale 1:75,000

Weller Cartographic Services, www.mapmatrix.com, Honduras Road Map

Honduras Camping

Location	Description	GPS Coordinates	Cost
Copán	Camping at the balnearios a few miles past the ruins. Small Balneario Escondido, and the larger Hacienda El Jaral.		Pay
Copán	Possible to park at the fuel station on the highway just outside of town.		
Gracias a Dios	Camping at the Finca Bavaria on the corner one block NW of the Iglesia La Merced. Walk in the front gate and ask permission to drive in the back gate.		Pay
Gracias a Dios	Also able to park on the main square in front of the police station		Free
Lago de Yojoa	Finca Las Glorias. Great location on the lakeshore. Ask to camp near the hacienda. Possible camping along the hwy at Los Remos Hotel.	N14 56.787 W88 02.280	Pay
Trujillo	Campamento RV park, on the beach	N 15 54.317 W85 59.299	Pay
La Ceiba area	Camping/parking at Finca El Eden in Santa Ana about 12km west of the airport. We parked our truck here while we spent time on Utila. Easy bus access to the airport and La Ceiba.		Pay
Siguatepeque	Free camped at the Hotel Pasagio Turistico/Restaurante La Faltoria. Ask permission in the restaurant. The complex includes a market and bank. Possible to free camp at the large Shell Gas Station and truck stop about 1/2 mile south of the hotel.	N14 35.38 W87 51.48	Free
Choluteca	Camped at the Hotel Gualiqueme.	N13 18.86 W87 11.48	Free

Location	Description	GPS Coordinates	Cost
El Espino Border Crossing with Nicaragua	Best option is the no-name Club & Camping at KM189/190 about 15 minutes before the Nicaragua border at El Espino in the mountains.		Pay

Border Crossing Formalities

There are three vehicle crossings from Honduras into Guatemala, three with El Salvador and three more with Nicaragua.

<u>Arrival</u>
Our first crossing from Guatemala was at El Florido as it was closest to the ruins at Copán. At the border we once again grabbed our passports and the paperwork for the vehicle and headed to deal with officialdom. Once again, the immigration and customs people were polite and efficient and we were done with both sides of the border within 45 minutes.

The vehicle permit in Honduras is the *Permiso De Entrada Y Salida Temporal De Vehículo*. In addition to the vehicle permit the customs inspector will stamp your passport with an *Ingreso Vehículo* stamp with your vehicle details written on it. When you exit the country you must present your passport to get the *Salida de Vehículo* stamp.

You will need the original and one copy of the following documents:

- Vehicle Title
- Registration
- Driver's License
- Passport

This border between Guatemala and Honduras had all of the officials together in one set of buildings. After checking out of Guatemala at one end of the building, we walked a few feet and checked into Honduras. At the time of writing, entry fees payable at the border were $39.00US.

Remember, every time you enter a country, be sure to make a copy or two of your Temporary Import Permit. Again, don't give the police the original of your Import Permit, just a copy.

Traveling northward, we crossed back into Honduras from Nicaragua at the El Espino crossing. There were big signs in English stating that all immigration and customs services were to be provided at no charge. This actually meant that there were no charges over and above the required fee of $39.00US for your vehicle permit. This is to discourage officials from demanding "extra" payments (read: bribes).

This information came in very handy as the very next day when we arrived at the El Amatillo crossing from Honduras to El Salvador, one of the officials requested payment of a $10.00US fee. When pressed to show us the official fee list, he relented and told us to go away!

Departure

Departure fees payable at the Honduras border were $3.00US.

If you are unsure about where to surrender your vehicle document and pay your departure fee, simply drive right up to the border gate. The guard will tell you where to park and where immigration and customs can be found. There is no reason to just wander around looking for the right office. If you wander around you will just be asking for the *tramitadores* to surround you offering up their services.

There is no fee for the cancellation of your vehicle permit.

Chapter Twelve

Nicaragua

Routes
Maps
Camping
Border Crossing Formalities
- Arrival
- Departure

Routes

Most travelers visit only a small portion of Nicaragua, primarily the Pacific region, as the Caribbean side of the country is serviced by poor roads, when there are roads at all, or by boat.

For the overland driver, Nicaragua shares three border crossings with Honduras: Las Manos, El Espino and Guasaule.

If traveling along the coast, Guasaule is the most direct route to the Pacific coast and the city of León. However one of the mountain crossings will give you a break from the heat and humidity typically found in the lowlands. If traveling south from Tegucilgalpa, Honduras, Las Manos is the most direct route, while, if heading from the coast or from El Salvador, El Espino would be best. Both of these routes connect on the highway to Estelí.

Estelí was a focal point during the Sandinista's fight against the government run by the Somoza family. It is also a big tobacco region as well as the starting point for trips into the Reserva Natural Miraflor.

A Local Museum

In the town of Estelí we visited La Galeria de Heroes y Martires (The Gallery of Heroes and Martyrs) which is a museum set up by the mothers of the local soldiers (both men and women) who died fighting Somoza's National Guard. It was incredibly interesting. It contained the personal effects of many of the soldiers, photographs, stories and timelines.

Visiting places like this helps to understand the local viewpoint of why they felt the battles or wars were

> necessary, stories that we only hear one side of when
> reading news at home. We learned a lot from that one
> little museum.

From Estelí, travel down the Panamericana detouring off to the coffee producing highlands around Matagalpa.

From Matagalpa drive to León and, if you're feeling energetic try climbing one of the nearby volcanoes. Then head south crossing through Managua and on to Masaya.

Poison Gas and Gospel-Preaching Military
Parque Nacional Volcán Masaya is a small park with a pair of volcanoes having between them five craters. One of the craters is actually in the middle between the volcanoes and is active - sending up clouds of toxic gas. You can drive right up the side of the volcano and park at the edge of the crater. The gas swirls around the area and depending on which way the wind blows it can be pretty much unbearable to stay long. The rangers who are stationed at the crater are equipped with gas masks as standard equipment. Interestingly, there is a species of parrot that makes its nest on the cliffs inside the crater - despite the presence of the fumes.

After our visit to the crater, we were welcomed to set up camp for the night in the Visitor Center parking lot. We found a great spot overlooking the Laguna de Masaya and the town of Masaya. After we got ourselves set, we had a new friend stop by. Francisco is a sergeant in the military and guards the park with three other soldiers. What do you do when you have a person in military fatigues walk into your campsite and ask you if you want to see his AKA machine gun? Although we were a bit uncomfortable, we offered him a glass of ice tea and tried to chat. He then took out his bible and asked us if we believed in God. It turned out that after 10 years in the military, Francisco was lonely and a bit lacking in social skills but otherwise a nice fellow.

Circle around Laguna de Apoyo and enjoy the views of the volcanoes and Lago de Nicaragua, then look for a celebration in one of the villages of the "Pueblos Blancos" before driving into Granada.

Local Festival

Driving around the "Pueblos Blancos" (known for their white buildings) above Laguna de Apoyo, we came across a village that was holding a celebration for its patron saint. The saint was being carried on a float balanced on the shoulders of close to 30 men. The float was placed under a huge palapa built in the middle of the street while throngs of men, women and children, all holding lit candles, crowded in, trying to touch it, and offering prayers and asking for favors.

In the street around the palapa were cross-dressing, masked dancers as well as vendors selling candles, ice cream, food and sweets to the mob of villagers surrounding the saint. We were the only non-locals there but everyone welcomed us and didn't seem to mind as we took tons of photos of the procession and fiesta.

On your way south from Granada make camp in San Jorge on the shore of Lake Nicaragua. If you want to explore Isla de Ometepe you can take your chances with the ancient ferry or park your vehicle at one of the hotels and take a boat across to the island. From San Jorge you can reach the Costa Rican border in just a couple of hours.

Maps

ITMB, Nicaragua waterproof map, scale 1:755,000

Weller Cartographic Services, www.mapmatrix.com, Nicaragua Road Map

Ice cream vendor

Americas Overland

Nicaragua Camping

Location	Description	GPS Coordinates	Cost
León	Camping in the back of the Esso Gas Station, private and secure. Possible parking in the public parking lot two blocks west and one block south of the central park (height restriction of 10 feet).		Free
Masaya	Parque Nacional Volcán Masaya, good camping at the visitor center. Water available.		Pay
Granada	Camping on the street in front of Hotel Central.		Free
Granada	Centro Turistico de Lago Nicaragua. Along the shore of the lake just south of the malecon. A bit trashy, avoid on the weekends.	N11 54.773 W085 55.96	Pay
San Jorge	At the parking lot for the Ometepe ferry.	N11 27.62 W085 47.415	Pay
San Jorge	Free option is to park on the beach right next to the ferry terminal.	N11 27.61 W085 47.462	Free
San Jorge	Other option is at Hotel California just before you reach the terminal.		Pay
Masaya	Narome Resort off the road to Granada, 5 miles to the shore of Laguna de Apoyo, big parking area, free but order dinner. Full use of facilities, low hanging trees but doable. Wifi	N11 55.055 W086 3.475	Free
Matagalpa	Hotel Lomas de San Francisco (used to be Lomas de Guadalupe). Very steep entry, better to bypass town and drive 10km to Selva Negra.		
Selva Negra	At KM 140. Pay for entry and park away from office. Did not ask permission but nobody cared. Only for smaller campers.		
Selva Negra area	Other option nearby is Restaurant at KM 143, Great view but only good for low height vehicles.		

Location	Description	GPS Coordinates	Cost
Estelí	Club Campestre de Estelí. North of town approx 5km, big facility w/pool, toilets, water, electricity.	N13 8.895 W086 22.066	Pay

Border Crossing Formalities

Between Nicaragua and Honduras there are three vehicle border crossings. Heading south we chose to cross at Guasaule between El Triunfo, Honduras and Somotillo, Nicaragua. Northbound we used the El Espino/Las Manos crossing out of Estelí as we were intending to cross the isthmus and enter El Salvador. There is only one vehicle crossing with Costa Rica.

<u>Arrival</u>

There is a $7.00US fee to enter Nicaragua. There was a fumigation area on our way south but somehow we bypassed it with no spraying and no fees. When we returned north we did have to drive through the fumigation booth. Fumigation fees are $5.00US.

Upon arrival at the border the officer will provide you with a customs declaration form then direct you to the immigration and customs buildings. Complete the declaration and ask for the *Aduana* officer. The officer is generally wandering around the parking area, just ask anyone to point him out. *Aduana* must sign the declaration before you can obtain your vehicle permit. Then enter the bank to fill out your insurance application and pay the $12.00US fee for the mandatory liability insurance.

Traveling northbound, Nicaragua will be your entry point into the CA-4 Region. Get your passport stamped at

Immigration, which is located near the bus terminal. Your passport stamp will provide you 90 days to visit the region.

Then go back inside, past the bank to the *Aduana* window to obtain your vehicle permit, the *Certificado De Vehículos*.

Provide the official with your:

- Vehicle Title
- Customs Declaration Form
- Proof of Insurance
- Driver's License
- Passport

Gobierno de Recnocliliación
y Unidad Nacional
El Pueblo Presidente

REPÚBLICA DE NICARAGUA
MINISTERIO DE HACIENDA Y CRÉDITO PUBLICO
DIRECCIÓN GENERAL DE SERVICIOS ADUANEROS

No.2409

CERTIFICADO DE VEHICULOS

Clase de vehiculo	CASA RODANTE	Tipo de vehiculo	VEHICULO DE TURISMO	Días Autorizados	30

Aduana de Ingreso	Fecha de Ingreso	Destino	Fecha de Vencimiento
PEÑAS BLANCAS.	30/01/2008	NICARAGUA	29/02/2008

CONDUCTOR

Nombre	Apellido	País del Conductor
DONALD	GREENE	ESTADOS UNIDOS

Licencia No.	Identificación.	Dirección en Nicaragua
		HOSPEDAJE GRANADA GARANDA

VEHICULO

Marca	Modelo	Color	Año
MITSUBISHI	2004	BLANCO	2004

Motor No.	Chasis No.	Matricula	Origen	Procedencia
SIN NUMERO	JL6		ESTADOS UNIDOS	COSTA RICA

COMPLEMENTO

ID	Clase	Marca	Modelo	Motor No.	Chasis No.	Matricula	País	Año

OBSERVACIONES

02 PERSONAS VIAJANDO DECLARACION # 2547

Este vehículo no podrá ser objeto de enajenación o cualquier otra forma. En caso de incumplimiento se adoptarán las medidas establecidas en la Ley 42/1998

Usuario del Sistema: 5670210X8000005

que todos los datos contenidos en este Certificado son correctos y me comprometo a Re-exportar el vehículo a más tardar en la fecha de vencimiento, de lo contrario me haga acreedor de las sanciones que establezca la Dirección General de Aduanas, salvo casos plenamente justificado ante la misma.

FIRMA/SELLO

FIRMA Y FECHA

Departure

Southbound

There is currently only one border crossing open for vehicles to cross from Nicaragua to Costa Rica. Just before the border, the local municipality required us to pay $1.00US each to drive through their town to the border. Arriving at the border control area, we immediately had "assistants" running up to the Fuso, trying to jump up on our steps to have us hire them to help us through the border.

After parking on the Nicaragua side, an official came over to write down our vehicle information on a slip that would have to be stamped by other officials, and then surrendered to another official as we actually crossed the border. We then went into customs to clear our vehicle and breezed through the paper work. There are two immigration offices, one for individuals and one for buses. If the individual line is long, find the bus passenger line near where the buses park.

Northbound

Exiting Nicaragua into Honduras we crossed the border at El Espino where we had to pay a $4.00US exit fee, and then at the very next window a $3.00US Honduras entry fee. Nicaragua and Honduras immigration offices are combined in one building.

To surrender the vehicle permit, do not stand in line inside the building at the *Aduana* office. This office is the entry line to receive your permit. Go back outside and ask for the *Aduana* officer. He will take your permit and verify that the vehicle identification numbers are the same. After that you are free to drive to the Honduras side of the border.

Road sign in the Nicaragua highlands

El Espino border at Honduras/Nicaragua

Chapter Thirteen

Costa Rica

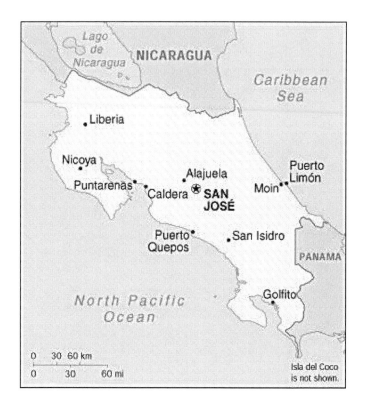

Routes
Maps
Camping
Border Crossing Formalities
- **Arrival**
- **Departure**

Routes

The choice of routes entering Costa Rica from Nicaragua is an easy one to determine, as there is only one way open to vehicles at the present.

Crossing the border at Peñas Blancas you drive through the Guanacaste Region. If you are lucky enough to have arrived during the turtle-nesting season, make the drive to Playa Tamarindo on the Península de Nicoya to view these lumbering creatures as they lay their eggs on the beaches.

Leatherbacks on the Beach
In search of Leatherback turtles, we drove to the Parque Nacional Marino Las Baulas on the Nicoya Peninsula of Costa Rica. Leatherbacks are known to come ashore here between October and March to lay eggs and this would be our best opportunity to witness this 100 million year old ritual. But Leatherback turtles are the most endangered of the sea turtles and only 50 females were recorded laying eggs at this main site during 2006-2007.

We arrived at the ranger station in time for sunset, put our name on a list and then waited with about 50 other people as the local guides and researchers patrolled the beach in search of nesting turtles. We understood that with so few turtles coming ashore we might not get the opportunity to witness this rare sight.

After about two hours of waiting, word came in by radio that a female leatherback had come ashore. We split into groups, scrambled into the available vehicles and drove a couple of miles down to the far end of the beach. From there our group hurried back about half a mile following the red light of our guide's flashlight. We arrived in time to watch as this nearly 5-foot long turtle laid her eggs, covered them up and began her trek back to the surf and the safety of the ocean.

As we walked back down the beach, we were all surprised, even the guide, when a second turtle crawled out of the surf right in front of us! We spent another 20 minutes watching as she pulled herself up the beach past the high tide line. This was a wonderful, awesome, once in a lifetime experience.

Make your way up the rough roads to Monteverde to explore the cloud forest in the Reserva Biologica. From here you can travel back towards Laguna de Arenal and drive around the lakeshore into the Parque Nacional Arenal.

From Arenal you can head towards San José or continue around the north side of the mountains to visit Volcán Poas.

Volcanoes of Costa Rica
Poas
Few volcanoes allow you to drive all the way to the rim but Volcán Poas lets you get to the very edge of one of the world's largest active craters (1.5km wide).

Looking down from the viewing platform, you can see Poas' bubbling sulphuric pool and fumaroles. That is, if it is clear. Typically the only time it is clear, is first thing in the morning, in the dry season. OK, it's 8:30am, it's the dry season, why is the crater fog filled? It was the strangest phenomenon. One side of the volcano was completely clear, while the other side was completely fogged in.

We decided we had nothing better to do than wait and see if the fog would lift. After about half an hour, the sky seemed to clear and get brighter and we were treated to just enough clearing of the fog to see the blue/green pool at the bottom of the crater and the steam generated by the fumaroles. The view only lasted a few minutes before the clouds returned to blot it out again.

Arenal
At Arenal Volcano Observatory Lodge we were charged about $3.00US each to enter their property where we found a nice, out of the way parking spot, and decided it was a good place to spend the night. We got to enjoy watching the volcano from the lodge's observation deck, and watch we did. For hours we watched and listened to the lava rocks rolling down the side of the volcano. Just before sunset the volcano made a very audible huffing and puffing sound and we saw a mini eruption and plume from the main crater with boulders of lava rolling down the mountainside sending up puffs of ash and smoke. After it got dark we watched as the boulders exploded into bright red showers of sparks. Very cool.

The layout of Costa Rica makes it difficult to see the entire country unless you want to double back or if you will be completing a return trip through Central America.

Back in the north, you can stop in Puerto Viejo de Sarapiquí from where you can travel by river (without your vehicle) along the Río San Juan to Barra del Colorado and Tortuguero.

If you continue eastward you will travel through Siquirres to the Caribbean coast. Be sure to take time for a rafting trip on the Río Pacuare. Heading towards the Panama border at Sixaola you can stop at Cahuita or detour through the banana plantations to the Refugio Gandoca-Manzanillo.

If you choose to head south from San José on the Panamericana detouring to explore the Orosi Valley. When you leave the mountains you can travel along the Pacific coastline detouring to explore the Osa Peninsula, before crossing into Panama.

Drive to Poas

The drive up the slopes of Poas Volcano took us through some beautiful countryside but as we got higher in elevation, the weather started to deteriorate. First it started raining off and on and patches of fog began to descend. And then we came over a hill and a truck was stopped at a strange angle, blocking both our lane and most of the other lane. Small cars and trucks were able to squeeze around the side, but we decided not to risk slipping off the wet grass into the gully on the far side.

So we 5-point turned around on the narrow road and headed back the way we came to find an alternate route. Following the map and a note in our guidebook about distances, we decided to chance a dirt road to get around. Suffice it to say, all's well that ends well, but it was a really lousy dirt road and the distances in the guidebook were incorrect.

We eventually ended up on the highway where we needed to be, but we'd lost a couple of hours drive time and darkness was quickly approaching, not to mention the rain and fog, and the narrow, winding mountain road. As the visibility became almost nil, we chanced upon a small store with a large parking lot off the side of the mountain. Which was actually a miracle because we hadn't seen anything with a big enough parking area anywhere on the steep mountain. Quickly pulling over, we decided that it was the perfect place to spend the night, providing it was OK with the owner. The owner had no problem with us spending the night there and we added another first to our camping experiences: just parking on the side of the highway.

Maps

Freytag and Berndt, Costa Rica with a scale: 1:400,000

Costa Rica Tourist Guide and Map by Jimenez and Tanzi, scale: 1:500,000

Toucan Guides, Waterproof Travel Map of Costa Rica at http://www.mapcr.com or the Digital PDF Atlas with a scale of 1:400,000

Rough Guides, Costa Rica and Panama scale of 1:550,000

Borch, Laminated Costa Rica Map, scale 1:650,000

ITMB, Costa Rica waterproof map, scale 1:300,000

Globetrotters Travel Map Costa Rica, scale 1:470,000

Rafting the Río Pacuare

Costa Rica Camping

Location	Description	GPS Coordinates	Cost
Cañas	Ask at the Las Pumas Cat Zoo.		
Liberia area	About 4 miles northwest of town is the Delfin Trailer Park.	N10 39.454 W085 28.154	Pay
Tamarindo	Playa Grande beach front parking w/security.	N10 20.18 W085 51.017	Pay
No name Lake Arenal Campsite, just past Nuevo Arenal, on the lake.	There was a "Camping" sign with an arrow, plus blue arrows painted down the center of the road.	N10 32.21 W84 53.54	Free
Arenal Observatory Lodge.	Pay entrance fee to the guard at the bottom of the hill. Park in lot at front of first gate below the resort. Don't ask to camp.		Pay
San Antonio de Belén	Belén RV Park, 15 minutes west of San José. American style RV Park with water, sewer and electrical hook-ups.	N09 58.801 W85 43.420	Pay
Pacuare River Camp	At the take-out for rafting the Pacuare River, free with payment of raft trip.	N10 5.722 W083 29.297	Pay
Puerto Viejo	Gavilon Lodge on the Río Sarapiquí, free camp, use of facilities with payment of a river boat tour.	N10 27.288 W084 0.092	Pay
Cahuita	La Piscina Natural in Cahuita. Private hostel, pay for camping. Also possible to free camp just down the road along Black Beach during high season. Low hanging trees throughout town.		Pay
Gandoca-Manzanillo Reserve	Refugio Nacional de Vida Silvestre Gandoca-Manzanillo. Camped at the end of the road across from the beach at Gandoca. Great drive through the banana plantations.	N09 35.828 W082 36.33	Free

Spectacled Caiman

Border Crossing Formalities

In addition to the one vehicle crossing with Nicaragua, Costa Rica has three crossings with Panama, with the border crossing at Río Sereno being a refreshing alternative from the hectic Panamericana crossing.

<u>Arrival</u>

<u>Southbound</u>
Arriving at the Costa Rican side after leaving Nicaragua, we had to pay about $4.50US to have the exterior of our vehicle fumigated, and then we drove to the immigration office. We parked and went inside and got our entrance stamps in just a couple of minutes.

We then walked to the vehicle permit window (next window down) to get our temporary import permit.

Provide the official with your:

> Vehicle Title
> Registration
> Proof of Insurance
> Driver's License
> Passport

Then it's outside to the customs office where we have to explain "It's not a truck, it's a camper", get a brief inspection and paperwork to take back to the vehicle permit window. The inspector will direct you to the office where you must buy a liability insurance policy for approximately $16.00US (if you don't have your own).

Costa Rican Proof of Insurance

Northbound

We crossed back into Costa Rica from Panama at Sixaola. We completed our tourist forms and got our passports stamped then went inside the same building to *Aduana* to get our vehicle permit.

The official was out getting his lunch so we had to wait until he returned, after about 20 minutes. By that time there were a bunch of truckers waiting and he took care of all the truckers first because all he had to do was stamp them in, but for us he had to type up paperwork. We also had to go across the street to purchase a liability insurance policy. All in all it only took about 1½ hours to do both sides which is pretty typical.

Americas Overland

CERTIFICADO DE IMPORTACION TEMPORAL PARA VEHICULOS AUTOMOTOR TERRESTRE, AEREO, Y MARITIMO PARA FINES NO LUCRATIVOS

No. CERTIFICADO: 91280033

MINISTERIO DE HACIENDA — ADUANAS

DATOS GENERALES

ANA: SIXAOLA	FECHA DE INGRESO: 22-01-2008	FECHA DE VENCIMIENTO: 21-04-2008	TIPO AUTORIZACION: TURISTA

TITULAR

PRIMER APELLIDO: GREENE	SEGUNDO APELLIDO:	NOMBRE: DONALD	NACIONALIDAD: U.S.A.	No. PASAPORTE O CEDULA DE RESIDENCIA:

DIRECCION Y TELEFONO DOMICILIO TEMPORAL EN EL PAIS DEL TITULAR: TODO EL PAIS

AUTORIZACION PARA CONDUCIR

PRIMER APELLIDO: XXXXXXXX	SEGUNDO APELLIDO: XXXXXX	NOMBRE: XXXXXXX	NACIONALIDAD: XXXXXX	No. PASAPORTE O CEDULA DE RESIDENCIA: XXXXXXX
PRIMER APELLIDO: XXXXXXX	SEGUNDO APELLIDO: XXXXXX	NOMBRE: XXXXXXX	NACIONALIDAD: XXXXXXX	No. PASAPORTE O CEDULA DE RESIDENCIA: XXXXXXX

CARACTERISTICAS DE LOS VEHICULOS

VEHICULO/AUTOMOTOR: X	AÑO: 2004	MODELO: (2004) F39	MARCA: MITSUBISHI	No. CHASIS O SERIE: JL6
CARRO CASA	No. MOTOR: NV		No. DE PLACA Y PAIS: CC U.S.A.	CAPACIDAD: 2

REMOLQUE:	SERIE:		MARCA:	No. DE PLACA Y PAIS:
EMBARCACION:	TIPO:	TAMAÑO:	MANGA: ESLORA:	MATERIAL DE FABRICACION:
CUBIERTAS:	No. MOTOR:		MATRICULA Y PAIS:	
MOTORES:	No. MOTOR:		TIPO:	
NAVE:	TIPO:	MODELO:	NOMBRE FABRICANTE:	
			No. MATRICULA Y PAIS:	

EQUIPO RECREATIVO

DESCRIPCION:	MARCA:	AÑO:	MODELO:	MOTOR:	No. MARCA O CHASIS:
DESCRIPCION:	MARCA:	AÑO:	MODELO:	MOTOR:	No. MARCA O CHASIS:
DESCRIPCION:	MARCA:	AÑO:	MODELO:	MOTOR:	No. MARCA O CHASIS:
DESCRIPCION:	MARCA:	AÑO:	MODELO:	MOTOR:	No. MARCA O CHASIS:

OBSERVACIONES: SEGURO 172544, SE CONFECCIONA A MAQUINA POR MAL ESTADO DE IMPRESORA. LEASE CORRECTO MODELO F39

DECLARO BAJO JURAMENTO QUE LOS DATOS CONSIGNADOS EN ESTE CERTIFICADO SON VERDADEROS ASI COMO QUE HE LEIDO Y ACEPTO LAS INSTRUCCIONES INDICADAS AL REVERSO DE ESTE DOCUMENTO. I DECLARE ON OATH THE INFORMATION I HAVE PROVIDED ON THIS CUSTOMS DECLARATION IS CORRECT. LIKEWISE, I STATE I HAVE READ THE INSTRUCTIONS ON THE BACK OF THIS CUSTOMS DECLARATION.

FIRMA DEL DECLARANTE

RODOLFO ES COE LEWIS
FUNCIONARIO DE ADUANA

ORIGINAL   No. 0378453

Departure

Southbound
We exited Costa Rica at the small Sixaola crossing into Panama, a very quiet, laid-back crossing with very little traffic. Its main claim to fame is that the bridge crossing

the Sixaola River into Panama is an old railroad bridge on which planks have been laid to allow cars to drive across it. It is also only one lane so one side has to wait for the other to finish crossing.

We obtained our Costa Rican exit stamp and surrendered our vehicle paperwork straight away, but just as we were getting into our vehicle to drive across, two cars came from the Panama side. It took about fifteen minutes for the drivers the complete their paperwork and then it was our turn.

Northbound
We exited Costa Rica into Nicaragua at the only border on the Panamericana Highway. We only had to get our exit stamps in our passports and surrender the vehicle permit.

Chapter Fourteen

Panama

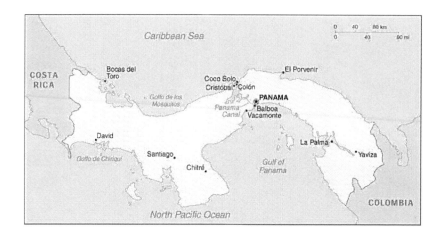

Routes
Maps
Camping
Border Crossing Formalities
- ## Arrival
- ## Departure
Shipping from Panama
Shipping into Panama

Routes

Arriving from Costa Rica there are three entry points into Panama, Sixaola/Guabito along the Caribbean, Paso Canoa along the Panamericana and Sabalito/Río Sereno a small mountain crossing north of the Panamericana.

The majority of vehicles enter at Paso Canoa since it is on the main highway. If you are coming from the Osa Peninsula in Costa Rica this will likely be the route you will be taking, although a detour into the mountains to Río Sereno may be a refreshing alternative after the humidity of the coast and away form the madhouse that is the border crossing on the Panamericana.

Continuing eastward into Panama you may consider detouring into the mountains to explore Volcán Baru or the area around Boquete. After passing through David you will connect with the road crossing Panama from the Caribbean.

Our favorite crossing into Panama is over the bridge at Sixaola/Guabito. From here you can ferry across to the islands Bocas del Toro for a relaxing few days. Following this route will take you over the mountains to the Panamericana near David.

One at a Time Please
The northern border crossing between Panama and Costa Rica is a unique one. The two countries are separated by a river that is spanned by an old railroad bridge. The train no longer runs and apparently the two countries didn't see any reason to build an additional vehicle bridge, so they modified the train bridge to accommodate vehicles. Sort of. Planks of wood have been laid down to raise the roadbed up to the level of the rails. Except some of them are missing or have moved and left big gaps for your tires to fall into. There is also a pedestrian walkway, but for some reason the pedestrians prefer to walk where the vehicles go.

Oh and did we mention that the bridge is only one lane wide? And that it has a limit of only one vehicle on it at a time? That means that you may have to wait your turn before crossing, but make sure that you don't wait on the raised platform on the Panama side where the immigration and customs offices are, because you'll be blocking the route for everyone else.

Rather than rushing through the country to Panama City, take time to explore the mountains north of the highway as well as the Península de Azuero south of the highway.

From Santiago, travel up to San Francisco and Santa Fé to explore for a few days. Locals indicate that the road across to the Caribbean from here may be completed within a few years, so check it out. Right now the route past Santa Fé degrades to a nearly impossible 4x4 trail before arriving at the coast.

The Península de Azuero has beautiful beaches and wildlife refuges where it is possible to see nesting turtles in season.

The drive from Penonome to Panama City passes by numerous beaches, all of which are being developed into resorts and are overrun with city refugees on the weekends and holidays.

If you want to bypass Panama City you can take the new road from La Chorrera which crosses the Canal near Gamboa. If you are intent on following the Panamericana into the Darien, the highway fades out into the jungle at Yaviza. Although the dream for a continuous land route still exists, the odds are stacked against it.

Regardless of which port you may ship your vehicle out of towards South America, be sure to leave yourself with at least a few days to explore the Canal Zone, Parque Nacional Soberanía and Portobelo where the old Spanish forts are worth the drive.

You could also take an expensive detour and fly to the Archipielago de San Blas, or you can learn about the indigenous Kuna inhabitants at any tourist location where they are selling their needlepoint and artworks.

The Canal

The Canal Zone in Panama is an interesting area. You can visit the locks and watch how the huge ships get moved from one side to the other. You can take a train through the zone and see the beautiful scenery along Lake Gatún or you can visit one of the premier bird watching areas of Panama called Pipeline Road. Pipeline Road is situated in Parque Nacional Soberanía, just above one section of the Canal. Interestingly, the entrance is just past some of the huge navigational markers that are situated on the hillsides.

We parked our truck between two of the markers and walked down Pipeline Road. Immediately we began to see birds including toucans, wood creepers, woodpeckers, cuckoos and ant shrikes. We saw a tremendous variety of birds and we were also fortunate to see an agouti and some spider monkeys.

Maps

Rough Guides, Costa Rica and Panama scale of 1:550,000

ITMB, Panama waterproof map, scale 1:450,000

Panama Camping

Location	Description	GPS Coordinates	Cost
Colón	El Rey Supermarket, security.		Free
Playa Lagosta	Restaurant and camping, on the road to Portobelo.	N09 28.185 W079 43.402	Free
Portobello	Ocean-side pull out on the main road, quiet.	N09 32.937 W079 40.212	Free
Pipeline Road	Past the Smithsonian Dock at the end of the road past Gamboa.		Free
Parque Nacional Soberanía	Ranger Station/entrance.		Free
Balboa Yacht Club	Close to water and city, some shade and occasional wifi.		Free
Playa Santa Clara	XS Memories, north side of the highway. American style RV Park with water, sewer and electrical hook-ups.		Pay
Santa Clara	The beach at Santa Clara, only good for short vehicles due to low trees.		
Pedasí	Playa El Arenel, fishermen launch on this extremely long beautiful beach. Buy fish from the fishermen.	N07 33.533 W080 1.213	Free
Playa Venao	Great swimming and surfing beach.	N07 25.955 W080 11.597	Free
Chitré	Playa El Aquillito, huge mud flats w/birds, buy shrimp from the fishermen.	N08 0.148 W080 24.272	Free
Santa Fé	Free parking in front of church or along the soccer field.	N08 30.683 W081 4.662'	
Santa Fé	Along the Río Santa Maria. Right at a swimming hole. The turn off for the river is at N08°31"38.4' W81°04"05.7'	N08 31.495 W81 4.025	
Santiago	Hotel La Hacienda.	N08 07.42 W80 58.75	
Playa Las Lajas	Nice campground at the very end of the road but right on the beach.	N08 10.33 W081 52.522	Pay
Boquete	City camp on Calle 2 Sur.		Free

Location	Description	GPS Coordinates	Cost
	Just down from the main square and market		
Willie Mazu Rancho Ecologico	KM 68 between Chiriquí Grande and Lago Fortuna.		Free
Chiriquí Grande	Parking area at the Police Sta at the entrance to town.		Free
El Paraiso Spanish School	Bocas Del Toro, Isla Colón, Parking space at language school.		Free with tuition
Playa del Drago	Bocas, Great spot on the beach only for one or two vehicles. Possible camping at end of road.	N09 24.953 W082 19.758	Free
Almirante	Bombaderos (Fire Station), just next to the ferry port to Bocas del Toro. Follow the RR from the hwy to the end of the line.		Pay

Border Crossing Formalities

<u>Arrival</u>
Arriving on the Panama side, we discovered that it was an hour later than in Costa Rica and the immigration officials were at lunch. Remember to move up your watches by one hour when you wake up on the Costa Rica side of the border. This will reduce your likelihood of running into this situation.

Fortunately the immigration/customs officials re-opened within a couple of minutes of our arrival; however, there was a long line of people who had crossed from Costa Rica during the hour that Panama was closed.

Having two people at this border was helpful as Kim got in line at immigration and Don went to the customs office to get the paperwork completed for the vehicle. As it turned out, Don finished just as Kim got to the head of the line, so the timing was perfect. But our truck sat on that one lane bridge blocking traffic for about 45 minutes because we couldn't move it off until we were allowed in the country. Sorry for the wait guys, but we don't make the rules.

Provide the official with your:

> Vehicle Title
> Registration
> Driver's License
> Passport

REPÚBLICA DE PANAMÁ
DIRECCIÓN GENERAL DE ADUANAS
FORMULARIO DE CONTROL VEHICULAR
VEHÍCULO EXTRANJERO - ENTRADA

Fecha: 02/01/2008

No. Permiso:	PE-08-01-02-CM-189			Fecha Permiso:	02/01/2008
1. DATOS DEL VEHÍCULO				No.Perm.Salida	
Marca	MITSUBISHI			No.Motor	S/N
Modelo	F39			No.Chasis	JL6
Año	2004	Eje		Placa-Remolque	S/N
Tipo	CARRO CASA			No.Puertas/Color	2 BLANCO
Placa No./Pais	S/N ESTADOS UNIDOS DE			No.Reg. Transp.	

Liquidación de Impuestos (Vehículos Nacionales)

Liquidación		Certificación	
Fecha		Fecha	
Observaciones			

2. DATOS DEL CONDUCTOR		Pasaporte/Cédula	
Nombre	DONALD GREENE	Nacionalidad	ESTADOS UNIDOS DE NORTEAMERICA

3. DATOS DEL PROPIETARIO (Si difiere del Conductor)		Pasaporte/Cédula/R.U.C.	
Nombre / Empresa	DONALD GREENE	Nacionalidad	ESTADOS UNIDOS DE NORTEAMERICA

Observaciones TURISTA

4. DATOS DEL VIAJE (Entrada)			
Procedencia	ESTADOS UNIDOS	Dir. Panamá	HOTEL COSTA INN AVE. PERU
Fecha Entrada	02/01/2008	Aduana Entrada	COLON MANZANILLO
Fecha Estimada Salida	1/4/2008	Aduana Esti. Salida	COLON MANZANILLO
DATOS DEL VIAJE (Salida)		Destino	
Fecha Salida		Aduana Salida	

Observaciones   TURISTA

5. PERMISOS	Funcionario	
Entrada		
Salida Sin Vehículo		
Salida		
Providencia		

El conductor o propietario declara que la información contenida en este formulario (Puntos 1-4) es verdadera y acepta los derechos y obligaciones que se detallan al reverso de este documento.

0 2 ENE 2008

Conductor o Propietario   Fecha

Jefe Control Vehicular

MINISTERIO DE ECONOMIA Y FINANZA
DIRECCION GENERAL DE ADUANAS
DIRECCION REGIONAL DE ADUANAS

Customs in Panama also stamps a miniature vehicle permit in your passport to prevent you from leaving the country without your vehicle.

If you are shipping from Panama, *Aduana* will cancel your permit once you show proof that your vehicle is booked on a ship.

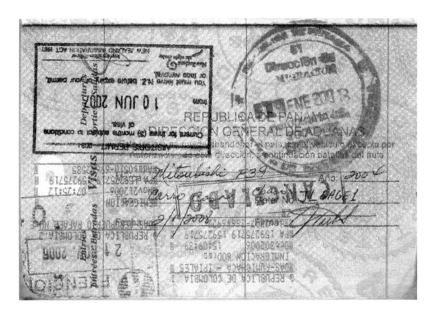

Shipping a vehicle from Panama

Shipping Southbound

Panamanian authorities require a document from the Policía Técnica Judicial to prove that the vehicle hasn't been in an accident, has no outstanding tickets and that the temporary tourist importation is still valid. You should leave half a day just in case there is a wait – going first thing in the morning is best.

Be sure you have lots of copies of your vehicle title, registration and passports available.

From the Police office, they will escort you across the street to where you will get a document from the Customs Office saying it is OK to ship your car from the port. This document is titled *Control de Vehículos*. Make at least three copies of the documents for the officials at the port.

VALOR B/.4.00

REPUBLICA DE PANAMA

VENCE=04=06=2005

MINISTERIO DE ECONOMIA Y FINANZAS
DIRECCION GENERAL DE ADUANAS   N° 145221

ADMINISTRACION DE ADUANA ZONA NOR , OCC

CONTROL DE VEHICULOS   12,50PM

El Infrascrito INSPECTOR DE ADUANA de GUABITO hace constar que el vehículo que a continuación se describe ha ingresado al país en esta fecha 05=07=2005 bajo el régimen de importación para turistas del Decreto Número 111 de 17 de marzo de 1969 por término de 30 días.

Conducido por DONALD BARRY GREENE de nacionalidad AMERICANO con

Pasaporte No. 9999999 Color BLANCO Año 2004 modelo MOBILE HOME Marca MITSUBICHI

Procedencia C,RICA No. Motor. 9999999 Placa No. 9999999 de C,RICA

Tipo de Vehículo CASA MOVIL de Puertas 2 Tonelaje Capacidad Pasajeros 2

Llantas de Repuestos 2 Indique si tiene Radio [S] Aire Acondicionado [S] Remolque [ ]

Otros detalles: TURISMO

Dirección de interesado en la Republica de Panamá CHIRIQUI, DAVID, COLON

Aduana por donde debe salir MANZANILLO con destino a VENEZUELA

Para los efectos legales consiguientes se extiende el presente certificado en la aduana de GUABITO

hoy 05=JULIO de 2005 y declaro que la naturaleza de la operación consignada en este certificado es verdadera.

El Conductor o Propietario   ALGARAS HILL
                                     Funcionario de Aduana

El señor _____   Fecha, _____
siguiente razón: _____, en cuanto a su automóvil, puede salir del país por la

Su automóvil pagó los impuestos [ ]   Liquidación No.

_____ [ ]

Ya salió el automóvil legalmente [ ]

REPUBLICA DE PANAMA
DIRECCION GENERAL DE ADUANA - ZONA NOROCCIDENTAL
1) Vencido el plazo de esta autorización el Vehículo será decomisado en poder de quien se encuentre.
2) Este Vehículo no puede ser traspasado sin previa autorización de la Aduana

Después de hacerse comparado la necesidad de la prórroga de este permiso la Dirección de Aduanas la autoriza por 30 días más.

REPUBLICA DE PANAMA
DIRECCION GENERAL DE ADUANAS
ADUANA - GUABITO

Entrada 05 JUL 2005 Salida

Firma del Jefe

For the Panama to Venezuela shipping, our shipping company was Wallenius Wilhelmsen Logistics. They are the largest RORO shipper in the world. Make sure you check other companies because schedules change often.

The agents we used were great. They were very helpful and knowledgeable about the ports. In Venezuela, especially because very few vehicles ship into the country on temporary import status, so no one is really familiar with the procedure.

Shipping Into Panama

When we arrived in Panama to collect our vehicle from the port, our first stop was to pick up a rental car. Having a rental car provided a place to store our personal items and suitcases while we were processing the necessary documentation to retrieve our vehicle.

After getting our rental, we visited our shipping agent, Barwil Agencies S.A. to collect the original Bill of Lading (BOL) properly stamped by the agents. Central America bureaucracy loves their stamps. The more stamps a document has on it, the more official it MUST be.

After getting our BOL, we went to the next stop – *Aduana*. This is the customs office and their main office is in Panama City near the national airport. At *Aduana* we collected our temporary import permit after surrendering a whole dollar for the cost of a few copies.

At *Aduana* you must provide the originals and one copy
of the following documents:

> Bill of Lading
> Vehicle Title
> Driver's License
> Passport

Then it was time to cross the isthmus to the Manzanillo
port in Colon. At the port, we met with a representative
of the shipping company, in our case it was again
Wallenius Wilhelmsen Logistics, to collect the
"Authorization to Release Vehicle" letter. Without this
document the port would refuse to give us possession of
our vehicle.

Then it was time to stand in line, first at *Cuarentena*,
then at *Aduana* to get copies of all of our papers and
more stamps on every one of them – including the
stamped copies. We paid our $3.00 for copies. Then
across the parking lot to *Aduana* #2 to get more copies
of everything and yes, more stamps on every page.
Here we thought we were finished and drove to the
RORO gate. Guess what – we missed one window with
more stamps.

So back to the main port gate and to the last window
that we missed, *Importación*, into another line to pay our
fees of $11.00 and collect two copies of stamped
receipts, and then to back to the window to have
everything checked. OK. Ready to go back to the
RORO gate. This is when it comes in handy to have a
rental car. If we had been relying on taxis to get around
we would have had a long walk back to the port
entrance as there were no taxis in the area.

Back at the RORO gate we had to go to yet another window, get the documents checked again and stamped again before they would bring out our Fuso.

But before we could leave we had to have the customs inspection. The customs agent checked the VIN number and then looked inside the door of the camper to make sure all was OK. No actual physical inspection was conducted.

One last stop, we had to drive through the fumigation spray booth where the underside of the truck was sprayed. We wondered why if the truck was already on Panamanian soil were they concerned about fumigating it, as any germs would already be in the country.

The entire process including the drive from Panama City and lunch took only four hours.

Bocas del Toro'beach camp

Chapter Fifteen

Venezuela

Routes
Maps
Camping
Border Crossing Formalities
- **Shipping Details into Venezuela**
- **Departure**

Routes

Venezuela is a wonderful country with great potential for tourism. There are not many areas set up for vehicle camping but we found it possible to park in guarded parking lots (arrive early enough to ask permission of the manager and not the security guard), hotel lots, beaches, National Parks and at tourist facilities in the Gran Sabana. We were able to city camp in the parking lot of the Isla De Margarita ferry terminal, the Ciudad Guayana airport and in front of the National Police barracks in Santa Elena and we wild camped on Isla De Margarita and in the Gran Sabana.

One possible route through Venezuela is along the Caribbean Coast on Route 9 with a detour to Isla Margarita, then along Routes 16 or 10. This will take you toward Ciudad Bolívar, from where you can fly to Parque Nacional Canaima and Angel Falls.

Angel Falls
Salto Ángel is the tallest waterfall in the world at 979 meters (3,230 feet) and has an uninterrupted drop of 807 meters (2,663 feet), 16 times the height of Niagara Falls. The waterfall is located in Parque Nacional Canaima and the only way to get to Canaima is to fly. After finding a secure spot to leave the Fuso (at Posada La Casita in Ciudad Bolívar), and making arrangements for a 3-day trip, we took off on a small 6-seater plane. Our first view of the park was a fly-by of the SIX waterfalls that flow into the lagoon at the foot of the village of Canaima. Our pilot then made a sharp turn and, rather than land on the paved runway, landed on the dirt strip that ran along its length. Very exciting.

Our first excursion was across the lagoon in a long

dugout canoe carved from a single tree. Landing on the other side, we began a hike to a waterfall called Salto El Sapo (salto means waterfall) where we were able to walk around the backside. We had been warned that we would be drenched by the time we were done and that was no lie. The amount of water was tremendous and the amount of wind that was generated behind it felt like a hurricane and the water was swirling so much that it looked alive. We walked all the way through the falls and then back again, 100 meters each way.

The next morning we boarded another dugout for the trip up the Río Carrao toward Angel Falls. It was a 5-hour trip, but the scenery was magnificent and there were some small rapids. It was a long, fun, wet ride.

Finally we came around a bend in the river and got our first unobstructed view of Salto Ángel. And what a magnificent view it was! We took several photos, but when we arrived at our camp, we realized that we were directly across the river from the falls and would be able to check the view often. What a great spot!

After lunch we set off to hike up the tepui for a closer view of the falls. We had to cross a small river on foot, which we did by linking hands (there were 12 of us) and crossing together. Then it was across, in this case, a literal rain forest as it started raining buckets, stepping over rocks and tree branches and trying to avoid the increasingly larger puddles. Very quickly our feet were soaked and sloshing around in our shoes. It was a tough hike but eventually we reached the mirador (viewpoint).

The waterfall is even more magnificent the closer you get, but clouds obstructed our view. So we sat in the spray and the wind that the waterfall generated and just experienced it. Finally we decided we needed to head back down before it got dark, but as we reached an

> earlier, smaller viewpoint, the clouds opened up and we could see the top of the falls!
>
> The night was spent swinging in hammocks and the next day saw us blasting back through the rapids to Canaima.

From Ciudad Bolívar you can head toward the Brazilian border at Santa Elena de Uairén taking time to explore the waterfalls and the tepuis of the Gran Sabana.

The Grand Gran Sabana
The Gran Sabana in Venezuela is a vast, beautiful area full of natural features such as rolling grassland, waterfalls and tepuis, and it encompasses the main route south through Venezuela and into Brazil.

Driving up a topographical feature called the *Escalera* (staircase), we climbed onto the plateau where the Gran Sabana is located. We came up out of the hot and humid jungle to an elevation of 800m (2,640ft). Not terribly high, but every little bit helps. With a little breeze and a cloud cover, the temperature was a lot more pleasant.

In the middle of the Sabana is the Pembóm village of Iberibo where we wanted to catch a boat to the waterfall Salto Aponguao. The village is about 43km (27mi) off the highway on a dirt road. The road wasn't in terrible shape, but there were some stretches that were really potholed and rough. Add to that the mud patches that we had to avoid and the going was pretty slow. As we turned off for the final six miles, we noticed that clouds were building on the horizon. We continued our steady pace and made our way toward the village, but the condition of the road deteriorated and many side roads split off from it, making it difficult to tell which direction to take.

The clouds opened and it started to rain. When it rains, the road gets really muddy so drivers go all over trying not to get stuck. We tried to find the best path but still had to drive through some nasty mud bogs. To make matters worse, the last two miles were driven in the pouring rain. The road deteriorated further and actually became a running stream, obliterating the tracks that we were using to find the right trail to the village. Using our best judgment and 4 wheel driving skills, we drove over rocks, across streams and through lots of wet sand to finally reach the village, three hours after we turned off the highway.

So after all of that, how was the waterfall? The waterfall on the Río Aponguao is 105m (347ft) high and in the rainy season can be as wide as 80m (264ft). We were able to hike down to the bottom where we were hit with the full force of the wind and spray that the waterfall generates. It was pretty impressive.

When we headed back out to the main highway, we slowly retraced our steps out the rutted road. Just before we made it back to pavement, we saw a track that lead off to an airstrip we had noticed on the way in. Thinking "Why not?" and looking both ways, we drove the final mile down a nice, smooth, paved airstrip. This was definitely a first for us, as we had never driven on a runway before!

Other routes lead to the border crossings into Colombia. You could choose to follow the Caribbean coast west through Maracaibo into Colombia, or if you are heading towards Bogotá, Colombia you have two choices.
You can wind your way through the Andes along Routes 1 and 7 to Mérida or explore the grassy plains of Los Llanos along Route 19 until you climb into the Andes.

Fuel in Santa Elena de Uairén

Venezuela has some of the cheapest gas in the world and in 2005 the price of regular unleaded gas was $.15/gallon. The price of diesel, which we use, was $.08/gallon. Yes, 8 cents. It cost us about $2.00 to fill the tank.

In Santa Elena, just before the border with Brazil, many Brazilians crossed over just to fill up their vehicle fuel tanks, as fuel in northern Brazil was about $4.00 per gallon. At the fuel station, there were two sets of pumps with two lines. The more expensive pump was for Brazilian vehicles and the less expensive pump was for locals.

Since we had been in Venezuela for the previous couple of weeks getting fuel at local prices we naturally got in line for the cheap gas. However once we got to the pump, the soldier "guarding" it insisted that all international vehicles had to pay the higher price for fuel. We disagreed and pleasantly argued our point that we should be able to buy the cheaper fuel. We started pumping the fuel and the soldier just walked away and let us finish.

Maps

We used the Venezuela Road Map by B&B. The publisher is Berndtson & Berndtson, and the map has a scale of 1:1,750,000. These maps are also sold as Borch Road Maps.

The maps by Freytag & Berndt are reputed to be good maps, but are published in Europe and are difficult to find in the United States. They can be ordered online. These maps have a scale of 1:1,000,000.

ITMB Publishing also has a folded map with a scale of 1: 1,750,000.

Angel Falls

Venezuela Camping

Location	Description	GPS Coordinates	Cost
Parque Nacional Henri Pittier	On the roadway in front of the Estacion Biologica Rancho Grande.		Free
Guatire	Hotel Las Cabinas parking lot.	N10 28.04 W66 33.93	Pay
Isla Margarita	Parque Nacional Laguna de La Restinga, at the embarkation pier A17.		Free
Isla Margarita	Parque Nacional Laguna de La Restinga, unnamed beach.	N11 04.02 W64 15.04	Free
Puerto La Cruz	Isla Margarita car ferry parking lot. Paid for 24 hour parking.		Pay
El Tigre	Large PDV Gas Station/truckstop at south end of town. Water and toilet.		Free
Ciudad Bolívar	Posada La Casita. Full services, tour services for Angel Falls trip.	N08 05.46 W63 29.37	Pay
Ciudad Guayana	Parking lot of the airport. Planes were not flying at night, quiet.		Free
El Dorado	Small park on the road into town, quiet. Town of El Dorado itself was a pit.	N06 44.73 W61 37.50	Free
Iboribo, Gran Sabana	Gran Sabana, waterfall and boat tours, grassy riverside location.	N05 35.25 W61 29.72	Pay
Gran Sabana Lagoon	Bush camp, quiet lagoon out of sight of the road.	N05 41.04 W61 32.63	Free
Santa Elena de Uairén	City camp in front of the Guardia Nacional Headquarters.		Free
Santa Elena de Uairén	Bush camp just north of town. Quiet.	N04 52.59 W61 05.40	Free

Border Crossing Formalities

Shipping Details into Venezuela

In Venezuela we had our agents draft a letter, in Spanish, that said that we wanted to temporarily import our vehicle according to *Articles 107/146/147 of the book of Organic Law.*

Your letter should describe the make, type, year, color, plate number and VIN of your vehicle. It should list the owner(s) and passport numbers, details of the shipping line, name of the ship, journey number, port of loading and port of unloading. It should list tourism as the reason for travel, and the city from which you plan to depart overland. SENIAT, which is the Venezuela Customs Agency, required our agent to pay a 100 Bolívar tax and have a tax stamp affixed to the letter to make it official.

At SENIAT you must provide the originals and one copy of the following documents:

> Temporary Import Letter (see above)
> Bill of Lading
> Vehicle Title
> Driver's License
> Passport
> Venezuela Tourist Card

It is likely that each office that you must visit will also require a set of copies of your documents so be prepared and bring along three extra sets, just in case.

Internacional Marítima c.a.

OPERADOR PORTUARIO N° A-010012

R.I.F.: J-07527303-6

PASE DE SALIDA

SERIE A 109804

1. PUERTO CABELLO

2. FECHA 18/03/05

3. NOMBRE BUQUE ROXANE 514	4. FECHA ATRAQUE 17/03/05	5. ALMACEN ZONA AREA III	6. TIPO CARGA O X
7. PUERTO PROCEDENCIA MANZANILLO	8. CONOCIMIENTO EMBARQUE PA32637	9. ACTA RECEPCION N° FECHA:	
10. CONSIGNATARIO DONALD GREENE	11. AGENTE ADUANAL DONALD GREENE	12. MARCA Y NUMERO	13. MANIFIESTO N° 1242
14. EMPRESA TRANSPORTISTA DONALD GREENE	15. VEHICULO MARCA MITSUBISHI PLACA S/P	16. CONDUCTOR NOMBRE DONALD GREENE C.I. N°:	

MERCANCIA AUTORIZADA PARA SALIR DEL ALMACEN DE INTERNACIONAL MARITIMA, C.A.

17. T. EMB.	18. DESCRIPCION	19. CANT.	20. PESO	21. OBSERVACIONES
10	K010907 VEHICULO CASA RODANTE	1		BAJO REGIMEN DE TURISTA

CLAVE DE EMBALAJE

1. Sacos	2. Cajas de Madera	3. Cajas de Cartón	4. Pipotes/Tambores
5. Garrafones	6. Paletas	7. Bobinas/Carretes/Rollos	8. Fardos/Atados
9. Contenedores	10. Vehículos	11. Maquinarias	12. Láminas/Tubos/Vigas
	13. Trailers	14. Otros	

22. OPERADOR PORTUARIO ALMACEN ZONA	23. CONFORME CONSIGNATARIO/REPR. LEGAL	24. CONFORME
Nombre: ARGENIS PETIT C.I.: Firma: Sello:	Nombre: C.I.: Firma: Sello:	Nombre: C.I.: Firma: Sello:

NOTA: Se autoriza la salida de la mercancía amparada bajo este documento del terminal de Internacional Marítima, C.A. UNICAMENTE.
El resguardo Marítimo permitirá la salida del recinto portuario si se ha cumplido con los requisitos exigidos por la Ley vigente.
ORIGINAL DPTO. CONTROL DE ALMACEN / ZONA (OFICINA MUNICIPAL)

Pto. Cabello 18 de Julio de 2.005

Ciudadano:
Gerente de la Aduana Maritima de Puerto Cabello
Servicio Nacional Integral de Administración Tributaria "SENIAT"
Su Despacho.

0027491

Estimado Señores:

Yo, **Donald Greene** muy respetuosamente me derijo a Usted, con el prososito de solicitar la
Autorización para introducir un vehiculo en **VENEZUELA, de** acuerdo a los articulos 107
146/147 de la Ley Organica.

Detalles del vhiculo: Marca: **MITSUBISHI – TIPO – CASA MOVIL – AÑO 2004 –
COLOR – BLANCO – PLACA- CC81941 – VIN- JL6AGE**

Propietarios del vehiculo: **Donald Greene No. Pasaporte. 1   9 USA**

Kim Greene No. Pasaporte 2   4 USA.

Detalles del transporte :   **WALLENIUS WILHELMSEM LINES**

Nombre del Buque: **ROXANNE**

Viaje   **BS-514**

Puerto de carga   **MANZANILLO – PANAMA**

Puerto de descarga   **PTO. CABELLO – VENEZUELA**

Motivo de la visita   **TURISMO**

Lugar de salida de

Venezuela   **SANTA ELENA DE UAIREN**

Damdoles las gracias por la atención prestada a la presente nos despidimos de Ud., con un
granto saludo

Atentamente,

Don Greene

100
Cien Bolivares

Día Mes Año

After you get your customs approval from SENIAT you
will need the agent to prepare a *Liberación de Carga* to
give to the storage lot where your vehicle is parked.
Again make sure you have copies of everything since

Americas Overland

everyone you will deal with will ask you for copies, including the gate agent as you exit the port.

PARAGUA MARITIMA, C.A.

Puerto Cabello, 19 de Julio del 2.005.

Señores.
INTERMARCA.
Puerto Cabello -

Atn. Capt. Cristian Casas.

LIBERACIÓN DE CARGA.

Estimados señores.

Por medio de la presente y por autorización de nuestros principales le comunicamos que las unidades descargadas de la M/V " ROXANNE " Viaje BS.514 fecha 17/07/05 bajo los BILL OF LADING #. PA.336977 consignados a los señores: **DONALD GREENE** Dicha carga pueden ser entregadas al cliente ya que este efectuo la cancelación correspondiente al USO DE SUPERFICIE.

Sin otro particular, nos despedimos de Uds., con un grato saludo.

Muy Atentamente.,

PARAGUA MARITIMA, CA

Legnis B. Marchena E.

Dpto. Trafico

Argenis Avila
C.I. 13.302.855

Sra. Carolina Diaz
Cc: Sr. Argenis Avila

Internacional Maritima, C.A.
(INTERMARCA)
Departamento de Despacho Area III
Puerto Cabello

19-07-05.
11:49 pm

C C C TAMANACO, TORRE C, PISO 6, OFIC. C-602, CHUAO, CARACAS - TLF.: MASTER (58 212)
APTO. POSTAL 64565, Z.P. 1064-A, E-MAILS: haydee7s@paramari.com / lerejesb@paramari
PUERTO CABELLO (58 242) 361.94.25 / 361.91.54 - FAX: (58 242) 2-1.89.48. E-MAILS: peramari

REPÚBLICA BOLIVARIANA DE VENEZUELA

SENIAT

SERVICIO NACIONAL INTEGRADO DE ADMINISTRACIÓN ADUANERA Y TRIBUTARIA
Adscrito al Ministerio de Finanzas

RÉGIMEN DE TURISTAS

SNAT/INA/APPC/DO/URAE/2005/   0001242

Puerto Cabello, '18 JUL 2005

Señor:
DONALD GREENE/KIM GREENE
Presente.-

En atención a su solicitud de fecha 18/07/2005, registrada en esta Gerencia
No. 0027491 de igual fecha, mediante la cual solicita autorización para introducir el
Vehículo descrito a continuación:

MARCA	MITSUBISHI
TIPO	CASA MOVIL
AÑO	2004
SERIAL-VIN No.	JL6AGE
COLOR	BLANCO

y un lote de mercancías usadas (equipaje), bajo el **Régimen de Turistas**. Esta

Gerencia le comunica que una vez cumplido con los requisitos previstos en

CAPÍTULO V, SECCIÓN II, y de acuerdo a lo establecido en el CAPITULO III,

SECCION II del Reglamento de la Ley Orgánica de Aduanas sobre los Regimenes

de Liberación Suspensión y Otros Regimenes Aduaneros Especiales; de

conformidad con la verificación documental y física, regulada en el CAPÍTULO III de

la Ley Orgánica de Aduanas, efectuada por el funcionario PEDRO J. RODRIGUEZ

R., portador de la C. I. No. V-7.272.857, adscrito a la Unidad de Regímenes

Aduaneros Especiales, decide otorgar el ingreso en forma temporal bajo el Régimen

"1805-2005 Bicentenario del Juramento del Libertador Simón Bolívar en el Monte Sacro".

Final Autopista Muelle, calle Puerto Cabello, Edificio SENIAT Nueva Sede- Aduana Principal de Puerto Cabello,
Ciudad de Puerto Cabello, Estado Carabobo.

RÉGIMEN DE TURISTAS

de Turistas, de acuerdo a lo previsto en la normativa citada. Asimismo, le informo

que de acuerdo a lo establecido en la Resolución del Ministerio de Hacienda No.

3235 de fecha 20/11/96, se le concede un plazo de permanencia dentro del Territorio

Nacional de seis (06) meses, es decir, hasta el día 14/01/2006, por lo que deberá

solicitar antes del vencimiento del lapso establecido, la autorización para la

reexpedición de los bienes ingresados, de no hacerlo, incurrirá en una infracción

aduanera tipificada el Artículo 115 de la Ley Orgánica de Aduanas.

Atentamente,

Lic. CARLOS SALIMA COLINA
Gerente de la Aduana Principal de Puerto Cabello
Providencia Administrativa N° SNAT-2004-0019 de fecha 09-01-04
Servicio Nacional Integrado de Administración Aduanera y Tributaria
Gaceta Oficial N° 37.865 de fecha 26-01-04

AEB/PRDI

NOTIFICACIÓN AL CONTRIBUYENTE:

NOMBRES	APELLIDOS	N° DE PASAPORTE

FECHA	HORA	FIRMA

Argenis Avila
C.I. 13.332.853

Internacional Marítima, C.A.
(INTERMARCA)
Departamento de Despacho Área III
Puerto Cabello

19-07-05
11:49 am

"1805-2005 Bicentenario del Juramento del Libertador Simón Bolívar en el Monte Sacro".

Final Autopista Muelle, calle Puerto Cabello, Edificio SENIAT Nueva Sede- Aduana Principal de Puerto Cabello,
Ciudad de Puerto Cabello, Estado Carabobo.

(In 2005) Our agent in Puerto Cabello was Paragua Maritima. Our contact there was Ms. Haydee Silva, haydee7s@paramar1.com. Their port agent was Gilberto Moncada, gilbertomoncada@cantv.net. All the shipping agents we met spoke English. On the Panama side, our agent was Barwil Agencies, S.A.

You would want to visit the Panama City office to complete all of your paperwork. Barwil does not have a presence in Puerto Cabello.

We did not have to pay any bribes to grease the wheels in either country.

Departure
We chose to depart Venezuela south into Brazil at Santa Elena de Uairén. The border is about fifteen minutes south of town, and when we arrived a soldier stopped us for a quick inspection/look inside the living quarters to see what it was. This was a common occurrence, as officials just didn't know what to make of us - truck or what? He looked at our Venezuela car documents and waved us through.

We didn't realize it right away, but that was apparently the border, we didn't even get our passports stamped or surrender our vehicle permit.

Gran Sabana

Chapter Sixteen

Brazil

Routes
Maps
Camping
Border Crossing Formalities
- Arrival
- Departure

Routes

From the border town of Santa Elena de Uairén, VZ, BR174 is the only route that heads south to Manaus and the Amazon River. This route passes through Boa Vista, the Equator and the Terra Indigena Waimiri Atroari – an indigenous reserve.

The famous Trans-Amazonia Highway from Manaus to Peru is nothing more than an abandoned dirt track that could take a week or more to travel by small, very well equipped 4x4s. For the rest of us, the only way to continue from Manaus is by riverboat or barge. It is possible to travel up river to Porto Velho or down to Belém. Most overlanders choose to go to Belém and then down the Atlantic coast.

Down the Amazon Without a Paddle
After a day of running around trying to set up our trip down the Amazon from Manaus to Belém, we were ready to board the barge. We had been told to be at the dock at 5pm to wait for loading, so imagine our surprise when at 10pm, we found out that the barges were full and we were not to be included! Apparently the people who had completed our paperwork had failed to put us on the list of vehicles that would be loaded that night, so we had to set up camp in the noisy and dusty parking lot at the port and wait until the next day.

In the morning our turn to board came and we were directed onto the barge, right into the middle and surrounded by massive semi-trailers. Fortunately the workers asked if we needed to go in and out and put us in the only row that would allow us to open the side door. Once our barge filled up, a second barge was loaded with trucks and we were connected together like a train. This took all day and into the evening and finally around

10pm we heard the sound of the tugboat's engine and felt the movement of barges - we were finally on our way down the Amazon River.

The company that runs the barges, Chibatao - Navegacao E Comercio Ltda, has a monopoly on the barge traffic on this part of the Amazon River. FYI, for other travelers who may wish to ship this way, their email address is jfoliveira@uol.com.br, be sure to write in Portuguese. They also ship up river.

The next three and a half days were spent going downriver at a speed of about 11mph. We read, ate, did some laundry and mostly just lay in our hammocks watching the world go by. The truck drivers were very friendly and always tried to include us in things that were happening on the barge. They even had their trucks set up with "chuck-wagon" type kitchen boxes where they could flip down the door to have a cook top complete with propane stove. They were very self-sufficient.

Occasionally, we watched as small dugout canoes paddled into the middle of the river to meet us, and the occupant would throw out a line to the crew to be pulled up behind. We were amazed that the river dwellers would risk coming alongside a moving ship, but we found that this was the way that commerce was conducted on the river. The dugouts were filled with an amazing variety of items. There were fish, shrimp, juices, fruits, furniture and things we couldn't identify. Sometimes things were traded and other times money was paid for the goods. We joined in and bought a big bag of dried shrimp.

As we neared Belém, we were surprised when the barge pulled up to the riverside and stopped. We finally figured out that because a drought had lowered the level of the Amazon, we had to wait six hours for the "high tide" so that we could get to the company dock. This meant

> another night spent on the barge. After all the delays,
> we finally arrived at the port in Belém early in the
> morning five days after we started our "three-day" trip.
>
> We then had to wait for about 5 hours before the dock
> employees could line up our barge with the dock so that
> the truckers could drive their rigs off the barge. Then we
> had to wait another hour while the trailers that had us
> blocked in were moved!

From Belém you can follow BR010 towards Brasília if
you are in a hurry to reach the south. By following
BR316 southeast, you can explore São Luís, then follow
the coast from Fortaleza, to Natal, João Pessoa and
Recife until you reach Salvador da Bahía. This route
provides many opportunities for exploring empty
National Parks and tons of beaches.

Brazilian Roads

Can you imagine a map that actually has a legend that
includes "bad pavement"?! Ours did. And our progress
through Brazil was significantly slowed by the long
stretches of potholed roadway that we encountered.
One hundred kilometers of potholes would take us more
than five hours to negotiate

We don't know how Brazil can function as a country
when the roads are in such bad shape. The trucks still
have to make their deliveries, but they must sustain
large maintenance bills from hitting the holes at high
speeds and their delivery times would have to be
delayed. On top of that, the trucks are required to stop
at police inspection points, we guess to pay taxes, every
time they enter AND exit a state. Luckily we just
zoomed through with a wave at the police.

Fortunately not all of the roads are this bad, just most of
the roads in the northern half of the country. In the south

> there are private toll roads that are great high-speed roadways, although you can end up paying some pretty high tolls but you get what you pay for.

South of Salvador, if you haven't had your fill of beaches, you can continue down the coast all the way to Rio de Janeiro. It is more interesting to head a bit inland to explore the mining districts of Ouro Prêto and Congonhas before heading to Rio.

Propane
In Brazil and in many other Latin American countries propane is referred to as butane. In our search to get our tank filled, we had found several small filling stations but all had refused to fill our tank. We received reasons from "sorry, we don't have the right fill valve" (although Brazil uses the same Acme fitting as in the US) to "no, we are not allowed to sell to individuals" to "you have to go to the main plant".

We finally learned that the main propane yards are only found in port cities where the gas is unloaded from ships into their tanks. The yards then fill thousands of small tanks that are loaded onto trucks and transported around the country. In the port city of Fortaleza, we were only able to find the main plant by hiring a motorcycle taxi to lead us through the winding streets. Once we arrived, we were finally given the good news that yes, they would fill our propane tank.

From Rio all roads seem to head through the insanity of São Paulo with its estimated 20 million residents. From there, there are three main routes you can choose from.

Heading to south to Curitiba you can then continue south to Uruguay or turn inland and go to Iguazu Falls before crossing into either Paraguay or Argentina.

Heading east from São Paulo will send you off to Campo Grande and the immense wetlands of the Pantanal. From the Pantanal, you can cross into Bolivia or head south to Iguazu Falls (Foz do Iguaçu).

Foz do Iguaçu
The National Park doesn't permit private vehicles to drive to the falls, so we walked from our camp to the park entrance where we took a bus to the falls. The closer we got to the falls, the more excited we got as we started to get glimpses of the falls through the trees.

We got out at the top of the falls to views of the wide river channel and the "smoke" that is really mist rising up from beyond the lip of the falls. The park provides really close access to the falls via a network of raised walkways built in the riverbed right along the edge of the falls! The views were just incredible, and we took a zillion photographs. We spent the next few hours walking the series of paths that go along the canyon's edge, stopping every few feet to see a new perspective of the falls. Depending on the time of year, the park claims to have nearly 270 falls along the Brazilian and Argentina sides of the canyon.

Maps

A good starting point in reviewing online road maps of each state in Brazil is the government transportation website, Ministerio dos Transportes at http://www.transportes.gov.br/bit/inrodo.htm or at http://www.transportes.gov.br/bit/mapas/mapclick/brs/RODCENTR.htm

Brasil Mapa Rodoviario by Guía Quatro Rodas. The scale on this map is 1:7,000,000. Remember that Brazil is a huge country and the maps will also be huge. This map includes in its legend a symbol for "road in poor condition".

Freytag & Berndt Maps has a combination Brazil, Bolivia and Paraguay map with scale of 1:4,000,000.

Automapa, Rutas de Brasil y Uruguay, scale 1:2,500,000. Website: www.automapa.com.ar.

Ouro Preto, BR

Brazil Camping

Brazil has a membership campground association that allows non-members to camp, although at higher rates. Their website has addresses but few directions to the camps. Check out Web Camping at http://www.webcamping.com.br/3campings.htm. However, many of the campsites that we found had low entrances that we could not fit through. Also, many "camping" areas do not have access for vehicles but are rather walk-in sites.

Brazil also has a great network of truck stops, called Postos, providing excellent places to spend the night for free. They usually have restaurants and bathrooms with showers. Security is also provided.

Location	Description	GPS Coordinates	Cost
South of Mucajai	Bush camp.		Free
Reserva Terra Indigena Waimiri Atroari	Bush camp near south entrance. Just off the road behind trees. The road through the reserve is closed between 6pm and 6am.	S01 16.69 W60 24.47	Free
Manaus	City camp. Across from the police station and behind the Central das Federacoes Desportivas do Amazonas (Stadium), Avenida Constantino Nery and Avenida Leonardo Malcher. Offer the guards a dollar or two.		
Manaus	Punta Negra, city camp. Suburb of Manaus, across from the amphitheater, police patrols.		Free
Manaus	Camp in the parking lot of the Amazon barge company, Chibatao - Navegacao E Comercio Ltda, Industrial District. Noisy with barges loading trucks but the only way to secure a place on a barge.		Free
Amazon River Barge	5 nights on the barge on the Amazon. See shipping info for details.		
Belém	BR gas station/truck stop on highway 316 about 10 miles south of Belém.		Free

Americas Overland

Location	Description	GPS Coordinates	Cost
São Luís	South of São Luís, Posto Marrecao on Hwy 135	S03 19.99 W44 26.79	Free
Praia (beach) Calhau	Praia (beach) Calhau, city camp, 8 km north of São Luís.		Free
Caxias	BR Truck stop, Hwy 316, 40 km wests of Caxias.		Free
Parque Nat'l de Sete Cidades	Camped in the park one night at Parque Hotel Sete Cidades.		Pay
Parque Nat'l de Sete Cidades	Camped at the Hotel Fazenda Sete Cidades outside the park entrance. Pool and restaurant.		Pay
Fortaleza	Truck stop west of the city.		Free
Canoa Quebrada	Two nights, beach camp and city camp on the main street. City camp a bit noisy due to location near restaurants.		Free
Natal	Camping Praias Belas - Rod. RN313, Km13, Colônia do Pium, turn off just south of Parnamirim. Camping ground just off the beach.		Pay
João Pessoa	Camping Club of Brazil at Praia do Ponta do Seixas. On the beach.		Pay
Recife	The Convention Center, located between Olinda and Recife. Enter through the west gate past the main entrance. 2nd night at a truck stop on the southern side of town.		Pay
Maceió	Praia do Frances 22km south of Maceió. Campground on the beach at the north end of town. Go to the beach and turn left until it ends at the campground.		Pay
Aracaju	Truck stop out of town.		Free
Salvador	Camping de Salvador - Praia do Flamengo about 20 km north of Salvador. On the beach. Bus service available.	S12 56.81 W38 20.46	Pay
Between Salvador and Ipatinga camped at truck stops.	Postos		Free

Location	Description	GPS Coordinates	Cost
Ouro Prêto	Camping Club Brazil-MG-01 - Rod. do Inconfidentes. Just past the west entrance to town, don't drive into the city, very narrow streets.		Pay
Congonhas	Camped in truck stop, but possible to camp behind the tourist office near the bus station.		Free
Teresopolis	Parque Nacional da Serra dos Órgãos. Very limited space, one or two campers only.		Pay
Rio de Janiero	Camping Verde Mar, Estrada do Bandeirantes, near Clube Aquatico Wet n' Wild. About 30 minutes from center, very quiet.		Pay
Rio de Janiero	Possible to camp at the yacht harbor or at a posto before the city. Camping on the beaches isn't recommended due to crime potential.		
Fredo	Behind the historical church, next to restaurants.	S23 01.54 W44 31.03	Free
São Paulo and Londrina at Postos (truck stops)			Free
Foz do Iguaçu,	Camping Club do Brasil, outside the entrance to the national park.		Pay

Border Crossing Formalities

Border crossing is possible into Venezuela, Paraguay, Bolivia, Uruguay and Argentina. We entered Brazil from Venezuela. You must have your Brazilian visa before you arrive at the border.

The border between Venezuela and Brazil is at Santa Elena de Uairén, Venezuela. The Brazilian Consulates throughout Venezuela were not willing to issue us visas the same day, or even the next day. But we were told that there was a possibility for same-day service at the consulate in Santa Elena, so we decided to roll the dice and try our luck at the border.

The consulate is located in a converted house right in town and across the street from the last petrol station in Venezuela. After waiting an hour for the consulate to open, we received the good news, that yes, we could get our visas here, we could have them by the end of the day, AND we were given a five-year, multiple entry visa for $100.00US.

Arrival
Arriving at the Brazil border post, we parked and went to get at the end of a long line of people waiting at a closed office. Isn't that typical of humans, we just get in line? While Kim saved our place, Don went off to find out how to import the Fuso. Carrying our lifeline, the Lonely Planet Brazilian Portuguese Phrasebook, Don found another office where an immigration officer stamped our passports and welcomed us into Brazil. We never did find out what the other closed office/long line was for.

Brazil/Venezuela Border

Another 50 yards down the road was the customs building where we stopped to get our new vehicle documents. The customs official never even looked inside the vehicle, but did ask us if our extra fuel containers were full. We replied that they were empty. We suspect that they might have made us pay some import duty on the fuel since the price in Brazil is about 39 times more expense than in Venezuela. Our first fill up cost about $3.37/gal, 89 cents/liter as compared to 8.2 cents/gal, 2.2 cents/liter in Venezuela.

We provided the customs officer with our Venezuela vehicle documents to help speed the import process, this way she could copy most of the necessary information from the old forms. The only twist here was that we were asked a value for the Fuso, so that they could calculate the tax that we would owe if we sold it in Brazil. The crossing was very quick, it only took us about an hour to cross both borders, get our paperwork and be on our way.

Provide the customs officer with the original and one copy of the following documents:

> Vehicle Title
> Registration
> Driver's License
> Passport

Departure
The border between Argentina and Brazil is called Foz do Iguaçu, on the Brazil side and Puerto Iguazú, on the Argentine side. The paperwork to release our car from the Brazil side was easy but time consuming. You have to surrender your vehicle permit before you go to immigration, but because we tried to do it the other way around, the customs officer "punished" us by taking our paperwork and disappearing for about 30 minutes.

When he returned he admonished us to surrender our documents first the next time we visit. Immigration was a breeze, just a stamp in the passport.

Below is a copy of our Brazilian vehicle permit, the *Declaracão Simplificada de Importação*.

MINISTÉRIO DA FAZENDA	Declaração Simplificada de Importação DSI	REGISTRO 0260151 - 216
Secretaria da Receita Federal		NÚMERO
Coordenação-Geral do Sistema Aduaneiro		06/08/2005
		DATA

1.IMPORTADOR

NOME/NOME EMPRESARIAL	ORF/CNPJ	MATRÍCULA NO MRE (número e sigla)
DONALD GREENE		

ENDEREÇO COMPLETO			
PO BOX	USA		
PASSAPORTE/CARTEIRA DE IDENTIDADE	NATUREZA DO VISTO	NACIONALIDADE	DATA DO DESEMBARQUE
USA		AMERICANA	06-ago-05
REPRESENTANTE LEGAL		CPF	NÚMERO DO REGISTRO

2.DESPACHO ADUANEIRO

VALOR TOTAL DOS BENS (US$)	VALOR DO FRETE (US$)	VALOR DO SEGURO (US$)	VALOR ADUANEIRO (R$)	TAXA DE CONVERSÃO (R$)
$ 000,00			R$ 302,00	2,3151

NATUREZA DA OPERAÇÃO		INFORMAÇÕES COMPLEMENTARES
☐ Missão diplomática ou semelhante		DE ACORDO COM A IN 155 DE 22.12.99 ART.4°
☒ Outra TURISMO		

3.DADOS SOBRE A CARGA

TRANSPORTADOR	IDENTIFICAÇÃO VEÍCULO	PAÍS PROCEDÊNCIA	DATA DE CHEGADA	TEMPO DE ENTRADA
	C :1	VENEZUELA	06-ago-05	
N° CONHECIMENTO/ETIQUETA DE BAGAGEM	QTDE. DE VOLUMES	PESO BRUTO (KG)	PESO LÍQUIDO (KG)	DEPÓSITÁRIO/ARMAZÉM
	0	0,00	0,00	

4.RELAÇÃO DE BENS

ITEM	QUANT.	UND	DESCRIÇÃO	VALOR FOB (US$)
1	1	UNID.	VEICULO MARCA MITSUBSHI, TIPO CASA MOVEL, ANO 2004, SERIAL JLE 7, COR BRANCO PLACA C 1	$ 000,00

CONTINUA EM FOLHA SUPLEMENTAR	DEMONSTRATIVO DE CÁLCULO DE TRIBUTOS ANEXOS	TOTAL	$ 000,00
☐ Sim ☒ Não	☒ Sim ☐ Não		

A presente declaração é expressão da verdade

Boa Vista-RR, 6 agosto, 2005　　　　　　Assinatura do importador (representante legal)

5.REQUISIÇÃO DO MINISTÉRIO DAS RELAÇÕES EXTERIORES | **6.CONTROLE SANITÁRIO, AMBIENTAL OU DE SEGURANÇA**

De acordo com o disposto nos artigos 153 e 234 do Regulamento Aduaneiro aprovado pelo Decreto n°91.030, de 5 de março de 1985, formulo a presente requisição ao titular da unidade de Secretaria da Receita Federal responsável pelo despacho aduaneiro, para fins de recolhimento da isenção dos impostos incidentes sobre a operação identificada nesta DSI.

Órgão responsável
Conclui-se a verificação, certifico
☐ a regularização da importação
☐ a irregularidade da importação em virtude _____ o que determina a adoção da seguinte providência em relação aos bens:

Nome da autoridade	Nome da autoridade
Data　　Assinatura	Data　　Assinatura

7.USO EXCLUSIVO DA SRF

ANÁLISE DO PEDIDO	DESEMBARAÇO ADUANEIRO
NOME DA AUTORIDADE LELIANA CONCEIÇÃO D... MIRANDA	NOME DO APRE CICERO HARNALDO MACIEL DE LIMA
DATA 06/08/2005　ASSINAT...	MATRÍCULA　ASSINATURA

OBSERVAÇÕES

O PRAZO DO REGIME DE ADMISSÃO TEMPORÁRIA EXPIRA EM 04/11/2008
DEVOLVER À ADUANA BRASILEIRA
QUANDO DA SAÍDA DO BRASIL

GIVE IT BACK TO BRAZILIAN
CUSTOMS WHEN LEAVING BRAZIL

Americas Overland

8. DADOS DO DESPACHO ADUANEIRO

Nº da DI ou DSI _____ 216

06/08/2005
Nº do Conhecimento de carga: _____

Data ____/____/____

Assinatura   Matrícula

9. BAIXA DO TERMO DE RESPONSABILIDADE

Regime extinto em virtude de:

☐ 1. Reexportação   Documento de despacho: _____   Data: ____/____/____

☐ 2. Entrega à Fazenda Nacional   Nº do termo: _____   Data: ____/____/____

☐ 3. Destruição   Nº do termo: _____   Data: ____/____/____

☐ 4. Transferência para outro regime   Nº do DTR _____   Data: ____/____/____

☐ 5. Despacho para consumo   Nº da DI/DSI _____   Data: ____/____/____

Data ____/____/____

Assinatura   Matrícula

10. EXECUÇÃO DO TERMO DE RESPONSABILIDADE

Tendo em vista o cumprimento do compromisso, encaminhe-se ao Sistema de Arrecadação para, nos termos da IN SRF nº 84/98, proceder-se à:

☐ 1. Notificação ao banco, com vistas à imediata conversão do depósito em renda da União.

☐ 2. Intimação do garantidor com vistas ao recolhimento do valor do termo.

Data ____/____/____

Assinatura   Matrícula

11. OBSER ESTA ADMISSÃO TEMPORÁRIA EXPIRA EM   04/11/2005

Chapter Seventeen

Argentina

Routes
Maps
Camping
Border Crossing Formalities
- **Arrival**
- **Departure**

Routes

Argentina shares borders with Uruguay, Paraguay, Brazil, Bolivia and Chile so needless to say there are numerous routes that can be driven around this long country. We'll simplify things a bit and describe what will basically be a long loop from Iguazu Falls at the Brazil/Paraguay border south to Buenos Aires all the way to Ushuaia then northward crossing back and forth into Chile until you cross out of Argentina for the last time from Salta or San Salvador de Jujuy.

Parque Nacional Iguazú – Argentina
Everyone has his or her favorite side of Iguazu Falls and we were determined to see for ourselves which was better. When we arrived at the entrance to the Argentine side we discovered that the most desirable area to explore in the park, the walkway to Garganta del Diablo (the devil's throat) and the best part of the falls, was closed. The walkway had been washed away in a flood several years ago and was in the process of being rebuilt. In recent years, boats had shuttled people to a still-existing portion, but that apparently was no longer the case. But we were told that the new walkway would open "maybe tomorrow".

A Disneyland-like train provides access around the park. Very slow (we later found we could walk the same distance faster), it brought us to the second-best walkways from which we could get very close to the tops of the falls themselves. Very nice, but the views were not as impressive (in our opinion) as on the Brazil side. But one unexpected delight was the tremendous numbers of butterflies. Large ones, tiny ones, colorful ones, some that looked like tree bark, some that were nearly psychedelic. They were really magnificent.

Upon leaving the park, we discovered that a second day ticket only costs half the price, so we decided to return the next day to see if the walkway was open (yeah, right).

The next morning on our way out of town, we stopped again to see if Garganta del Diablo was open. Miracle of miracles, it was! But we missed the train, and we didn't want to wait for the next one, so we walked 2kms to the new walkway. The walkway was then an additional 1km long. But when we finally arrived at the viewpoint, the view was magnificent. We don't believe there are very many places where you can get as close to a tremendous waterfall as you can on this walkway. This was an absolutely amazing experience, especially since this walkway hadn't been open for years and we got to be there at its inaugural.

From Iguazu Falls you can follow RN12/14 through the Jesuit mission province of Misiones then follow the Río Uruguay all the way to Buenos Aires. Along the way you can detour to the wetlands of Reserva Provincial Esteros del Iberá, the shrine of folk hero "Guachito" Gil, Parque Nacional El Palmar and the religious town of Luján, which is the site of a tremendous pilgrimage to view a statue of the Virgin Mary.

After dancing the tango in Buenos Aires, take any of the routes heading south until you enter the Patagonia

Region when you cross the Río Negro into Viedma. Argentina has two main north/south routes, *Ruta 3* along the Atlantic coast and *Ruta 40* following the Andes along the Chilean border.

The details of the routes from Puerto Madryn south to Ushuaia then north through San Carlos de Bariloche are to be found in the Patagonia Chapter.

Driving back into Argentina from Chile via the tunnel at Paso del Cristo Redentor, you are treated to magnificent views of the highest peak in the Americas, Cerro Aconcagua (6,962m, 22,975ft). This is the main route from Santiago, Chile. From there you can head down to the wine country of Mendoza and San Juan. Leaving *Ruta 40* behind, visit the shrine of the Difunta Correa then explore the desert badlands of Parque Provincial Ischigualasto.

Further north explore Tafi del Valle before arriving in another wine producing area, Cafayate. After replenishing your wine supply, take your time exploring the Quebradas del Cafayate, an area of beautifully carved canyons and interesting landforms.

From here it is still northward, as you have to decide from which border you plan to cross out of the country. From Salta you can follow the amazing Tren a las Nubes (Train to the Clouds) crossing multiple passes over 12,000 and 14,000 feet high. This dirt and gravel route leads you to the starkly beautiful Paso de Sico before dropping out of the Andes into Chile's Atacama Desert.

North of Salta you can follow the paved road over the Andes out of Jujuy all the way to San Pedro de Atacama, Chile. Along this route you can detour to the World Heritage listed Quebrada de Humahuaca. Continuing northward out of the Quebrada will have you crossing into Bolivia.

Argentina Folk Heroes

Gauchito Gil

Outside of Mercedes in the state of Corrientes, you can visit the shrine of "Gauchito" Antonio Gil. As the story goes, in the 1850's, Gil made a name for himself by robbing from the rich and giving to the poor. When he was finally caught, he was sentenced to execution. Just before his sentence was carried out, Gil told the sergeant in command that the sergeant's son was dying and that the child would be spared if the sergeant prayed for Gil's soul. When the boy recovered, the sergeant placed a cross at the site of Gil's death. Now the site is a shrine filled with tributes and exhortations of thanks from the many, many people who claim miracles from "Gauchito" Gil. Red flags symbolize adherence to the "cult" of Gil and they can be found along roadsides across the country.

Our experience was one of awe at the numbers of people who claim that Gil has helped them and the devotion of his followers. There were thousands of plaques attached to every flat surface surrounding the shrine and candles and offerings and ribbons adorned the ground. We were even able to buy a red ribbon requesting "Gauchito" Gil to protect our truck. It was quite an amazing sight.

Difunta Correa

The Difunta Correa is a popularly venerated soul who, according to legend, has performed miracles. Legend has it that during the civil wars in the 1840's, Deolinda

Correa and her baby followed her husband from battle to battle. Eventually succumbing to hunger and thirst, Correa died.

When found by passersby, Correa was dead, but her baby still suckled at her breast. This is considered her first miracle. Since then, people have come to the site where she was found and prayed for whatever they need. Small chapels have been erected on the site to house the offerings that people bring to express thanks for favors received. The most popular offerings include models of houses, license plates and gifts of flowers and notes, however some offerings are quite elaborate including a car and a motorcycle. One of the stranger items was a stuffed dog!

One of the chapels has a life size rendering of the defunct (difunta) Correa in repose with her baby at her breast. People enter the chapel and touch the statue with the same reverence as they would a statue of Christ. This has the Catholic church quite annoyed. The Difunta is not a saint and there is no proof that she even existed. The church has even gone so far as to erect a church on the site to combat the popularity of the Difunta.

The site, which started as a simple cross on a hillside, has grown in size to include 17 chapels, vendors, restaurants, the church and even a gas station. The day we visited was a Sunday and hundreds of families were visiting and picnicking. There even appeared to be a group who had charted fourteen buses to visit the shrine and party complete with a band. Quite a sight. One of the down sides to the veneration of the Difunta is that at small shrines in both Argentina and Chile, people leave bottles of water to quench the Difunta's thirst. This has created a huge trash problem as the thousands of bottles of water get scattered to the four winds.

Maps

ACA, the Automovile Club Argentino has great maps available for the entire country on a state-by-state basis. If you are a member of a reciprocal automobile association, like the AAA (United States) or the CAA (Canada) you should be able to purchase the maps at discounted prices, although in practice you will likely be charged full price. The maps are not inexpensive. Check out the map page of the ACA website at http://www.aca.org.ar/servicios/cartografia/framecartogra.htm

ITMB has maps available for Argentina and Patagonia, however we found our copies to be out-dated. Newer editions may have better information.

Freytag & Berndt Argentina Road Map has a scale of 1:1,900,000.

Rough Guides Argentina Map has a scale of 1:2,000,000.

Automapa, Rutas de la Argentina, scale 1:2,000,000. Website: www.automapa.com.ar.

Instituto Geografico Militar has road maps of the entire country by Province. www.igm.gov.ar/descargas/mapas_escolares

Argentour has lots of maps and information. http://www.argentour.com/en/

Argentina Camping

Argentina is a wonderful place for camping as nearly every community will have a municipal campground. Many of the campgrounds will be free while others will charge only a minimal fee of a few dollars.

Location	Description	GPS Coordinates	Cost
Puerto Iguazú	Camping El Pindo, just west of the roundabout before entering town.		Pay
River camp spot on RN12	Private campground right on the river.	S28 24.98 W56 32.63	Pay
Esteros del Iberá, Northern entry	Eastern entry, radio tower camp.	S28 25.28 W56 20.41	Free
Colonia Pellegrini	Municipal campground on the lagoon.		Pay
Mercedes	El Guachito Gil Shrine.	S29 08.60 W58 08.07	Free
Colón	Municipal campground on the Uruguay River.		Free
San Antonio del Areco	Municipal campground, on the river at west side of town.	S34 14.38 W59 28.35	Free
Buenos Aires	Puerto Madero, northeast side of the Hilton Hotel (on the street).		Free
Las Flores	Municipal campground at El Parque Playa Montero.		Free
Patagonia Argentina			
Bahia Blanca	Municipal campground on RN3, Complejo Recreativo Maldonado. Pool		Pay
Viedma	Camp along the Río Negro near the tourist office.		Free
Península Valdés	Municipal campground at Puerto Pirámides.		Pay
Punta/Playa Ninfas	Wild camp past the lighthouse.	S42 58.72 W64 18.55	Free
Gaiman City Park	Street camp		Free
Cabo Raso	Ghost town south of Punta Tombo, wild camp.		Free
Rada Tilly	Municipal campground, Avenida Capitan Moyano.		Pay

Location	Description	GPS Coordinates	Cost
Puerto Deseado	Municipal campground, Camping Refugio de la Ria.	S47 45.31 W65 53.27	Pay
Monumento Natural Bosques Petrificados	Wild camp	S47 39.64 W67 55.02	Free
Parque Nacional Monte León	Park campground near the Grotto.		Pay
Río Gallegos	Chakra Daniel	S51 40.49 W 69 14.92	Pay
La Frontera	Chile Magallanes and Argentina Tierra del Fuego.	S53 19.30 W68 39.63	Free
Ushuaia	La Pista del Andino campground.	S54 48.71 W68 20.97	Pay
Parque Nacional Tierra del Fuego	Free wilderness campsites at Río Pipo and Camping Laguna Verde.		Free
San Sebastian	Camping on the beach near the police stop.		Free
Back into Argentina from Chile			
Tapi Aike	Wild camp in the steppe off Hwy 40 about 10 km north of Tapi Aike.		Free
Los Glaciares Nat'l Park	Free camp in the parking lot at the Moreno Glacier.		Free
El Chaltén	Around the corner from the official campground. Low entry for campers.	S49 19.08 W72 53.69	Free
Estancia La Angostura	Private ranch, but they didn't charge us. Meals available.	S48 38.05 W70 38.92	Free
Cueva de las Manos	Wild camp above cave entrance at pull out on the road.		Free
Estancia Telken	Private ranch that welcomes guests. Meals available.	(Entrance at) S46 48.28 W70 47.35	Pay
Los Antiguos	Municipal campground		Pay

Location	Description	GPS Coordinates	Cost
Back into Argentina from Chile			
Río Mayo	Riverside campsite.	S45 40.98 W70 15.92	Free
Esquel	Nahuel Pan Camping, east side of town across from the Petro Bras Station.		Pay
Esquel	PN Los Alerces	S42 53.13 W71 36.20	Free
El Bolsón	Camping La Chacra	S41 58.28 W71 31.54	Pay
Colonia La Suiza	Unofficial camping at the Bomberos on Arroyo Goya, near San Carlos de Bariloche.	S41 05.24 W71 30.76	Free
Parque Nacional Nahuel Huapi	RN231 Km 48, West of San Carlos de Bariloche.	S40 50.40 W71 32.29	Free
Back into Argentina from Chile			
Mendoza	Vina de Vieytes Campground, Chacras de Coria exit, west of RN 40 in Luján.	S33 00.77 W68 50.39	Pay
Mendoza	Municipal campground in the park in the city center. Noisy bar.		Free
Pocito	South of San Juan, KM 154 RN 40, Petro Bras Service Station.	S31 38.58 W68 32.34	Free
Chucuma	Desert Wild camp RN 510 south of Chucuma.	S31 16.48 W67 14.39	Free
Ischigualasto Prov. Park	Parking area, dusty but free.	S30 09.90 W67 50.66	Free
Catamarca	Municipal campground, off Av República 4km w of centro.	S28 27.89 W65 49.98	Pay
Río Seco (South of Tucuman)	YPF Service Station, grassy area	S27 16.61 W65 32.89	Free

Location	Description	GPS Coordinates	Cost
Tafi del Valle	Wild camp on the lakeshore closer to El Mollar	S26 55.39 W65 40.97	Free
Cafayate Municipal Campground	Limited space for large overlanders, south side of town on RN 40. Other campgrounds nearby.		Pay
Quebreda de Cafayate	15 km north of Cafayate; wild camp.	S26 01.26 W65 48.16	Free
Embalse Cobre Corral	Approx. 50 km south of Salta, Municipal campground.	S25 17.32 W65 26.42	Pay
Cachi	Municipal campground, south side of town.		Pay
PN de Los Cardones	Wild camp approx. 37 km west of Cachi on RP33.	Turn off at S25 09.44 W65 59.44	Free
Salta	Municipal campground south side of centro.	S24 48.79 W65 25.18	Pay
San Antonio de los Cobres	Approx 15km west of town, Indigenous farmhouse, private residence, 13,134ft elevation.	S24 14.34 W66 24.68	Free

Iguazu Falls, La Garganta del Diablo

Border Crossing Formalities

<u>Arrival</u>
Crossing to the Argentine side at Puerto Iguazú there was a HUGE line of cars waiting to cross from Brazil. Uncertain as to what they were waiting for, and knowing that we needed to do paperwork, we drove up the shoulder to where a policeman was directing traffic. He directed us to where we needed to go and our paperwork took about ten minutes. I'm sure some of those cars in line are still waiting.

Provide the customs officer with the original and one copy of the following documents:

>Vehicle Title
Registration
Driver's License
Passport

The vehicle permit in Argentina is called the *Declaración Jurada Admisión Temporaria Vehículos de Turistas.*

Argentina and Chile have numerous border crossings back and forth. In fact, in the Patagonia Region, the only way to reach some parts of Chile is to exit into Argentina then transit around the part of Chile where there are no roads, and then cross back into Chile. We have described the border crossings that we used between these countries in the Chile Chapter.

REPUBLICA   ARGENTINA
ADMINISTRACION FEDERAL DE INGRESOS PUBLICOS
DIRECCION GENERAL DE ADUANAS

DECLARACION JURADA
ADMISION TEMPORARIA VEHICULOS DE TURISTAS

SOLICITUD Nº (1)

1	PROPIETARIO	AUTORIZADO

Apellido y Nombres: .....
Domicilio en el
País de origen: .
Domicilio
transitorio en el País: ....

Nacionalidad: ....

Tipo y Nº Doc.: ....

Registro Nº: ....

Apellido y Nombres: ....
Domicilio en el
País de origen: ...
Domicilio
transitorio en el País: ....

Nacionalidad: ....

Tipo y Nº Doc.: ....

Registro Nº: ....

2	DATOS DEL VEHICULO Y OPCIONALES

Título Propiedad Nº: .... Marca .... Tipo: ....

Modelo: .... Año: .... Motor Nº: .... Carrocería-Bastidor Nº: ....

Opcionales: Aire acondicionado - pasacassette - otros (Tachar y agregar lo que corresponda) (*) ....

.... Valor del vehículo en $ (Pesos) (2) ....

3	DETALLE DE ELEMENTOS QUE LLEVA EL TURISTA COMO EQUIPAJE ACOMPAÑADO

1	Acoplado Nº Identificatorio: ....
2	Motocicleta Nº patente y marca:
3	Motoneta Nº patente y marca:
4	Motobicicleta Nº patente y marca: ....
5	Lancha con/sin motor Nº: ....
	Marca: .... Modelo: ....
6	Bote:

7	Casa rodante patente Nº:	....

Equipada con:

A	x	Cocina	D	X	Equipo de radio	G	x	Radio
B	X	Heladera	E	X	Ventilador	H	X	Pasacassette
C	X	Aire acondicionado	F	X	Televisión	I	X	Otros

CODIGOS OBJETOS	DETALLE DE OBJETOS TRANSPORTADOS COMO EQUIPAJE				
	CODIGO	MARCA	NUMERO	ESTADO	CANTIDAD OBJETOS
01 -Máq. fotográfica					
01a -Objetivos					
01b -Fotómetro					
01c -Flash electrónico					
02. -Proyector					
02a -Objetivos					
03 -Filmadora					
04 -Grabador					
05 -Máq. escribir					
06 -Escopeta					
07 -Radio					
08 -Televisor					
09 -Prismáticos					
10					
11			Total de elementos		

4	COMPROMISO DE RETORNO

Me comprometo a retornar al exterior con el vehículo y los elementos detallados precedentemente dentro del plazo acordado o en su defecto a pagar los derechos y gravámenes que correspondan. Me obligo a cumplir las instrucciones que figuran al dorso y medio por notificado que la salida fuera de término constituye una infracción penada por la Legislación Argentina con una multa cuyo valor será de 1 a 5 veces el importe de los tributos que gravan la importación para consumo y que no podrá ser inferior al 30 % del valor en Aduana del vehículo, aún cuando no estuviere gravado (Ley Nº 22415 - art. 970).

5	AUTORIZACION

Aduana de Entrada:

27	01	08	26	07	08

Fecha de Ingreso   Vencimiento

Firma y Sello Autoridad Aduanera

Firma del Propietario o del Autorizado

PERMISO PARA CIRCULAR	6	PRORROGA	7	RETORNO

ESTE VEHICULO Y EL EQUIPAJE DEL TITULAR PUEDEN CIRCULAR POR TODO EL PAIS HASTA EL PLAZO INDICADO EN EL SECTOR 5 Y SU EVENTUAL PRORROGA.

Lugar y Fecha: ....

Se concede hasta el .... bajo las mismas

previsiones determinadas en oportunidad de su ingreso.

Providencia Nº .... de ...

Firma y Sello (3)

Fecha: ....

Aduana de Salida: ....

Firma y Sello Guarda Interviniente

OF. ALM. - MARZO/00 - 30.000

VER INSTRUCCIONES AL DORSO

OM - 1867/A

DUPLICADO: Para el Interesado - ORIGINAL: Para la Aduana, Argentina Argentina de Entrada

Departure

When exiting the country you need to go into the
Customs office and surrender your vehicle permit. Go
to the Immigration window/desk and get an exit stamp in
your passport. As you drive through the border gate
you may have to show your passport exit stamp.

Cueva de las Manos

Chapter 18

Patagonia

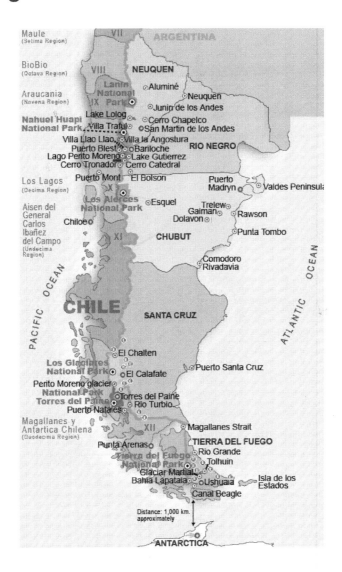

The Patagonia Region is an area that covers the southern portions of both Argentina and Chile.
We are covering Patagonia in a separate section due to its geographical uniqueness and the fact that to adequately explore the region an overlander must cross back and forth across the Argentinean and Chilean Borders no less than four times.

Routes
Maps
Camping
Border Crossing Formalities

Routes

Patagonia is a diverse region complete with mountains and glaciers, rivers and lakes, broadleaf and coniferous forests, temperate rain forests and arid steppes. A major characteristic of Patagonia is the constant wind that blows in the summer months. The region has a low population density and a high number of nature reserves.

Along the Atlantic coastline are reserves where you can wander among penguins and their young, and view whales and elephant seals. Inland you can explore the extremes of desert-like petrified forests to glaciers and ice fields.

Heading south on Argentina's RN3, you arrive at the must-see Reserva Provincial Península Valdes with its stark beauty and huge numbers of marine animals.

Then on your way to the penguin-breeding colony at Punta Tombo, you can detour to Trelew to visit its excellent dinosaur museum.

Penguins

Reserva Provicial Punta Tombo is South America's largest single penguin colony. Half a million penguins come ashore here in the spring (October to December) to nest and give birth. The park is remote, but worth the drive. Immediately after passing the entrance gate, we began to see penguins. Penguins on the road, penguins in burrows, penguins on hillsides, penguins walking, penguins swimming, penguins everywhere.

People are supposed to stay on the marked path so as not to disturb the penguins, but nobody told the penguins the rules. And they are everywhere! There is no way that you could come here and not have an up-close and personal penguin encounter. One curious penguin actually grabbed Kim by her pant leg and refused to let her go! They are incredibly inquisitive and are as interested in you as you are in them. And when you get ready to leave, it is imperative that you check under your car before driving away, because they'll be checking out the underside of it.

Crossing hundreds of miles of windy, barren steppe, there are other wonders such as the Monumento Natural Bosques Petrificados and Parque Nacional Monte León to explore. Crossing through a narrow strip of Chile and the Strait of Magellan you reach Tierra del Fuego as the southernmost road ends at Ushuaia and Parque Nacional Tierra del Fuego.

When you turn back northward, traveling past beautiful Chilean fiords you'll arrive at the stunning Parque

Nacional Torres del Paine. You'll be amazed as you sit and watch the changing moods of Patagonia in the views of the jagged mountains and their glacial lakes.

Crossing back into Argentina you travel on the lonely and legendary *Ruta 40*. Beware of the high winds dropping off of the Southern Ice Field. Set up camp in front of the Perito Moreno Glacier and then climb Cerro Fitz Roy in the northern sector of the park. Visit some of the remote sheep estancias and view the mysterious handprints at the World Heritage site of Cueva de las Manos.

Parque Nacional Los Glaciares is a UNESCO World Heritage Site that contains more than 750,000 hectares (over 1.6 million acres) of glacial ice fields.

The southern sector of the park contains the Glaciar Perito Moreno where you can park your car within view of the glacier. A ten-minute walk took us to the first viewing area. This first view was enough to take our breath away. You could see the entire face of the glacier where it advances into the lake, as well as looking up the glacial valley with its crevasses all the way up to the ice-covered mountains in the background.

A short walk further and we reached the face of the glacier. The walkway leads right down to the face so that we were standing about 50 feet away with only an iceberg filled pond separating us from tons of ice. Perito Moreno is an oddity in the age of global warming as it is an advancing glacier. As it advances it blocks the flow of water out of Lago Argentino, causing the lake level to rise. Every few years, the water erodes the ice dam, causing it to collapse and the water to pour out into the adjoining portion of the lake.

We brought our chairs down to the face so that we could just sit, listening and watching the glacier. For a day and a half we were content just to sit across from the 150-foot high ice walls, watching as huge chunks would crash down into the lake and sending ripples and waves across the water. We hated having to leave to eat or go to the bathroom for fear of missing some giant calving off of the face. At night we could lie in bed listening to the sounds of the glacier.

We'd recommend crossing back into Chile to drive its legendary road, the Carretera Austral. Glacial lakes and rivers, ice fields, waterfalls and fiords await you. From here you can choose to take a ferry through the fiords, cross to the Isla Grande de Chiloé or travel back into Argentina and up to the Lake District. We explored the Lake District and San Carlos de Bariloche before crossing the Andes to Puerto Montt and taking a ferry to Chiloé. This road passes through even more incredible scenery and you might get lucky and view one of the smoking volcanoes on either side of the border.

> **Wind on Ruta 40**
> Driving from the Perito Moreno Glacier to the Fitz Roy
> sector of the park at El Chaitén requires that you drive
> around Lake Argentino. When crossing in front of an ice
> field you have to be aware of the possibility of high winds
> being generated from the cold air as it falls off of the
> glacier.
>
> Even knowing this we were caught by surprise by the
> ferocity of the wind. Visibility was terrible and we had to
> slow down to 10 miles per hour as we continued down
> the road, all the while trying to stay out of the way of
> oncoming traffic and the rocks they were likely to throw
> up at our windshield.
>
> At one point a wind gust hit us so hard it knocked us up
> onto two wheels! We were so scared at that point that
> we drove on the shoulder of the wrong side of the road
> just so that our vehicle would be tilted into the wind.
> Finally getting around the lake we were treated to
> incredible views of Cerro Fitz Roy and its rocky
> pinnacles.

Maps

Automapa, Rutas de Patagonia and Tierra del Fuego,
scale 1:2,000,000. Website: www.automapa.com.ar.

ITMB Patagonia Travel Reference Map, scale
1:2,000,000.

Nelles Guides & Maps has a Chile & Patagonia Map
with a scale of 1:2,500,000.

Patagonia Camping

Patagonia has many opportunities for quiet wild/bush camping. You can also choose to stay in municipal campgrounds or National Park camping areas.

Location	Description	GPS Coordinates	Cost
Patagonia Argentina			
Viedma	City camp along the Río Negro near the tourist office.		Free
Península Valdés	Municipal campground at Puerto Pirámides.		Pay
Punta/Playa Ninfas	Wild camp past the lighthouse.	S42 58.72 W64 18.55	Free
Gaiman City Park	Street camp		Free
Cabo Raso	Ghost town south of Punta Tombo, wild camp.		Free
Rada Tilly	Municipal campground, Avenida Capitan Moyano.		Pay
Puerto Deseado	Municipal campground Camping Refugio de la Ria.	S47 45.31 W65 53.27	Pay
Monumento Natural Bosques Petrificados	Wild camp	S47 39.64 W67 55.02	Free
Parque Nacional Monte León	Park campground near the Grotto.		Pay
Río Gallegos	Chakra Daniel	S51 40.49 W 69 14.92	Pay
Chile Magallanes and Argentina Tierra del Fuego			
La Frontera	At the border crossing from Chile Magallanes into Argentina Tierra del Fuego.	S53 19.30 W68 39.63	Free

Americas Overland

Location	Description	GPS Coordinates	Cost
Ushuaia	La Pista del Andino campground	S54 48.71 W68 20.97	Pay
Parque Nacional Tierra del Fuego	Free wilderness campsites at Río Pipo and Camping Laguna Verde.		Free
San Sebastian	Free camping on the beach near the police stop above the beach.		Free
Punta Arenas	Reservas Nacional Magallanes (expensive campground).		Pay
Puerto Natales	Wild camp on the shores of Seno Ultima Esperanza, approximately 3 miles past the ferry dock.		Free
Torres del Paine	Free camp in the parking lot of the Salto Grande trailhead.		Free
Into Argentina			
Tapi Aike	Wild camp in the steppe off Hwy 40 about 10 km north of Tapi Aike.		Free
Los Glaciares Nat'l Park	Free camp in the parking lot at the Perito Moreno Glacier.		Free
El Chalten	Around the corner from the official campground. Low entry for campers.	S49 19.08 W72 53.69	Free
Estancia La Angostura	Private ranch but they didn't charge us. Meals available.	S48 38.05 W70 38.92	Free
Cueva de Manos	Wild camp above cave entrance at pull out on the road.		Free
Estancia Telken	Private ranch that welcomes guests. Meals available.	(Entrance at) S46 48.28 W70 47.35	Pay
Los Antiguos	Municipal campground		Pay
Into CHILE			
Embarcadero	60km west of Chile Chico.	S46 41.32 W72 26.68	Free

Location	Description	GPS Coordinates	Cost
Río Bravo	8km south of Puerto Bertrand.	S47 05.36 W72 46.52	Free
Puerto Río Tranquilo	Wild camp off highway, lots of choices.		Free
Río Correntoso Campground	KM 21 Puerto Aisen Road from Coyhaique.		Pay
Quelat	Waterfall camp, 7km south of Queulat Lodge.	S44 33.41 W72 28.38	Free
Río Cisnes camp	4.5 miles toward La Tapera, east of Villa Amenqual.	S44 43.60 W72 07.48	Free
Coyhaique, Camping Alborada	KM2 north of Coyhaique on the Puerto Aisen Rd.		Pay
Into Argentina			
Esquel	Parque Nacional Los Alerces	S42 53.13 W71 36.20	Free
El Bolson	Camping La Chacra	S41 58.28 W71 31.54	Pay
Colonia La Suiza	Unofficial camping at the Bomberos on Arroyo Goya, near San Carlos de Bariloche.	S41 05.24 W71 30.76	Free
Parque Nacional Nahuel Huapi	RN231 Km 48, west of San Carlos de Bariloche.	S40 50.40 W71 32.29	Free
Into Chile			
Puerto Octay	Camping Molino on the lakefront		Pay
Chacao, Chiloé	Town square city camp	S41 49.68 W73 31.59	Free
Tin Tin, Chiloé	10Km north of Castro, YPF station		Free
Ancud, Chiloé	Playa Gaviotas, 3km North of town		Free

Parque Nacional Torres del Paine

Border Crossing Formalities

For border crossing procedures and documentation refer to the information in the Argentina and Chile Chapters.

Cerro Fitz Roy

Chapter Nineteen

Chile

Routes
Maps
Camping
Border Crossing Formalities
- **Arrival**
- **Departure**

Routes

This long, skinny country runs north to south for over 2,600 miles (4,200km) yet its average width is a mere 125 miles (200km).

In the far north, Chile shares only one land crossing with Peru near Arica. There is one major and several minor crossings into Bolivia, and numerous crossings with Argentina. In some instances you will find that the best way from A to B will be to cross the border into Argentina.

If you are traveling along Highway 5, the Panamericana, you will travel through Arica on your way into or out of Peru. Near the border you can detour to see the Lluta geoglyphs.

Should you be crossing on the main route to La Paz, Bolivia you will have a stomach-churning ride up and over the Andes through Parque Nacional Lauca before reaching the Andean summit and border crossing at Paso Chungara – Tambo Quemado at 15,145 feet (4,660 mts).

Detouring from the Panamericana will lead you to San Pedro de Atacama from where you can explore one of the largest geyser fields in the world, walk along some smaller salars or salt lakes and view volcanoes and flamingos. You can also cross into Bolivia at tiny border posts to explore the Southwest Circuit on your way to Uyuni, Bolivia.

El Tatio Geysers

The El Tatio Geyser field is the largest such field in South America and the third largest field in the world, following Yellowstone, USA and Dolina Geirerov, Russia. It seems that everybody in San Pedro de Atacama runs a tour out to the geyser field at sunrise to see the geysers erupting in the cold morning air. If you take the tour you have to leave the town at 3am and drive to the geyser field in the dark. We felt it best to drive there in the afternoon after all the tours had returned so that we could have the place to ourselves and make camp.

The drive to the geyser field was 84km of mostly dirt road. The scenery was gorgeous and the road wasn't too awful. We saw lots of vicuna (a type of camelid, similar to a llama) and greater rheas (ostrich-like birds). We also passed a steaming volcano and we could see right into the crater as it apparently had blown a little to the side when it had last erupted.

The drive continued to climb in elevation, going up and up until finally reaching the geyser field at over 14,000ft! As we expected, there was absolutely no one else there. We arrived at about 4:00pm and wandered around until the sun went down around 6:00pm. We had a great time exploring and the color at sunset was wonderful.

We got up early in the morning and beat the tour groups

out to the geysers. It was very cold, we even had ice on our windows, but we wrapped ourselves up and spent a couple of hours admiring the huge plumes of steam that the geysers send out into the cold air. Every steam vent regardless of how small, added to the overall steamy view, creating a somewhat hellish effect.

Within 30 minutes of sunrise, thirteen tour buses had arrived. We decided that this was a good time for breakfast and by the time we were done cleaning up, the tours were all gone and we had the place once again to ourselves. What a great experience!

From San Pedro there are two passes over the Andes into Argentina, the Paso de Jama at 12,000 ft. and the Paso de Sico at 14,000 ft. Many overlanders choose these crossings so as to avoid the 400 miles or so, of the sparsely populated Atacama Desert and semiarid transition zone of Norte Chico dotted with old mining towns and small fishing communities.

On your way south you can visit the grape growing areas near La Serena from where Chile's Pisco is produced. Then continue south on the Panamericana to Valparaíso with its port and colorful hillside neighborhoods accessed via funicular.

North of Valparaíso and Santiago is the main border crossing leading to Mendoza, Argentina. This route follows an amazing train-route, now abandoned, up to the Paso Cristo Redentor, elevation over 12,500 feet, where you cross under the border through a long tunnel. South of Valparaíso we preferred to follow the coastal route down to Pichilemu to take a break from the Panamericana. If you visit Santiago, then you can continue south along Highway 5 meeting up with the road from the coast at Teno.

Don't forget to detour off the highway to one or more of the Rutas de Vino in any of the wine growing regions you will be passing. There are the wines of the Colchagua Valley near Santa Cruz as well as through Chile's biggest wine producing region – the Maule Valley near Talca.

Then comes Chillán with its huge colorful local market, the perfect place to enjoy a good meal and stock up on the freshest of fruits and vegetables.

Passing through Temuco brings you into the Lake District. The District runs on both sides of the border and there are two major routes and a couple of minor ones across the Andes between Chile and Argentina. In addition to the lakes, there are volcanoes, thermal springs, rivers and no less than 15 National Parks and Reserves on both sides of the border to explore.

When you finally pull yourself away from the Lake District you'll drive through Puerto Montt on your way to the Isla Grande de Chiloé. Chiloé will be full of surprises as you travel the island and great scenery and excellent seafood abound.

Shingles and Shellfish
Driving around the Island of Chiloé we were taken by the beauty of the island and the slow pace of life there. We passed by many milk canisters waiting by the side of the road to be collected and emptied.

In the villages we walked around enamored by, and taking photos of, the shingle patterns on the wood

---

> homes and churches that Chiloé is famous for. There were many different styles and colors and they seemed to reflect the uniqueness of their owners.
>
> We traveled via a tiny ferry across to another island in the archipelago where we had a fabulous lunch of the biggest oysters and mussels that we have ever seen. While we enjoyed our lunch, we watched as local fishermen waited for boats to take them out to the commercial salmon farms in the bay.
>
> Along the roadways we passed a way of life from the past - ox carts hauling firewood.

From Chiloé, you can loop back northward through the Lake District and across the border to Argentina or catch a ferry across to Chaitén where you can start south on the Carreterra Austral.

Routes south from here are discussed in the Patagonia Chapter.

Maps

Mapa Rutero De Chile available at COPEC Fuel Stations is the map to have. This is a handy publication with all of the maps printed by the Servicio Nacional de Turismo (SERNATUR).

Rough Guides Chile Map has a scale of 1:1,600,000.

Freytag & Berndt Chile Road Map has a scale of 1:1,500,000.

Automapa, Rutas de Chile, has various scales, Website: www.automapa.com.ar.

Nelles Guides & Maps has a Chile & Patagonia Map
with a scale of 1:2,500,000.

Viaje Por Chile, great downloadable maps.
http://www.viajeporchile.cl/vers_eng/mapas.htm

Valparaiso

Chile Camping

Location	Description	GPS Coordinates	Cost
La Frontera	Chile Magallanes and Argentina Tierra del Fuego.	S53 19.30 W68 39.63	Free
Punta Arenas	Reservas Nacional Magallanes (expensive campground).		Pay
Puerto Natales	Wild camp on the shore of Seno Ultima Esperanza, approximately 3 miles past the ferry dock.		Free
Parque Nacional Torres del Paine	Free camp in the parking lot of the Salto Grande trailhead.		Free
Back into CHILE			
Embarcadero	60km west of Chile Chico.	S46 41.32 W72 26.68	Free
Río Bravo	8km south of Puerto Bertrand.	S47 05.36 W72 46.52	Free
Puerto Río Tranquilo	Wild camp off highway, lots of choices.		Free
Río Correntoso Campground	KM 21 Puerto Aisen Road from Coyhaique.		Pay
Abandoned Homestead on the Río Cisnes	Route 25 toward Puerto Cisnes.	S44 40.04 W72 26.43	Free
Queulat	Waterfall camp, 7km south of Queulat Lodge	S44 33.41 W72 28.38	Free
Río Cisnes camp	4.5 miles toward La Tapera, east of Villa Amenqual	S44 43.60 W72 07.48	Free
Coyhaique, Camping Alborada	KM2 north of Coyhaique on the Puerto Aisen Road		Pay
Back into CHILE			
Puerto Octay	Camping Molino on the lakefront.		Pay
Chacao, Chiloé	Town square city camp.	S41 49.68 W73 31.51	Free

Location	Description	GPS Coordinates	Cost
Tin Tin, Chiloé	10Km north of Castro, YPF station.		Free
Ancud, Chiloé	Playa Gaviotas, 3km north of town.		Free
Paillaco	Rt 5, Carabineros parking area south of town.		Free
Los Angeles	Copec Station, Rt 5 approx 16 km north of Los Angeles, wifi.		Free
Talca	Secure but unattractive parking across from Hostal del Puente, corner of 1 Sur and 3 Poniente.		Pay
Pichilemu	Beach parking at Punta de Lobos 6km south of town.	S34 25.63 W72 02.38	Pay
El Quisco	Beach camp about 5km north of Isla Negra.	S33 23.61 W71 42.23	Free
Con Con beach camp	Behind the restaurant La Pica de Emeterio.	S32 55.19 W71 30.69	Free
(Great camping possibility at Parque Nacional La Campana near Ocoa)			Pay
Portillo	Camp in parking area at Hotel Portillo overlooking Laguna del Inca, 9,434 ft elevation/ 2,871 mt.	S32 50.14 W70 07.79	Free
Back into CHILE			
San Pedro de Atacama	Street camp in front of Hostal Katarpe.		Free
Monturaqui Meteor Crater	Wild camp	S23 56.90 W68 17.86	Free
Valle de Luna overlook, San Pedro de Atacama	West of San Pedro de Atacama	S22 55.05 W68 15.17	Free
Geysers de Tatio	North of San Pedro de Atacama. Open parking area at the middle geyser field.		Free
San Pedro de Atacama	3 km west of town, the Cordero del Sal,	S22 53.12 W68 12.46	Free

Americas Overland

Most of the COPEC Fuel Stations have free WiFi available from their parking area.

Border Crossing Formalities

The island at the bottom of South America is called
Tierra del Fuego and it is split in half between Chile and
Argentina. We had to cross out of Argentina and into
Chile and then cross back out of Chile and into
Argentina. These two countries have so many border
crossings that the list could take up an entire page.
We've described all of the crossings that we made.

At each of the Chile/Argentina borders you need to
provide the customs officer with the original and one
copy of the following documents:

> Vehicle Title
> Registration
> Driver's License
> Passport

The vehicle permit you will receive is called the *Título
De Importación Temporal De Vehículos.*

GOBIERNO DE CHILE
SERVICIO NACIONAL DE ADUANAS
TITULO DE IMPORTACION TEMPORAL DE VEHICULOS

REPUBLICA DE CHILE

15.04.0

NUMERO   FECHA VENCIMIENTO

DATOS CONDUCTOR

☑ PROPIETARIO   ☐ AUTORIZADO

Apellido Paterno	Apellido Materno	Nombres

| Cédula de Identidad | N° | Nacionalidad | Código |
| Pasaporte ☑ | De | | |

| Domicilio País de Origen | Teléfono |

| VEHICULO | EQUIPAJE ACOMPAÑADO |

VEHICULO
☐ AUTO   ☐ MOTOR HOME   ☐ OTRO   Código
☐ JEEP   ☐ STATION WAGON
☑ MOTOCICLETA   ☐ CAMIONETA

Matrícula o Patente	Código	N° Pasajeros
N°	De	
Marca	Modelo	

N° VIN / CHASIS

| Año de Fabricación | N° de Motor |

EQUIPAJE ACOMPAÑADO

DESCRIPCION	MARCA

VEHICULO DE ARRASTRE
☐ VIVIENDA   ☐ BOTE/LANCHA
☐ PORTAVEHICULOS
☐ OTRO

| N° | PATENTE ☐ |
| | MOTOR ☐ |

DECLARACION JURADA

Declaro que los datos consignados en este documento son fidedignos y me comprometo a retornar el vehículo, vehículo de arrastre y demás mercancías individualizadas, importarlos o entregarlos a la Aduana más cercana dentro de los plazos de validez de este documento (hasta la fecha de vencimiento). Además, declaro conocer que el incumplimiento de la obligación precedente será sancionado de conformidad a lo dispuesto en el Art. 154° de la Ordenanza de Aduanas, sin perjuicio del delito de fraude en que pudiera incurrir.

ISMAEL BELTRÁN ROJAS
ROL. 02915
ADUANAS - CHILE

Firma Propietario   Firma Autorizado

ADUANA

ADUANA DE INGRESO		ADUANA DE SALIDA	
Aduana VALPARAISO	Código	Aduana	Código
Avanzada/Resguardo SERVICIO DE ADUANAS	Código	Avanzada / Resguardo	
FECHA INGRESO 1 6 ENE		N° Pasajeros	FECHA SALIDA
RODOLFO		Nombre y Firma Funcionario	
Nombre y Firma Funcionario Nombre / Sello		Timbre / Sello	

...KA GARRIDO PASMINO
ROL N° 9670 Cód. 157
ADUANAS DE CHILE

OBSERVACIONES

025604

1ª COPIA - INTERESADO - ADUANA DE CANCELACION   (Dirección Nacio

After finishing up at the border you can head either to Punta Arenas or towards Tierra del Fuego. We headed toward the ferry crossing that would take us across the

Strait of Magellan and onto the island of Tierra del Fuego, the southern tip of South America.

Strait of Magellan ferry

The ferry runs every hour and a half and amazingly we were the last vehicle allowed to board. We just drove up and followed a big truck onto the ferry and left. Unfortunately, because of our timing, when Kim drove the vehicle onto the ferry, the Fuso was sandwiched so close between two other vehicles, that Kim couldn't get out of the truck and so spent the 15 minute crossing staring at other vehicles. Don, who had gotten out of the Fuso before boarding, reported that the scenery was relatively uninteresting and Kim didn't miss much.

Throughout the Patagonia region we went back and forth, crossing the Argentine/Chile border some four times. Then we crossed back and forth twice more before crossing into Bolivia near San Pedro de Atacama.

Torres del Paine, Natl. Park border crossing

The roads in Chile stop about 40 miles north of the park so in order to head further north we had to cross back into Argentina. Luckily there is a border crossing just outside the park. This border station was the smallest station that we crossed on this journey. Two little windows in a small building where we got our passports stamped and surrendered our Chilean vehicle permit, and another little building on the Argentine side. Paperwork was straightforward and took about 30 minutes total.

Chile Chico/Los Antiguos border crossing

The Chilean border at Los Antiguos included a thorough food inspection with a dog. Luckily we had failed to stock up with food in AR otherwise the meats, cheeses and vegetables would have all been confiscated.

Los Antiguos, Chile does have a number of small stores where we were able to stock up on a few supplies. From here you are driving on the Carretera Austral, the famous road that opened up Chile's Patagonia to settlement.

Coyahique, Paso Coyahique border crossing west of Río Mayo, AR

Border crossings seem to get easier the longer you are on the road. You just park, go into the immigration building, get your passports stamped, surrender the vehicle permit and wave (a temporary) goodbye to Chile.

A few miles down the road, you stop at the Argentina Immigration building and basically do the same thing, only in reverse. The only difference is that it should take about five minutes for the customs agent to copy your vehicle information onto a new vehicle permit - and away you go! So simple.

Coyahique has big supermarkets to stock up on everything you may need, and the Argentine inspectors aren't known to search vehicles for food. It appears that only the Chilean inspectors search.

Bariloche, AR, Paso Cardenal A. Samore to Osorno, CH border crossing

The border is at the top of the Paso Cardenal Samore at the height of about 3,000mt (9,900ft) - just a short little mountaintop. The drive was beautiful, going up, up and up through the mountains until we nearly reached the snow line. Then after crossing into Chile it was down, down, down but at a much quicker pace. We had a great view of the Volcano Puyehue which erupted in 1960 the day after Chile suffered a major 8.6 (Richter Scale) earthquake.

Exiting Argentina and then entering Chile, again the same formalities which went quickly and smoothly, even though the Chilean guards once again did a quick inspection of our Fuso looking for contraband meat and vegetables! They even checked our storage compartments, but we satisfied them with our responses that they contained only truck parts and camping equipment.

Los Libertadores Tunnel/Paso Cristo Redentor: border crossing between Santiago, CH and Mendoza, AR

The elevation at the pass is 3,863mt which is 12,671ft! In order to reach the pass, the road switchbacks up the mountain with at least 24 hairpin curves (we lost count after 24). It was also a very stark landscape, but nonetheless impressive.

This drive is even more impressive as it follows the tracks of a railway that was completed in 1910. Guidebooks describe this line as a marvel of engineering. As we drove we lost count of the number of tunnels cut through the rocky sides of the canyon and the number of bridges over the river.

When the builders crossed rubble strewn alluvial deposits or old landslides, they either tunneled under the loose rock, or built free standing "tunnels" to deflect both rock and snow from the tracks. (We also got to drive through some of these tunnels on the car road.) We could understand why this line was constantly being worked on as we saw areas where the tracks had been wiped away by landslides, sometimes leaving the tracks hanging over washed out canyons. You guessed it, the train no longer runs.

We checked out of Chile and entered the 3km long Los Libertadores/Cristo Redentor tunnel (the name depends on which side of the border you are on) that passes through the mountain and under the border with Argentina. This was a first, crossing under a border. When you emerge on the other side you are in Argentina.

Before reaching the official immigration point, there is a turnoff for the tallest mountain in the Americas, Cerro Aconcagua at 6,962 meters (22,835 ft).

At the immigration stop, you will have to go through all of the same paperwork as with all of the other CH/AR crossings. At this stop however, the Argentines wanted proof of insurance. If you don't have an insurance document, you will have to buy short term insurance, with a broker conveniently located right there.

Salta to the Chilean border at Paso de Sico

From Salta there are two border crossings to Chile. One is through Jujuy and along the paved road to the Paso de Jama. We wanted to follow the famous train route, Train to the Clouds (without actually taking the train). This is a rougher route, all dirt, that travels through the altiplano, passing pre-Inca ruins and takes two days to reach San Pedro de Atacama, Chile.

Americas Overland

Along this route you will pass through several very high Andean passes, the highest of which showed up on our GPS at 14,700ft (4,523mts)!

The roads are more washboarded and speeds slow down, but you will drive through gorgeous scenery. The landscape was very stark, but the altiplano vegetation of yellow grass gives the appearance of spring wildflowers. Closer to the border we passed through a region of high volcanic activity with craters and cinder cones and multi-colored soil.

The Argentina border post is in the middle of nowhere, just a building with a gate across the road. Just park in front of the gate and go inside to surrender your vehicle permit and get your passport stamped. When you leave you will probably have to open and close the gate yourself.

Paso de Sico

When we arrived at the Chilean border, we found that it was actually only an agricultural stop where the inspectors look for, and will seize, any meats, cheeses and vegetables.

In order to pass through customs and immigration we were told that we must be in San Pedro that day or be considered as illegally in the country.

This changed our plans from wild camping in a park along the way. So we had to rush down the mountain, on the bad road for another 100km until we met up with a paved road, then we rushed another 70km into town. We're not sure it this was actually necessary, but we don't know what kind of hassles we would have gotten if we showed up the next morning. The immigration office is located on the south/eastern edge of town just off of the main highway to the Paso de Jama.

The authors at Torres del Paine Natl. Park, Chile

Chapter Twenty

Bolivia

Routes
Maps
Camping
Border Crossing Formalities
- **Arrival**
- **Departure**

Routes

The Southwest Circuit

As the name suggests, this route explores the southwest corner of the country. The route can be entered from the Bolivian border near San Pedro de Atacama CH, or from Tupiza on the road to the Argentine border or from the city of Uyuni.

The roads here are little more than tracks in the altiplano as you drive over various salars, including the Salar de Uyuni, the world's largest salt flat, and through the Reserva Nacional de Fauna Andina Eduardo Avaroa. Be prepared for cold nights, sandy tracks and a total lack of fuel stations. This route stays consistently above 12,000 feet elevation rising as high as 16,500 feet as you head toward the Sol de Mañana Geyser Basin.

The Southwest Circuit

The road out of San Pedro de Atacama heads up the Andes mountains toward the Argentina border at the Paso de Jama. Near the top of the first pass is the turnoff for the Bolivian border.

The scenery was spectacular as we passed numerous volcanoes, lagoons and salt flats. In one area, huge, house-sized rocks appeared surrealistically just sitting by themselves in a valley. These rocks have been named Dali Rocks, after Salvador Dali and his painting style. Continuing another 40km further to Laguna Colorado we arrived just as the sun set, finding the unmarked campsite using some GPS way points that we had collected from other travelers.

The morning was spent enjoying the fabulous numbers of flamingos at the lagoon. The lagoon gets its name from the red color of the algae and plankton that grow off of the minerals in the water. The color of the flamingos is also enhanced by the algae. There are three different types of flamingos that live at the lagoon, the Andean, the Chilean and the James (or Puna) and there were thousands of them, eating, walking, flying and sleeping. They didn't seem to be very disturbed by our presence, but as soon as we would get too close, they would slowly start walking away. These birds are very elegant looking and we really enjoyed visiting with them.

Later in the morning we continued on our way, bumping and sliding and tilting our way across the altiplano at 15,000+ ft. It was a real challenge to find our way because there really wasn't what we would call a road, but rather multiple sandy tracks going in the same direction (or in slightly different directions, but joining together later.) The original road was cut many years ago, but it has not been maintained. Because it is in such bad shape, people have chosen other paths across the altiplano, so there are dozens of tracks all going in more or less the same direction. Sometimes the routes even take different paths around a mountain, but they always seem to find each other again.

Periodically we would see a road sign so we would know we were still heading in approximately the right direction. Four wheel drive and high clearance was very helpful. The going was very slow however, as none of the roads were in particularly good shape. It took us 1½ hours to go 18km. That is averaging 12km/hr. (7mi/hr).

We took a lunch break at some rocks that had been sculpted into weird shapes by the sand and wind. Several 4x4's filled with backpacking tourists drove by, giving us reassurance that we were in fact heading the right direction. We stopped for the night near a small lagoon unnamed on our map.

> The new day dawned very bright in the high altitude but turned into our toughest day of driving. When we asked other drivers about the quality of the road ahead, we were told that it was ok with a rocky patch. We usually get very accurate information from other travelers. Well, it turned out the road was in fact one of the hardest 4x4 trails we have ever tackled. It involved quite a bit of rock hopping and steep angles.
>
> When all was done and finished we were proud of our vehicle as it handled everything exceptionally! We on the other hand, came through with frayed nerves. There apparently was an easier route beginning near our campsite, however it was an unmarked intersection.

Amazonia and the Eastern Lowlands

This route follows a loop northeast from La Paz down into the jungles of the Amazon Basin to Trinidad, the regional capital. The roads are poor and the major transportation corridors are the rivers. From November to April the roads may be impassible.

Continue around to Santa Cruz, Bolivia's most populous city. From here you can head into the Pantanal, crossing into Brazil at San Matías or Puerto Suárez – both poor quality roads.

The alternative is to head west back up into the highlands to Cochabamba.

Central Highlands

If you are in a hurry to travel from La Paz to the south, or vice versa, you will likely travel the newly paved road from Oruro to Potosí. Potosí, the highest city in the world at 4,090mt (13,497ft), is an attractive colonial town built around the silver mountain named Cerro Rico.

If you have more time, you can travel through Cochabamba to Sucre, Tarabuco and Potosí before heading to Uyuni or Tupiza. The Cordillera de Los Frailes near Sucre have numerous trekking possibilities that rival the famed Inca Trail in Peru.

Tarabuco has a large Sunday indigenous market to explore.

Begging Fuel

While driving through the altiplano in southwestern Bolivia we found that we were running low on fuel. We had already added to the tank, the fifteen gallons that we carry in our extra fuel cans but due to the high altitude, our vehicle was running rough thereby using more fuel than we anticipated. There are no fuel stations in this area but it is often possible to buy fuel in villages from 50-gallon supply drums. We stopped in each pueblo that we came across but were told that they didn't have any diesel available. We were promised that the provincial capital would have some.

Arriving at the provincial capital, Colcha K, we set off on foot in search of fuel. A soldier offered to help and took us to a couple of houses where the residents usually have extra fuel. But neither of the places we went to had fuel available. We were starting to get concerned as we calculated that we didn't have enough fuel to reach the next "big" city, Uyuni. We were finally able to purchase about 30 liters (7 1/2 gallons) of fuel from the municipal supply.

When we finally crossed the salt deserts of the salar to reach Uyuni we made a bee-line for the fuel station and found that we would have been able to just reach town with our original fuel capacity, but we sure wouldn't have wanted to run out in the middle of a trackless desert!

To or from Peru you have two options for travel. The main overland route to the border at Desaguadero passes by the large pre-Inca ceremonial site of Tiahuanaco. The vastly more interesting route takes you and your vehicle across Lake Titicaca on incredibly small, outboard engine powered barges to Copacabana.

From your camp spot on the shore of Lake Titicaca you can explore the famed Inca islands of Isla del Sol and Isla de la Luna. After you get your vehicle blessed at the church in Copacabana you can stop at one of the many indigenous villages along the lakeshore on your drive to La Paz.

The Salars of Bolivia
Salar is Spanish for a dried salt lake or salt flat. Driving across the salt flats is a strange experience as all you can see is flat and white. Following the tracks of other vehicles is advisable as some areas of the flats are not as solid as they appear.

After getting directions to the "on ramp" for the Salar de Uyuni - the largest salt flat in the world at over 3,000 square kilometers, we headed off. The "on ramp" turned out to be a mile long raised roadway that ended abruptly in salt water! We could not even tell how deep this ford was, but luckily a full size bus happened to be exiting just as we arrived. After talking with the driver and getting instructions on how to proceed, we nervously put the Fuso in four-wheel drive and set off slowly through the water. It turned out to be really easy as the water was only 6 or 8 inches deep even though it looked bottomless.

Exiting the water, we followed the bus tracks and set off across 40 miles of very white salt flats. Other than our GPS way points, the only guidance was the occasional pile of rocks or old tire left on the ground as markers. The air was so clear that we could see all the way across. It was strange to drive toward mountains but not seem to get much closer.

The "off ramp" at the other side of the Salar was similar to the on ramp, only the water portion was much shorter. It did turn out to be trickier though and when we first tried to take a drier path, we broke through the surface and had to quickly reverse our course. Two-wheel drive probably would have left us stranded.

Arriving at the town of Uyuni, we immediately set out to get our car washed. This was important to remove the salt that was splashed onto the chassis. The carwash did a terrific job and the process took about two hours. Can you imagine, a high pressure rinse, soapy wash, lube and rust treatment - all for just $10.00.

Maps

Freytag & Berndt has a combination map including the countries of Bolivia, Ecuador, Guyana, Colombia, Peru and Venezuela with a scale of 1:4,000,000).

Freytag & Berndt has another combination map including the countries of Brazil, Bolivia and Paraguay with a scale of 1:4,000,000).

Borch has a Bolivia Road Map with two scales: Bolivia Oeste 1:1,750,000, Bolivia Este 1:2,500,000.

ITMB has a Bolivia Travel Reference Map with a scale of 1:1,250,00

Flamingos at Laguna Colorado

Americas Overland

Bolivia Camping

Location	Description	GPS Coordinates	Cost
Laguna Colorado	Right on the lagoon next to hot springs and flamingos.	S22 12.81 W67 47.86	Free
Laguna Honda	Actually just over the hill to the next unnamed lagoon, elevation 4,115 mts (13,580ft).	S21 37.77 W68 04.34	Free
Salar de Chiguana	2 miles past the military checkpoint along the RR tracks.	S21 01.06 W67 55.06	Free
Uyuni	Out front of the Tonito Hotel and Minuteman Revolutionary Pizza, great food, lots of info from the owner Chris.	S20 27.93 W66 49.50	Free
Potosí	Petrol station on north side of town on road to Oruru, OK due to our large size. Better option, but only for small vehicles, is the Hostal Tarija.	S19 35.07 W65 45.35	Free
Pasna	Half way between Oruro and Challapata, EU Project building.	S18 35.67 W66 55.46	Free
La Paz	Hotel Oberland, in Mallasa, Zona Sur. Not central but taxis are cheap and you don't really want to drive into central! If you get to the zoo you've gone too far.	S16 34.08 W68 05.36	Pay
Copacabana	On the beach near the fresh trout restaurants. 12,541 ft elevation.	S16 10.07 W69 05.42	Free

Border Crossing Formalities

<u>Border crossing east of San Pedro de Atacama, CH</u>
We tried to get an early start out of San Pedro de
Atacama but first we had to wake up the immigration
person to stamp us out of Chile. The road out of Chile
heads up the Andes Mountains toward the Argentina
border at the Paso de Jama. The going is really slow as
you are climbing straight up starting from about 8,000
feet. Along the way are shrines made up of pieces of
the vehicles that have run off the highway. Near the top
of the first pass is the turn off, on a dirt road, for the
Bolivian border.

At the simple immigration building we got our passports
stamped and found out that we would have to stop at
the customs office some 50 kilometers down the road to
get our vehicle permit. Oh yes, this border was at
15,000 ft elevation! Taking this route into Bolivia it is
very important to get a hold of GPS waypoints for the
drive ahead as you will be venturing into an area with
poorly marked roads.

When we reached the customs office, our GPS showed
an elevation of 16,528 ft., a new personal record for us!
It may be an option to bypass this customs post and
finish your paperwork in Uyuni, but check first.

This customs office was little more than a shell of a
building and did not have a copy machine available so
be sure to have some extra copies of your documents
just in case they may be requested.

Provide the customs officer with the original and one copy of the following documents:

> Vehicle Title
> Registration
> Drivers License
> Passport

<u>Exiting Bolivia to Peru, there are two main routes.</u>
One is past the Inca ruins at Tiahuanaco to the crossing at Desaguadero. The other, more interesting route is through Copacabana, along Lake Titicaca crossing at Yunguyo. We crossed at Yunguyo.

We made the obligatory visit to Bolivian immigration to get our passports stamped, and where we refused the officials request for a "few dollars". After crossing through the gate we drove to the Peruvian side, where we had been warned that crossing could be difficult (unfounded). We pulled up to the chain across the road and went to take care of business.

Ferry crossing towards Copacabana

Espíritu Santo celebration near Copacabana

Chapter Twenty-one

Peru

Routes
Maps
Camping
Border Crossing Formalities
- **Arrival**
- **Departure**

Routes

Driving into Peru from the south, the choice of routes will be either from Arica, Chile or from La Paz, Bolivia. Unless you find yourself in a hurry, we would recommend that you do not skip Bolivia. You can follow the routes in the Chile Chapter that will lead you along RN11 west from Arica, or through the Southwest Circuit from San Pedro de Atacama.

Both routes entering Peru from Bolivia meet up along the shore of Lake Titicaca and will lead you into Puno. Puno is the jumping off point for trips to the Floating Islands. This route continues to Cuzco and the Sacred Valley. From Cuzco you can continue down to the coast at Nazca, cross the altiplano to Ayacucho or retrace your path towards Puno turning off at Sicuani to visit the Cañón del Colca and Arequipa.

From Arequipa on your way to the coast, detour to the Toro Muerto Petroglyphs. Once on the coast you can take a break and explore the ruins at Puerto Inca before heading to Nazca.

Inca Trash Middens

The small ruins at Puerto Inca are of a residential community that supplied the Inca emperors in Cuzco with ocean seafood. Fish and shellfish were harvested from around the area, then dried and carried over the mountains to Cuzco. Legend has it that runners would carry fresh fish to Cuzco, but this is unlikely.

We explored the ruins and found that in addition to the residences, the entire area had underground rooms that had been sealed off. We couldn't find any explanation for these rooms other than that they were likely tombs as they were small and completely buried, that is, buried until they were dug up by tomb robbers.

On one side of these tombs we found the trash midden for the community. Erosion of the midden provided us with a window into their lives and we spent quite a while viewing their cast-offs. We saw discarded textiles and rope, broken pottery and tools, corncobs and shells of marine animals, and other items unidentifiable to us. It was all very interesting.

If you decide to skip Bolivia and follow the Panamericana north from Arica, Chile you can detour to the Toro Muerto Petroglyphs before heading to Arequipa.

Petroglifos de Toro Muerto
As we continued our drive down to the Peruvian coast from Arequipa we made a detour to the Petroglifos de Toro Muerto. We have never seen a petroglyph site quite like this one anywhere else. The glyphs are carved onto volcanic white boulders spread over an area of about 2 square kilometers.

When we arrived at the site headquarters, we were told of the suggested route to explore the boulders and which number boulders were the recommended ones to try and find to view. Well, we thought there would just be a handful of boulders, but when we started to explore, we found there where well over 1,300 different boulders with carvings of "dancers", animals and geometric patterns. And to top it off, more than just a few of the boulders contained nearly a hundred carvings on individual boulders alone!

We spent so much time exploring the area that the entire afternoon passed by, so we decided to stay right there and make camp for the night. It was an eerie experience camping out in this lunar-like landscape.

From Arequipa on the road to Puno, detour off to the
Cañón del Colca. After watching the condors over the
canyon, continue to Puno and Lake Titicaca.
Afterwards you can follow the route to Cuzco and the
Sacred Valley.

The altiplano route from Cuzco to Ayacucho is stark and
beautiful. However this route causes you to bypass the
coastal desert from Nazca to Pisco. The coastal route
is highly recommended so that you can explore the
Nazca Lines, stop off in Ica or Huacachina and then visit
the islands in the Reserva Nacional de Paracas.

A Whale in the Desert
Heading north on Hwy 1 towards Nazca, we stopped off
to visit a museum in the desert oasis at Sacaco. Here,
we had read, the museum contains a fossilized whale
found right there in the middle of the desert and that it
was possible to find fossilized crocodile teeth.

Well, unfortunately when we arrived, the museum was
closed but we decided to explore anyway. Pulling off the
dirt track, we found that the ground was covered, not by
sand but with fossilized shells.

This was such an interesting find that we wandered
around for about an hour and a half just looking at the
ground. Things got even more interesting when we
found our very first fossil bones! Protruding from the
ground were a couple of whale rib bones and an even
larger bone, possibly a pelvis. We didn't disturb the
bones, but we continued to look around and eventually
started to find the fossilized teeth we had read about.
Once we knew what we were looking for, they became
quite obvious to us. It was a fun afternoon of discovery.

From Paracas and Pisco you can head back up to Ayacucho where you can drive through the altiplano to Huancayo before dropping out of the Andes into Lima.

While in Lima, find a secure parking lot to leave your vehicle for a week and fly to Iquitos on the Amazon River.

North on the Panamericana from Lima, stop and explore the ruins at Paramonga. Then head into the mountains to explore the region around Huaraz. A detour to Chavín de Huántar is worthwhile before returning to the coast via the spectacular Canon del Pato with its multitude of rock-hewn tunnels.

The Canyon of the Duck
El Cañón del Pato is famous for its approximately 50 tunnels, 35 of which are in a stretch of only 12 miles. The tunnels are carved right out of the mountainside and are not reinforced with concrete, nor are they necessarily consistent in height. As the Fuso is 3.5m (11.5ft) tall, we were concerned about height and there were no signs on any of the tunnels. We used our best judgment and experience and slowly moved through the tunnels with no problems. The fact that the roadway is dirt and rock, helped to slow our travel to about 15mph as well. The tunnels range from short singles, to very long singles, to doubles and even triple tunnels. Exiting one tunnel we found ourselves on a bridge over the river!

Although the canyon is only about 130km (80mi) long, our slow pace meant that we were only able to get about half way through it before night fell and we made camp off the road for the night.

The next day, after driving 4 more hours over rocks and dodging rock falls, we finally reached pavement.

The coast north from Trujillo to Chiclayo is strewn with ruins, temples, pyramids and wonderful museums. Take your time and don't miss the Museo Tumbas Reales de Sipán in Lambayeque.

If you choose to explore the Chachapoyas region, you can do a loop (rough roads) from Cajamarca through Chachapoyas. The alternative is to follow the route north and east from Chiclayo to Chachapoyas, before returning to Jaén for the back route border crossing at La Balsa to get to Zumba in Ecuador.

If you don't want to take a back route into Ecuador you can cross the border at Macara to reach Loja, or you can enjoy more of the Peruvian coastal desert as you follow the Panamericana through Tumbes and across into Ecuador.

A Grand Inca Festival
Inti Raymi is an ancient Inca celebration of the winter solstice in the southern hemisphere. Because it was an Inca festival, the Spanish banned it after their conquest. The holiday was resurrected by the City of Cuzco in the 1970's and is celebrated today as a pageant. Nearly 200 people portray Incas in various roles. The finale is the mock sacrifice of a llama. It is the greatest of all the Inca festivals.

We started the day early in order to watch the "opening ceremonies" at a church that was built atop a holy Inca pyramid. The Incas came out of the church and filled the courtyard in their colorful costumes. The main event in the morning was when the Inca ruler made an offering to the Sun God. By getting there early, we had a great vista to watch the show. Our luck in this regard held all day, as we were able to get good viewing spots all along the procession route. The pageant moved from the church down narrow walkways to the main town square and later in the day, the whole show moved 5km out of town to the ruins of Sacsayhuamán (pronounced like "sexy woman").

The ruins themselves are quite spectacular just for the quantity of large boulders cut and fitted together by the Incas. In the midst of the ruins, the pageant continued surrounded by thousands of onlookers, including us. We were all perched along the ruins and the terraces looking down on the show. In addition to the pageant, the festival put on by the local people was a show in itself. There were carnival rides, clowns and food vendors going throughout the day and into the night. We didn't have the stamina to last through the whole thing. It was an amazing spectacle and definitely worth braving the crowds.

Maps

Freytag & Berndt has its Peru Road Map with a scale of 1:1,200 000).

Freytag & Berndt has a combination map including the countries of Bolivia, Ecuador, Guyana, Colombia, Peru and Venezuela with a scale of 1:4,000 000).

Borch has a Peru Road Map with a scale of 1:1,750,000.

ITMB has a Peru Travel Reference Map with a scale of 1:1,500,000.

The Peru Rough Guide Map has a scale of 1:500,000.

Globetrotters Travel Map Peru, scale 1:1,600,000.

Huanchaco tortola reed fishing raft

Peru Camping

Location	Description	GPS Coordinates	Cost
Arequipa Highway	Approx 80km west of Juliaca. Off the main hwy. 13,544 ft elevation	S15 38.18 W70 41.50	Free
Arequipa	Hotel Las Mercedes, secure, full facilities and walking distance to city center. Very popular, arrive early in the day to get a space.	S16 24.05 W71 32.53	Pay
Toro Muerto Petroglyphs	Near Corire, wild camp in the park.	S16 13.45 W72 30.13	Free
Puerto Inca	North of Chala	S15 50.32 W74 18.77	Pay
Nazca	Hotel Nido del Condor, across from the airport Condor Hotel, next door.	S14 51.09 W74 57.54	Pay
Pisco	The Hostal San Jorge Residencial, *May have been damaged/destroyed in the earthquake of 2007*	S13 42.39 W76 12.17	Pay
Paracas	Yacht Club Peruviano at Paracas, on the beach.	S13 50.07 W76 15.20	Free
RN Lomas de Lachy	Campground	S11 21.23 W77 22.08	Pay
Fortaleza de Paramonga	Behind the fort in the sugarcane fields.	S10 39.34 W77 50.40	Free
Machac	7km from Chavín ruins, great spot overlooking the river.	S09 37.99 W77 11.97	Free
Huaraz	Hotel Andino, secure parking in back.	S09 32.074 W77 31.387	Pay
Caraz	Los Pinos Lodge and Camping, street camp in the front along the Parque San Martin.		Free
Lago Paron	Overlooking the lake, rough road access. 13,780 ft 4,240 mt.	S08 59.96 W77 41.09	Free
Cañón del Pato	West of Huallanca	S08 47.39 W77 53.03	Free
Viru	South of Trujillo, Grifo Camp	S08 24.72 W78 47.98	Free
Huanchaco	Huanchaco Garden Hostal, camping next to the pool. Space for maybe 4 campers.	S08 04.386 W7907.108	Pay

Location	Description	GPS Coordinates	Cost
Santa Rosa	On the beach sw of Chiclayo.	S06 51.63 W79 56.10	Free
Waterfall camp, near Pedro Ruíz	Wild camp	S05 55.34 W78 00.51	Free
Chacahapoyas	Public car park	S06 13.70 W77 52.15	Pay
East of Chamaya crossroads	Government Weigh Station	S05 43.90 W78 38.34	Free

Huacachina Dunes, Peru

Toro Muerto camp

Border Crossing Formalities

<u>Arrival from Bolivia</u>
We parked our car in the road next to the chain and made our visits to the officials. First to immigration for our passport stamp and visitor's cards, then across the street to customs for our vehicle permit, the *Libre Circulación y Salida*.

Then to the police (we don't really know what for other than for them to ask for a $5.00 fee (bribe), which we declined to pay) and finally to SENASA who are the people who check to make sure you aren't bringing any meat, cheese, fruit or vegetables into the country. It all took less than an hour and despite what we had heard, wasn't any more of a hassle than any other border. Just goes to show, "don't believe everything you hear."

SUNAT

ADUANAS

SUPERINTENDENCIA NACIONAL DE ADMINISTRACION TRIBUTARIA

No. 2 - LIBRE CIRCULACION Y SALIDA
(PARA SER ENTREGADO EN LA ADUANA DE SALIDA)

CERTIFICADO DE INTERNACION TEMPORAL N°.....................

Plazo de validez hasta el...

(PARA SER LLENADO POR EL TURISTA)

Nombre del Titular...

....

Nacionalidad...

N° de Pasaporte..

Domicilio en su país de origen..

....

Domicilio temporal en el Perú...

....

Clase de vehículo..Color..

Marca...Modelo...Año............

Motor N°...Chasis N°..

Placa N°.................Monto de Tributos Liquidados US$.......................................

Equipos, repuestos, accesorios y/u opcionales...

....

....

....

....

Peruvian vehicle permit (front)

Declaro, que conforme a lo dispuesto en el D.S. N° 015-87-ICTI-TUR, que norma la internación temporal de vehículos con fines turísticos, constituyo como garantía prendaria a favor del Estado Peruano (ADUANAS), el vehículo automotor de mi propiedad así como sus equipos, repuestos, accesorios y/u opcionales, cuyos datos consigno en el documento N° 1 "INGRESO" a fin de resguardar los derechos de aduana y demás tributos que pudieran originarse por el incumplimiento de las obligaciones derivadas del destino especial citado.

En caso que tuviera que ausentarme del país sin el vehículo, me comprometo a dar cuenta inmediatamente del hecho a la Autoridad Aduanera y Policial mas próxima, depositando por mi cuenta y riesgo el vehículo en un garaje o depósito a orden de ADUANAS.

NOTA.- De no efectuarse la reexportación del vehículo dentro del plazo concedido este caerá en comiso de modo automático.

_____
Firma del interesado

(PARA SER LLENADO POR ADUANAS)

AUTORIZACIÓN DE INGRESO Y CIRCULACIÓN

INTENDENCIA DE ADUANA DE INGRESO....................................

FECHA..

_____
Funcionario de Aduana - Sello y Firma

CONTROL POR LA INTENDENCIA DE ADUANA DE SALIDA

INTENDENCIA DE ADUANA DE...

FECHA..

_____
Funcionario de Aduana - Sello y Firma
(DEVUELVASE A LA ADUNA DE INGRESO)

Peruvian vehicle permit (back)

Exiting to Ecuador

We chose the least used route of the three available to reach the border. It was only opened a few years ago after Peru and Ecuador made peace following their 1995 war over border issues. Originally there was only a ferry to take cars across the river, but recently a bridge was built. This is the border at La Balsa/Zumba.

The other border crossings are at Tumbes on the Panamericana, and La Tina/Macará.

The La Balsa crossing is more convenient if you intend to explore the Chachapoyas region. The road from San Ignacio to the border is claimed to have been paved, and maybe it will be by the time you arrive there, but when we drove it, the road across the border and on to Vilcabamba in Ecuador is some 90% dirt and best to avoid after heavy rains. However, the scenery is fantastic.

After a couple of minutes of formalities on the Peru side (we had to get the immigration official out of his house), we had our passports stamped and surrendered our vehicle permit, the gate was then unlocked and lifted for us to cross the bridge.

Chapter Twenty-two

Ecuador

Routes
Maps
Camping
Border Crossing Formalities
- **Arrival**
- **Departure**

Routes

The most exciting, and fortunately, the main route
through Ecuador is along RN35/the Panamericana from
Loja through Quito then to the Colombian border at
Tulcán/Ipiales. To reach Loja from Peru you can
choose from three routes, the most interesting is the
"back-road" through Zumba across the new bridge at La
Balsa. If you have the time, and if you visited
Chachapoyas in Peru, then this is the best route to
enter the country and will pass through incredible
scenery as you travel to Vilcabamba before meeting up
with the Panamericana near Loja.

Your other options are to cross into Ecuador at Macará
or follow the coastal Panamericana from Tumbes in
Peru.

A Back Route into Ecuador
The road crossing the border at La Balsa/Zumba is not
paved and because we have friends who had difficulty
driving this road in the rain, we thought we would check
the conditions before committing to this route. The police
at the turnoff (in Peru) told us that the road was "pista"
(paved) all the way to the next main town. Sounded
great. Except that it wasn't quite true.

The road might have been "pista" at one time, but after
less than 50 miles the good pavement turned to bad and
then to non-existent. And then it started to rain. Hmmm.
We decided to take our chances because we have four-
wheel drive in case we need it (our friends didn't) and
besides, we were already more than half way to the
border. Fortunately the choice turned out to be the right
one when the rain stopped and the road dried out.
We reached the border on the river without further
incident and after a couple of minutes of formalities on

each side, we continued on our way. And immediately found where our friends must have had their problems. The road rising up from the river was incredibly steep and narrow, and would have been extremely difficult to negotiate in wet weather. Fortunately for us, we were able to just drop the gears into low and slowly climb and climb and climb.

In the late afternoon we found a fabulous spot to spend the night on the banks of another river and all the trucks and buses that drove by us honked their horns and the drivers waved to us in greeting. As the sun went down we sat outside and enjoyed the birds and the sound of rushing water. What a nice welcome to Ecuador.

From Loja you can stop off at the indigenous town of Saraguro, where market day is the day to visit.

Cuenca is worth a couple of days to relax and explore the colonial heart of the city. You can even take a break and soak in the hot springs at the smaller, "other" Baños just a few miles away.

The route north to Quito is through a beautiful corridor ringed by volcanoes. Stop off for thrills where you can ride on the roof of a train through the Devil's Nose at Alausí.

The Devil's Nose
The town of Alausí is the last stop along the train line before heading down over El Nariz del Diablo (the devil's nose) a railway-engineering feat that was completed in 1902. The round trip train ride, which is now just for tourists, leaves the Alausí station and heads down the "nose" by a series of switchbacks where the train has to pull forward onto a spur line so that it can back up onto another line, so that it can then go forward again. Quite

amazing. But the fun part about the trip is the fact that the riders sit ON TOP of the train cars. Cushions are provided and there are rails to hang on to.

On the way out of town all the little kids waved at the crazy tourists sitting on top of the train and we all waved back. We had a fun time taking photos of the beautiful scenery and the other train cars as we went around curves.

On our return trip, just after the engine had crossed over a bridge nearing Alausí, there was a horrible grinding noise and the train came to a halt. Assuming some minor problem had occurred, we kept our seats and started looking around. The conductors had gotten off and were looking underneath and then started picking up rocks and placing them under the train.

At this point we got more curious and started asking others that had gotten off to look, just what the problem was. Well, the problem was that the train had actually jumped the tracks and some of its wheels were six inches off! Knowing that we could walk back to town from this point if we had to, we were able to make jokes about how they would get the train back on the tracks.

Apparently there was a bad spot on one portion of the track and even though the engine and the first car made it across OK, the second car derailed. Somehow or another, using rocks and plants, the conductors were able to get the wheels back aligned and by moving very slowly were able to coax the rest of the cars across the bad spot. All in all it only took about a half an hour. I guess those guys know what they're doing.

Further north you can loop west through Chimborazo on the new road from Riobamba. Detouring eastward off the main route, you can soak in the hot springs at the popular resort town of Baños set on the slopes of an active volcano. From Baños you can make a loop over rough roads to Tena and then drive to the end of the road at Coca in the Amazon. This drive can also be undertaken from Quito.

If you continue north from Riobamba you can stop off at Volcán Cotopaxi before heading into Quito.

There are lots of things to see and do in Quito, one of which is to make arrangements for a tour of the Galápagos Islands, if that is part of your plans.

The last major stop on this route is at the indigenous town of Otavalo. Make plans to visit on market day. There are other interesting towns to visit in this area as you drive towards Quito.

You can wander around the quirky cemetery at Tulcán with its tremendous display of strange topiary before crossing the border into Colombia.

Maps

Freytag & Berndt has its Ecuador Road Map covering Ecuador and the Galapagos Islands with scales of 1:600,000 and 1:800,000 respectively.

Freytag & Berndt has a combination map including the countries of Bolivia, Ecuador, Guyana, Colombia, Peru and Venezuela with a scale of 1:4,000 000).

Borch has an Ecuador Road Map with multiple scales of
Ecuador West 1:1,000,000, Ecuador East 1:2,000,000,
The Galápagos at 1:1,300,000.

ITMB has its Ecuador Travel Reference Map with a
scale of 1:1,700,000.

Otavalan women in the market

Ecuador Camping

Location	Description	GPS Coordinates	Cost
Zumba River camp	Wild camp on river.	S04 53.59 W79 07.65	Free
Vilcabamba	Casa Tinku Restaurante.	S04 15.62 W79 13.18	Pay
Saraguru street camp	Just pick a quiet street.		Free
Cuenca	Baños, Hosteria Duran parking lot, free camping with paid admission to the hot springs.		Free
Cuenca	Cabanas Yanuncay, address Calle Canton Gualaceo 21-49	S02 54.34 W79 01.68	Pay
Alausí Train Station	City camp on street in front of depot.	S02 12.08 W78 50.87	Free
Reserva Faunistica Chimborazo	Elevation 12,800 ft	S01 31.58 W78 50.24	Free
	Better campsite at the Chimborazo Refugio about 6km west of above location.		Free
Cotopaxi Nat'l Park	Laguna Limpiopungo, elevation 12,640 ft.	S00 36.89 W78 28.41	Pay
Quito	Hotel Quito. Ask a taxi driver to lead you there, or ask them to take you to a "parqueadero" for 24 hr secure parking. We parked here and went to The Galapagos.		Pay
Tena	Hostel Limoncocha, $6pp but that includes use of a room. Hostal has a travel agency good for rafting, etc. Tight parking for long rigs, limited space for one or two vehicles. Possible camping on street in front.	S01 00.02 W77 48.49	Pay
Misahuallí	Great beach camping spot	S01 02.11 W77 39.90	Free
Papallacta	Free camp on Plaza 24 de Noviembre in front of the church	S00 22.66 W78 09.06	Free

Location	Description	GPS Coordinates	Cost
Otavalo	Great central parking lot, 2 choices. We stayed in the Lavadora/Parqueadero on Calle Quito. Other choice just one block west on same street	N00 13.86 W78 15.69	Pay

Bartolome Island, Galapagos

Camping Extortion

We arrived at a balneario/hot springs resort early in the afternoon and hoped that after using the pools that we could spend the night in the parking area. We asked around and sought out the person in charge. After being directed to the person collecting the entrance fee we asked for and received permission to park overnight for no additional fee other than our entrance fees. This was not unusual and we said our thank you's.

After enjoying the pools for the afternoon, we returned to our vehicle. We prepared our dinner and later got ready for bed. Just as we turned off our lights there was a knock on our door. Expecting that the security guard was merely introducing himself, we were surprised to be told that camping was not permitted. We explained that we had been given permission but we were now told that it wasn't possible. Unfortunately we didn't get the individual's name who gave us permission. After a while the guards relented and called the owner for permission. The owner told us that we cold stay only if we agreed to pay $12.00. Considering that by this time it was after 10pm, we reluctantly agreed to pay.

The moral is, when you've been given permission to camp, introduce yourself to the person so that you can get their name. We would have gladly paid up front, but we would have liked having the choice of staying or not. At 10pm you don't have much of a choice.

Border Crossing Formalities

<u>Arrival from Peru</u>
Just after the end of the bridge but before the gate on the Ecuador side, we snagged a low-hanging electrical wire on the roof of the truck. Fortunately we were able to grind to a halt before ripping it down and thus ending any chance of us getting into the country!

Moving over to a spot with greater clearance we passed safely under the wire and came to a stop at the Ecuador gate.

After immigration formalities, we were greeted very warmly by the two customs officials and welcomed into the country after filling out one piece of paper and giving them copies of our passports, driving licenses and vehicle title.

Be sure to have copies of your documents before crossing at this border as the customs office did not have a copy machine at the time we crossed.

Let me repeat. Only one piece of paper was required to be filled out and the copies of our documents. **NO CARNET IS REQUIRED TO ENTER ECUADOR WITH A VEHICLE.** This had been a worry even though we had found official documentation that said it hadn't been necessary for several years, but we hadn't met anyone who had crossed recently without one.

The road rising up from the river at this border is very steep. Do not attempt it after heavy rain if you do not have four-wheel drive.

Americas Overland

DECLARACION PARA INGRESO DE VEHICULO PARTICULAR DE TURISMO NO SUJETO A CONVENIO INTERNACIONAL VIGENTE
Formulario N°DJT: 073-23-07-08-001

Señor
Gerente Distrital de la Corporación Aduanera Ecuatoriana
Ciudad.-

De mi consideración:

Yo, **RICHARD**   , de país de origen **UNITED STATES**, con **IDENTIFICACION N°** , solicito la autorización para la **INTERNACIÓN TEMPORAL DE UN VEHÍCULO CON LA INTENCIÓN DE REALIZAR TURISMO EN LA REPUBLICA DEL ECUADOR** de conformidad a lo establecido en el Artículo 82 del Reglamento General a la Ley Orgánica de Aduanas, constituyéndose mi vehículo como garantía prendaria especial y preferente, facultando a la Corporación Aduanera Ecuatoriana, de hacer efectiva la misma en caso de incumplir con el fin para el cual fue autorizado o exceder de los **60** dia(s) calendario de permanencia en el país, de acuerdo a lo estipulado en el Artículo N°74 de la Ley Orgánica de Aduanas.

Declaro bajo juramento que el vehículo destinado a turismo a ser autorizado tiene las siguientes características:

Placa:
Marca: **CHEVROLET**
Clase y Subclase: **CASA RODANTE**
Año del modelo: **2007**
Color: **BLANCO**
Chasis o VIN: **1GBH**
N°de Motor: **1GBH**
Capacidad: **2**
Tonelaje: **0.01**
País de origen: **ESTADOS UNIDOS**
Matrícula N° y País otorgante: **1W   UNITED STATES**

Así mismo, me comprometo a presentar la copia original de la presente declaración juramentada, al momento de la salida del vehículo particular de turismo del territorio nacional.

Atentamente.

RICHARD
IDENTIFICACION N°

Este formulario constituye una declaración juramentada y declaro bajo juramento que la información aquí considerada es correcta y ajustada a las disposiciones legales vigentes. Conozco que cualquier omisión pueda dar origen a los procesos legales y acciones establecidas en la Ley Orgánica de Aduanas.

Fecha de Ingreso: 23-07-2008	Fecha de Salida:
Autorizado por 60 días	Por Distrito de:
Por Distrito de: TULCAN	
Código N°: 073	
CORPORACION ADUANERA ECUATORIANA VIII DISTRITO TULCAN	
Sello y Firma del Distrito de Entrada	Sello y Firma del Distrito de Salida

Revisar al reverso, las condiciones que la Aduana ecuatoriana necesita que cumpla usted como turista.

Ecuadorean Vehicle Permit
(Provided by Rick & Kathy Howe, www.travelin-tortuga.com)

Departure

Our last Ecuadorian stop was at the town of Tulcán, about 6 kms from the border, then onward to the Colombian border. Ecuador immigration officials stamped our passports (although they were surprised to find our entry stamp from the remote border crossing at La Balsa) and we surrendered our temporary vehicle permit to *Aduana* and drove across the border.

La Balsa border crossing

Chapter Twenty-three

Colombia

Routes
Maps
Camping
Border Crossing Formalities
 • **Arrival**
Departure
Shipping From Colombia

Routes

The thought of driving through Colombia often conjures up stories of drug runners and killings, paramilitary/rebel conflicts and kidnapping. That said, the government and the people are tired of the violence and are working hard to bring peace into their daily lives. Additionally, tourists are rarely affected by these problems and in our opinion you do not want to skip visiting this beautiful country. The cities are clean, the people friendly and the attractions numerous.

Ipiales, the first town in Colombia coming north out of Ecuador, makes a great stop and excellent introduction to the country. Just on the edge of town you must visit the religious pilgrimage site of Santuario de Las Lajas. Getting through town is a bit of a challenge due to the traffic and narrow one-way streets.

The drive north from the border is through stunning scenery as you drive up and down and through the Andes until you arrive in the "white city" of Popayán; white due to the white-washed facades of the colonial buildings.   In time, the road across the mountains to the pre-Columbian sites at San Agustín and Tierradentro may be considered safe for travel, but until then you must travel a huge loop north through the coffee growing region of Armenia and back south. Ask the police if the mountain road is safe to travel.

The Panamericana takes you north through Cali and into the coffee heartland around Pereira and Armenia.

Hotel Bambusa

Driving through Colombia is not high on many people's list of things to do, but we had a wonderful time there. The scenery was beautiful, the roads well maintained and clean and the people very friendly.

We were invited to visit a Colombian overlander/hotelier that we had met online and we took him up on his invitation. The directions to his hotel had us wandering some back roads and wondering if we were out of our minds. But the locals were friendly and helped us with the directions and we finally found the beautiful hotel located in the middle of banana fields. We spent three days exploring and enjoying the beauty and tranquility of the area.

From Armenia you can travel inland towards the Andes and the capital, Bogotá. From Bogotá you can drive along the Andes northward either to Cartagena or the Venezuela border. You could also choose to loop back to the Panamericana and the city of Medellín.

Medellín is a great city made beautiful by a law that requires all public buildings to display art, and the city is full of sculptures.

At the top of the list of Colombia's attractions is the walled, coastal city of Cartagena. This world heritage listed site is not a museum but rather a living, breathing, wonderful place to explore. It is also a major port so you may arrive or depart South America from Cartagena. From Cartagena you can travel northeast along the coast to explore National Parks on the road towards Venezuela and explore the northernmost point in South America located on the Península de la Guajira.

Cartagena
Visiting Cartagena is an absolutely beautiful experience and one that any visitor to Colombia should experience. As it is one of the few walled cities remaining in the world, we weren't able to drive into it, but we were able to find a very nice, large parking lot just outside one of the entrances where we could park overnight. We were then able to explore the city and delight in its charm, color and beauty. Just a few miles down the road are beaches where you can also find overnight parking lots.

Maps

We found it very difficult to find up-to-date maps for Colombia. Most of the maps we found had a very large scale and were usually combined with either Ecuador or Venezuela.   While it may seem to be a good idea to buy one map with multiple countries on it, in reality the scale tends to be so large that there is very little detail for a driver.

In this case we found that the Colombia government highway website, *Instituto Nacional de Vías* had the best maps.

We downloaded the maps into our laptop computer and also printed out separate maps for each Colombia Territory. The page is entitled *Mapas Red Vial* and the website address is: http://www.invias.gov.co/invias/index.php?option= com_wrapper&Itemid=87&lang=es

The other thing that we did was, every time we stopped for fuel, we asked if a map was available. Eventually we found a country map and bought it. The map was not high quality, but it was a good supplement to our Territory maps since it did show the entire country on one page. This was the *República de Colombia Mapa Vial y Guía Turistica.*

Freytag & Berndt has a combination map including the countries of Bolivia, Ecuador, Guyana, Colombia, Peru and Venezuela with a scale of 1:4,000,000).

ITMB has a Colombia Travel Reference Map with a scale of 1:2,000,000.

Nelles Guides and Maps has a Colombia/Ecuador Map with a scale of 1:2,000,000.

Cartagena

Santuario de Las Lajas

Colombia Camping

Location	Description	GPS Coordinates	Cost
Santuario de Las Lajas	Free camp in parking area.	N00 13.86 W78 15.69	Free
Popayán	Terbal Fuel Station just south of town, 1st station you come to from the south.		Free
Piendamo	Truck stop with security 6km north of town, near Piaje.	N 02 41.94 W76 32.01	Free
Uribe exit, Panamericana	Parador Rojo Restaurant, 70km south of Armenia (Hwy 25), nice shaded parking area with restaurant, garden and security.	N04 15.42 W76 06.95	Free
South of Armenia	Hacienda Bambusa, beautiful grounds owned by former overlander. Email ahead for directions and to give notice of arrival.	Hacienda N04 24.00 W76 46.51, Gatehouse N04 25.30 W75 45.68	Free
Salento	Restaurante El Roble, just north of Salento turn-off, buy dinner, good food.	N04 39.76 W75 35.79	Free
Salento	Secure camping also available on a river in Boquia on the road to Salento just south of El Roble.		Pay
La Pintada	2 hrs south of Medellín, Hotel Parton de la Pintada, restaurant and pool.	N05 45.51 W75 36.51	Pay
Medellín Parqueadero	Calle 50 (Colombia), just west of Centro.	N06 14.51 W75 34.36	Pay
Llanos de Cuibe	50 miles north of Medellín, Mobil Fuel Station.	N06 49.01 W75 28.87	Free
Taraza	Terbal Gas Station, free riverside camping behind station, restaurant.	N07 35.24 W75 23.70	Free
Sahagun	South side of town, no-name fuel station with Restaurante Las Villas. Big secure parking area.	N08 55.24 W75 26.66	Free
Los Naranjos	Playa Grande Camping. On the beach 6km east of PN Tayrona entrance.	N11 16.71 W73 51.93	Pay

Location	Description	GPS Coordinates	Cost
Cartagena locations			
Old Town	Guarded parking lot on the east side of the city just outside the gate at Plaza Santa Teresa.		Pay
Bocagrande	Guarded parking lot across from the beach.		Pay
	Empty dirt lot next to the Hilton Hotel at the end of the Peninsula on the water.		Free
	Another spot recommended is near the airport called Hotel Derust, camping for 20000 peso per night. It consists of many small bungalows but OK if self contained and it is right on the beach. It has toilets and open showers.		Pay

Border Crossing Formalities

<u>Arrival from Ecuador</u>
We parked under the sign that read "Colombia" and walked over to immigration to have our passports stamped into the country. We didn't even have to fill out a visitor's card. Then we went to *Aduana* to get our vehicle permit.

The officials were so quick that we were finished in less than 15 minutes. Welcome to Colombia!

The Colombian vehicle permit is called the *Solicitud Y Autorización de Importación Temporal de Vehículo de Turista.*

ADMINISTRACION DE ADUANAS NACIONALES DE IPIALES
CUSTOMS SERVICES ADMINISTRATION OF IPIALES

SOLICITUD Y AUTORIZACION DE
IMPORTACION TEMPORAL DE VEHICULO DE TURISTA
TEMPORARY IMPORTATION OF A TOURIST VEHICLE

No. AUTO *REQUEST*	774
FECHA *DATE*	30-Oct-06

CONFORME LO ESTABLECEN LOS ARTICULOS 158, 159, 160 Y 161 DEL DECRETO 2685 DE 1999, SE DA TRAMITE A LA PRESENTE SOLICITUD DE IMPORTACION TEMPORAL DE VEHICULO DE TURISTA
ACCORDING TO ESTABLISHED IN ARTICLES 158, 159, 160 AND 161 DECREES 2685, OF 1999, THE FOLLOWING TEMPORARY IMPORTATION OF A TOURIST VEHICLE REQUEST IT IS PROCESSED.

NOMBRE TURISTA SOLICITANTE *TOURIST NAME*	NUMERO PASAPORTE *PASSPORT No.*
GREENE DONALD	

NACIONALIDAD *NATIONALITY*	DIRECCION EN EL PAIS DE ORIGEN *ADDRESS IN THE COUNTRY*		DIAS AUTORIZADOS POR EL D.A.S ó DIAN *IMMIGRATION DAYS AUTHORIZED*
ESTADOUNIDENSE	AZ	ARIZONA, ESTADOS UN	60

DATOS DEL AUTOMOTOR
VEHICLE DATA

CLASE DE AUTOMOTOR *KIND CAR*	No DOCUMENTO DE PROPIEDAD *PROPERTY DOCUMENT NUMBER (IDENTIFY CAR NUMBER)*	MARCA *BRAND*
MOTORHOME	0504085	MITSUBISHI
TIPO *MODEL*	AÑO - MODELO *MODEL YEAR*	COLOR *COLOR*
F39	2004	BLANCA
PLACA *COUNTRY OF ORIGIN PLATES*	NUMERO CHASIS *CHASIS NUMBER*	NUMERO MOTOR *ENGINE NUMBER*

VALOR DEL AUTOMOTOR *COST VEHICLE*		ADUANA DE SALIDA
	4500	CARTAGENA

TRIPTICO U OTRO ☐	EMISOR	NUMERO	FECHA VENCIMIENTO

AUTO Y ACTA PARA LA AUTORIZACION DE IMPORTACION TEMPORAL DE VEHICULO DE TURISTA.
AUTORIZATION OF A TOURIST VEHICLE TEMPORARY IMPORTATION.

SE AUTORIZA ☑	DATE ENDING HASTA 28-Dic-06	**IMPORTANTE** Informe a la Aduana la salida del vehiculo. Si vencido el termino autorizado no se ha producido la reexportación procederá la aprehension y decomiso del vehiculo.

3 0 OCT. 2006

OBSERVACIONES (observations).

FIRMA
NOMBRE
TURISTA O INTERESADO
TOURIST OR OTHER CONCERNED

FIRMA
NOMBRE
MARINA CARREÑO DE OCHOA
JEFE DIVISION COMERCIO EXTERIOR
HEAD OF EXTERIOR COMMERCE DIVISION

FIRMA
NOMBRE
LEONARDO MORA
FUNCIONARIO INSPECTOR
CUSTOMS INSPECTOR

PARA SU VALIDEZ EL FORMATO Y LOS DATOS CONSIGNADOS EN ESTE ESTAN DILIGENCIADOS COMPLETAMENTE EN COMPUTADOR

ILHV1   774   37/5830/10/2006 03:14:45 p.m.

Shipping Out of Cartagena

When we arrived in the port city of Cartagena it was raining and many of the streets were flooded. We needed to contact our Customs Agent so we found a place to park and attempted to find a telephone. We had to walk quite a ways to avoid the flooded streets, but we finally found a phone and contacted the Customs Agent.

The Customs Agent agreed to meet with us so we found a taxi (also difficult in the rain) and headed over to the Manga section of the city. The Customs Agent then introduced us to the Cartagena Shipping Agent (who spoke English). The Shipping Agent arranged for the Customs Agent to start our document processing that afternoon, and invited us to wait in his office. After waiting 2-1/2 hours for the man to return with our documents, we decided to call the next morning to find out when they would be ready.

Not to go into too much detail, we ended up making countless trips to Manga and the port and waiting for four working days for the Customs Agent to finish the paperwork that we felt we could have completed in one or two days.

On the last day before we were supposed to fly out of Cartagena, we were instructed to bring the truck to the port at 8:00am for its final inspection by the police before being shipped out. Only the Customs Agent hadn't made an appointment for the inspection, so when we showed up, the police said, no, we'll inspect you in two days. Well, that obviously wouldn't work since the boat was to leave the next day and so would we. Don finally convinced the police to do the final inspection, but they wouldn't do it until 5:00pm. Since the Fuso had already been allowed into the port area, it wasn't allowed to leave, so we were stuck without our home/transportation for the rest of the day and Don had to return in the late afternoon, again, to finally finish up the paperwork. And for all this "help" we had to pay $100.00 to the Customs Agent, in addition to the $120.00 in port fees.

The moral of the story is that it is always best to handle as much of the paperwork yourself as you possibly can.

Below are copies of the documents required to clear Colombian customs and to enter the port.

R_OTE_10	CONTECAR S.A.		Page 1 of 1

Centro de Servicio al Cliente y Operaciones Aduaneras.
Autorización Ingreso Terrestre de Carga Suelta

Autorizacion		Fecha	Usuario
21711063613		17/11/2006 11:11:21	ASANCHEZ

Carga	Descripción Carga	Cantidad	Peso	BL
21711063613	CARRO CASA	1	5464	....

Propietario		Puerto	Linea
GREENE DONALD		PAMIT	WALLENIUS

Operador		Transportador
800116164 TERMINAL DE CONTENEDORES DE CARTAGENA	1	POR SUS PROPIOS MEDIOS

Embarcación	Conductor	Placa	Ubicación	IMO
NAESBO - BR618 - N	GREENE DONALD	CCi	DH DH	

Empaque	Producto	Clase de Carga	Pendiente
VEHICULOS EN GENERAL	VEHICULOS 20 A 40	NORMAL	....

Sia	Observaciones
	CUBICAJE DE LA CARGA: 53,82 METROS CUBICOS
Lote	SE RECIOE OL VEHICULO

Embarcador	Bascula Ent	Bascula Sal	Auxiliar
	Ever Castro Auxiliar de Radicación CONTECAR S.A.	Ever Castro Auxiliar de Radicación ...... S.A.	

- IMPORTANTE: **NO se permiten** enmendaduras ni anotaciones que modifiquen el contenido del documento originalmente emitido. Se debe anotar unicamente placa, cédula del conductor y nombre del conductor.

- **NOTA ACLARATORIA CONTENEDORES REFRIGERADOS:** El servicio de Contecar se limita al suministro de energía. El control técnico y mantenimiento de la temperatura es responsabilidad del exportador ó la SIA designada.

- Recuerde que en caso de solicitarse la inspección de Antinarcóticos deberá hacerse presente, ya que de lo contrario su mercancía no se embarcará.

Americas Overland

TERMINAL DE CONTENEDORES DE CARTAGENA S.A

SOLICITUD PARA INSPECCIÓN DE AFORO DE CARGA SUELTA

FECHA DE LA SOLICITUD DIA [26] MES [11] AÑO [2006] TIEMPO ESTIMADO DE OPERACIÓN

No. CONSECUTIVO DE AFORO	TIPO DE AFORO						MODALIDAD	MOTONAVE	No VIAJE
974	DIAN	ICA	DASA	ANT	RECO	T. IMP	IMPO / EXPO X	MAESTBORB	BR613

NOMBRE DEL CONSIGNATARIO   MARCA DE LOS BULTOS   CANTIDAD DE BULTOS   NUMERO B/L

GREENE DONALD B   GREENE DONAL   1   2071063613

SOLOCITADO POR: GREENE DONALD   SIA
NOMBRE Y C.C.   Jose Luis
1253333(5

PERSONAL AUTORIZADO POR EL CLIENTE

OPERADOR PORTUARIO   Cootecas N.I.   DOCUMENTACION CONTECAR

COOPERATIVA   NOMBRE DE ESTIBADORES

NOTA LA PRESENTE SE REALIZARA HOY PM [ ]   MAÑANA AM [ ]

FECHA DE LA INSPECCION: DIA [20] MES [11] AÑO [06]   HORA DE INICIO 16:55
HORA FINAL 17:15

INSPECTOR 1   NOMBRE   AUTORIDAD 01

INSPECTOR 2   NOMBRE   AUTORIDAD

OBSERVACIONES Énsp. Antinarcotica, No utilizo Né maquina, né
Estibadores, solamente Verificación de contenedo

REVISIÓN DE LA CARGA: PARCIAL [ ]   TOTAL [ ]   [X]   REG FOTO [ ]

AUXILIAR CONTECAR S.A   FIRMA CLIENTE O FUNCIONARIO DE LA SIA

Forma 600-MFF-044-02/04

Chapter Twenty-four

Information Index
a. Equipment and Supplies List
  - Cab/Camper Equipment
  - Camping Equipment
  - Truck Equipment
  - Parts
  - Tools
b. Document Checklist
c. Embassy Websites
d. Conversion Tables

Equipment and Supplies List

Cab/Camper Equipment
- 1 mattress, 2 sheets, 1 duvet cover, 2 pillows, 4 pillowcases
- 1 internal ladder
- Personal clothing, hats, footwear and toiletries
- First aid kit
- Towels, washcloths, shower curtain
- 3 fire extinguishers
- Utensils, pots, pans, melamine plates and bowls, plastic glasses, coffee pot, pressure cooker
- Radio/CD player
- Computer
- Digital camera
- Binoculars – one pair per person
- Batteries, battery charger, 2 headlamps, 2 flashlights (torch)
- Games, playing cards, books

Americas Overland

- 12V fan
- 2 hiking day sacks
- Walking stick
- Soft sided cooler
- 2 folding bicycles, helmets, tire pump, bike bags
- Inflatable kayak, life preservers and paddles
- Camper leveling blocks
- 2 hoses, 50' & 25' with faucet adapters in 1/2", 1" and a hose thief
- Tabletop gas BBQ
- Entry door insect screen
- Toilet oxidizers, no chemicals
- Disposable gas lighters and matches
- Snorkeling equipment: mask, fins, snorkel, booties, wet suits (2 sets)
- Clothes line
- Locks and cable
- Candles
- Insect/mosquito coils and repellant
- Whisperking water pump
- Solar Boost 2000E
- Powered roof vent
- Interior 12v fluorescent lighting
- 2000 Watt Inverter and remote
- C200 Thetford Cassette Toilet
- Propane and CO_2 alarms
- 30lb horizontal propane tank
- AC/DC refrigerator/freezer
- 35 amp power inlet, Day/night 2000 solar/12v exhaust fan
- 62 gal water tank, 14 and 11 gal gray-water holding tanks
- 2 burner stove top

- Instant/tankless electric water heater
- 1 instant hot water dispenser
- Naturepure water purifier
- Airtop 2000 diesel powered air heater
- ByCool Camper 12v evaporative air cooler
- Electrical fuse panels
- 100' electrical extension cord, 3-prong to 2-prong adapter
- 2 12-Volt 225 Amp Hour GEL Batteries 8G8D
- 2 roof mounted 120watt solar panels
- 12 foot long Horizon Awning

Camping Equipment
- 1 small folding table and 1 rollup table
- 2 folding chairs and 2 tripod chairs
- 1 folding shovel
- Screened tent
- Outside light
- Tarps, clamps & stakes
- Hammocks
- Small rake

Truck Equipment
- 1 windshield sunscreen
- 2 spare tires
- Proper sized lug sockets for tires
- 10 ton bottle jack
- Hi-lift jack
- Jacking plate
- 4 *Maxtrax Recovery Device* – sand ladders
- 3 Safety Triangles – mandatory in most countries
- Folding shovel
- 3' long shovel

Americas Overland

- 3-step ladder
- Windshield squeegee
- CD Changer and receiver with speakers
- Fog and driving auxiliary lights and wiring harnesses
- 100% duty air-compressor, air hose, and 2 gal pressure tank
- 3"x30' HD Snatch/Recovery/Tow strap and D shackle
- Recovery points front and rear
- 5 step Hijacker folding aluminum camper step
- Center Cab Console and safe
- Cab roof rack and mounts
- Diesel and water 5 gal/20lt containers
- RV cover
- Weather Guard underbed mounted storage box
- 1 *MaxAx* Multipurpose tool

Parts

- Puncture repair set
- Extra headlights
- Extra windshield wipers
- Replacement filters: oil, fuel, air, transmission
- Fan belt and hose repair kits
- Extra bulbs for interior lights

Tools

- Rechargeable Drill
- Eye protection
- Tire pressure gauge
- Sockets and ratchet, 1/4", 3/8" and 1/2"
- Breaker/power bar for sockets/lug nuts
- Extension bar/pipe for power bar

- Screwdrivers
- Pliers, needle nose and flat
- Wire cutter
- Adjustable crescent wrenches
- Wrenches/spanners
- Hammers, claw and ball peen
- Rubber mallet
- Hacksaw
- Pipe wrench
- Allen wrench set/keys
- Tire valve key/ deflator
- Vice grips
- Voltage meter
- Battery jumper cables
- Electrical tape/duct tape
- Assorted fuses, screws, nuts & bolts
- Electrical wire and connectors
- Glues, sealants, silicone and caulk
- Multiple pairs of leather gloves
- Bungee cords
- Ratchet tie downs
- Soldering iron and solder
- Drill and drill bits
- Rivet gun and assorted rivets
- Bolt cutters
- Extra rope/line
- Weather-stripping tape
- Windshield washer concentrate
- Brake fluid
- Cable ties, various sizes
- Electrical adapters, 3 pin to 2 pin
- Assorted hose clamps

- Miscellaneous cables, bolts and screws, wire, etc. that can be used when necessary to improvise repairs and modifications

Document Checklist

- Make sure you have at least one set of photocopies of all documents for each country you plan to visit.
- Original Driver's License, plus 6 color copies
- International Driver's License, if required
- Vaccination papers
- Vehicle Insurance docs, or purchase liability insurance at borders where required
- Vehicle Registration docs
- Vehicle Title docs
- Copy of vehicle license plate
- Carnet, if required
- Extra passport photos
- Credit card and ATM/cash card
- Passport, do not carry original on you, only a photocopy
- 2 sets of extra keys
- Maps
- Guidebooks

Embassy Websites

Mexican Embassy to the United States
http://portal.sre.gob.mx/usa/

Embassy of Belize
http://www.embassyofbelize.org/

Embassy of Guatemala
http://www.guatemala-embassy.org/

Embassy of El Salvador
http://www.elsalvador.org/home.nsf/home

Embassy of Honduras
http://www.hondurasemb.org/

Embassy of Nicaragua
http://www.cancilleria.gob.ni/

Embassy of Costa Rica
http://www.costarica-embassy.org/

Embassy of Panama
http://www.embassyofpanama.org/cms/index2.php

Embassy of Venezuela
http://www.embavenez-us.org/

Embassy of Brazil
http://www.brasilemb.org/

Embassy of Argentina
http://www.embassyofargentina.us/espanol/home/home.
htm
Embassy of Chile
http://www.chile-usa.org/

Embassy of Bolivia
http://www.bolivia-usa.org/

Embassy of Peru
http://www.peruvianembassy.us/en.html

Americas Overland

Embassy of Ecuador
http://ecuador.org/main.htm

Embassy of Colombia
http://www.colombiaemb.org/opencms/opencms/

Embassy of Uruguay
http://www.uruwashi.org/

Embassy of Paraguay
http://www.embaparusa.gov.py/index_english.html

Guyana – no official website at the time of research
http://www.guyanaconsulate.com/

French Guiana
French Guiana is an overseas department of France with no diplomatic office in the USA, at the time of research.

US State Department – Travel Warnings
http://travel.state.gov/travel/cis_pa_tw/tw/tw_1764.html

Conversion Tables

To Convert	Multiply by	To Get
Length/Distance		
inches	2.54	centimeters
centimeters	0.4	inches
feet	0.3	meters
meters	3.3	feet
miles	1.6	kilometers
kilometers	0.62	miles
Weight		
pounds	0.45	kilograms
kilograms	2.2	pounds
Volume/Liquid		
cups	0.24	liters
pints	0.47	liters
quarts	0.95	liters
gallons	3.8	liters
liters	4.2	cups
liters	2.1	pints
liters	1.06	quarts
liters	0.26	gallons

Americas Overland

Temperature	
Fahrenheit to Celsius	Subtract 32, then multiply by 0.56
Celsius to Fahrenheit	Multiply by 1.8, then add 32

Celsius	Fahrenheit
0	32
5	41
10	50
15	59
20	68
25	77
30	86
35	95
40	104
45	113
50	122

Crossing a bridge on a banana plantation, Costa Rica

Crossing a bridge in the Gran Sabana, Venezuela

Americas Overland

The Equator in Brazil (equador is equator in Spanish)

Kim at Ushuaia, Tierra del Fuego, Argentina

Penguins at Reserva Provincial Punta Tombo, Argentina

Cerro Aconcagua, the tallest mountain in the Americas, AR

Parque Nacional Torres del Paine, Chile

Parque Provincial Ischigualasto, Argentina

Heading toward Paso Seco, Argentina

Americas Overland

The salt flats at Uyuni, Bolivia

Tatio Geysers, Chile

Chachapoyas, Peru

Navigating a landslide, Cordillera Blanca, Peru

Waiting at a one lane tunnel, Huaraz, Peru

Cañón del Pato, Peru

A variety of overland vehicles in Chile

Don & Kim Greene and the pyramids at Teotihuacán

About the Authors

Kim and Don Greene are travel soul partners, working and traveling together for the past 18 years. One of their first journeys together was a two-month driving trip through Mexico. This was followed by a four-month backpacking journey around the world. After taking countless chicken buses and more than a few third-class trains filled with animals and non-functioning toilets the thought occurred to them that it would be nice to travel in their own vehicle. Later came the idea to drive around the world. They got their feet wet with a 16-month journey through Mexico, Central and South America.

Made in the USA
Las Vegas, NV
26 March 2023

69676018R00210